THE NORMATIVE GROUNDS
OF
SOCIAL CRITICISM

THE NORMATIVE GROUNDS
OF
SOCIAL CRITICISM

Kant, Rawls, and Habermas

Kenneth Baynes

STATE UNIVERSITY OF NEW YORK PRESS

Published by
State University of New York Press, Albany

For information, address State University of New York
Press, State University Plaza, Albany, N.Y. 12246

Production by Ruth East
Marketing by Theresa A. Swierzowski

Library of Congress Cataloging-in-Publication Data

Baynes, Kenneth.
    The normative grounds of social criticism : Kant, Rawls, and
    Habermas / Kenneth Baynes.
        p.   cm.
    Includes bibliographical references and index.
    ISBN 0–7914-0867–1 (alk. paper) . — ISBN 0–7914-0868–X (pbk. :
    alk. paper)
        1. Justice. 2. Kant, Immanuel, 1724–1804—Contributions in
    justice. 3. Rawls, John, 1921– —Contributions in justice.
    4. Habermas, Jürgen—Contributions in justice. I. Title.
    JC578.B39   1992
    320'.01'1—dc20

90–27204
    CIP

10 9 8 7 6 5 4 3 2

In memory of my mother,
Barbara Clare Spock

CONTENTS

Contents

LIST OF ABBREVIATIONS

BL   Rawls. The "Basic Liberties and Their Priority," in *The Tanner Lectures on Human Values*, v. 3, ed. S. McMurrin. Salt Lake City: University of Utah Press, 1982.

BS   Rawls. "The Basic Structure as Subject," in *Values and Morals*, ed. A. I. Goldman and J. Kim. Boston: Reidel, 1978.

DE   Habermas. "Discourse Ethics," in *Moral Consciousness and Communicative Action*, trans. C. Lenhardt and S. Nicholsen. Cambridge: MIT Press, 1990.

GMS   *Groundwork of the Metaphysic of Morals*, trans. H. J. Paton. New York: Harper and Row, 1964.

KC   Rawls. "Kantian Constructivism in Moral Theory," *The Journal of Philosophy* 77 (1980): 515–572.

KPW   *Kant's Political Writings*, trans. H. B. Nisbet, ed. H. Reiss. Cambridge: Cambridge University Press, 1975.

KpV   *Critique of Practical Reason*, trans. L. W. Beck. Indianapolis: Bobbs-Merrill Co., 1982.

KU   *Critique of Judgment*, trans. J. Meredith. Oxford: Clarendon, 1978.

LC   Habermas. *Legitimation Crisis*, trans. T. McCarthy. Boston: Beacon Press, 1975.

MCCA   Habermas. "Moral Consciousness and Communicative Action," in *Moral Consciousness and Communicative Action*.

MdS   *Metaphysik der Sitten*. Hamburg: Meiner, 1966.

ME   Habermas. "Morality and Ethical Life," in *Moral Consciousness and Communicative Action.*

TCA   Habermas. *The Theory of Communicative Action*, vol. 1 and 2, trans. T. McCarthy. Boston: Beacon Press, 1984, 1987.

TJ   Rawls. *A Theory of Justice.* Cambridge: Harvard University Press, 1971.

ACKNOWLEDGMENTS

The following work began as a doctoral dissertation submitted to the Department of Philosophy at Boston University in 1987. I am grateful for the support and criticism I received at that time, especially from Thomas McCarthy and Seyla Benhabib. In the process of rewriting the manuscript for publication, I have also benefited from discussions with Jürgen Habermas, Axel Honneth, Dick Howard, Michael Kelly, James Bohman, and the graduate students in two seminars on Kant and Habermas at Stony Brook in 1988 and 1989. I would also like to acknowledge the financial support for research provided by the State University of New York (Faculty Research Grant) and by the Alexander von Humboldt Foundation (for a year's study in Frankfurt). Chapter 1, section III first appeared in a special issue of *The Monist* devoted to Kant's Practical Philosophy and is reprinted here with the editor's permission. Last but not least, I thank Peggy Cohee, Galen, and Nora for their patience and good humor while I worked to complete the manuscript.

INTRODUCTION

My aim in the present study is to provide a clarification of the normative grounds on which the practice of justifying and/or criticizing social norms and institutions rests, at least within a democratic regime. It is widely assumed that such grounds (or foundations) are necessary if criticism is to express anything more than the subjective preferences or particular interests of the critic. A clarification of its normative grounds should help insure that the criticism is objective or reflects generalizable interests. At the same time, however, it has been forcefully argued by others that such grounds do not exist and that social criticism can be more effective if pursued "without foundations."[1] It has also been claimed that a continued search for the normative grounds of social criticism reflects a failure to appreciate our "postmodern condition" and, according to Richard Rorty, an unfortunate "urge to see social practices of justification as more than just such practices."[2] What is needed in our time is rather a greater sense of irony and toleration of diversity in view of the contingency that surrounds our social institutions and practices.

In the following I attempt to mediate between the extremes of "foundationalism" and "relativism" by developing what can be called a (Kantian) constructivist defense of the grounds of social criticism.[3] Constructivism parts with stronger foundationalist projects which assume that the grounds of social criticism must consist of (self-evident) principles that are absolute and immune to revision.[4] It also parts with those foundationalist strategies that seek to establish an objective standpoint by appealing to a morally neutral notion of rational self-interest.[5] As I understand it, Kantian constructivism attempts to account for the objectivity of our normative assessments by relating the ideals and principles employed in our critical practices to an expressly normative conception of practical reason or, what I shall argue amounts to the same thing, to a conception of ourselves as free and equal moral persons.[6] There is no further claim that these principles or ideals correspond to a prior moral order that exists independently of this conception of practical reason or that these principles cannot be revised in the light of subsequent criticism and renewed argument. Rather, the justification of this normative ground is ultimately reflexive or recursive in the sense that there can be no

1

higher appeal to something beyond the idea of that to which free and equal persons can rationally agree.[7]

Following Michael Walzer, however, I also believe that when it is most effective social criticism (or "collective reflection on collective life") takes the form of "immanent critique."[8] Good criticism draws attention to the discrepancy between ideology and practice, or between what is claimed for a given social practice and how that practice is actually conducted. Nevertheless, in suggesting that criticism is best pursued as a kind of storytelling, Walzer unnecessarily limits this practice in at least two respects. First, the distinction Walzer makes between the path of interpretation, on the one hand, and the paths of discovery and invention, on the other, is overdrawn. Just as all good storytelling also involves elements of invention and discovery, even the most contrived inventions deployed for the purpose of social criticism (such as Rawls's original position) acquire a critical edge only because of their role within a larger narrative in which we recognize ourselves.[9] Second, Walzer invokes precisely the normative ground that stands in need of further clarification when he states that the "effective authority" of an interpretation is, in the last analysis, "the reader":

> The interpretation of a moral culture is aimed at all the men and women who participate in that culture—the members of what we might call a community of experience. It is a necessary, though not a sufficient, sign of a successful interpretation that such people be able to recognize themselves in it.[10]

Although Walzer does not state why self-recognition is not sufficient for a successful interpretation, presumably it is because (at least in part) a successful interpretation, especially one that is to serve a critical purpose, must involve a recognition of a certain sort, that is, it should not be based on self-deception or illusion and it should come about in a way that regards other members of the "community of experience" as free and equal cointerpreters. The idea of an ideologically undistorted agreement among free and equal persons thus seems to be the unacknowledged ground in Walzer's model of social criticism.

These two considerations suggest that the practice of social criticism involves stronger justificatory claims than Walzer's model of storytelling initially suggests. My own strategy will be to attempt to clarify the ground or basis of these claims with reference to a normative conception of practical reason or, in the case of Habermas, a model of communicative reason. That is, I hope to show that a suitable basis for the public justification and criticism of social norms and practices can be developed by reflecting upon the capacity for practical reasoning and deliberation that agents engaged in those practices exhibit.

The approach that will be pursued in this study can thus be broadly described as Kantian.[11] It begins with a set of arguments found in Kant which undergo further refinement, though in different ways, in the writings of John Rawls and Jürgen Habermas. Kant, it will be recalled, sought to derive the "supreme moral principle" (or categorical imperative) from an analysis of the structure of pure practical reason. The idea of the social contract, or notion that laws are legitimate only to the extent that they could receive the consent of citizens regarded as free and equal moral persons, is also introduced as an idea of pure practical reason. Thus, in both his moral and political theory, the criterion of legitimacy is related to a concept of practical reason that is normative in character rather than to a notion of self-interested rational choice.

Similarly, Rawls's *A Theory of Justice* can be viewed as a sustained attempt to continue Kant's project by introducing a procedural (and "detranscendentalized") interpretation of the categorical imperative and concept of autonomy and by providing a more convincing justification for them via the method of "reflective equilibrium." Moreover, the principles of justice are defended not with reference to a neutral (game-theoretic) model of rational choice, but with reference to a "model-conception" of the person as a free and equal moral being.

Finally, Habermas's theory of communicative action and his model of discourse ethics also continue Kant's project in its detranscendentalized form. The strategy now becomes that of clarifying the basic idea of discourse ethics—"only those norms can claim to be valid that meet (or could meet) with the approval of all affected in their capacity as participants in a practical discourse"—not with reference to the rational faculties of a monological subject, but with reference to a concept of communicative reason:

> What is paradigmatic for the latter is not the relation of a solitary subject to something in the objective world that can be represented or manipulated, but the intersubjective relation that speaking and acting subjects take up when they come to an understanding [*Verständigung*] with one another about something. (*TCA* 1:392)

Habermas's claim is that an analysis and reconstruction of the conditions of *Verständigung* (or mutual understanding) can provide a normative foundation for social criticism. In this sense, he pursues by different means Kant's attempt to develop normative principles for social criticism from a notion of practical (communicative) reason.

Despite the common strategy found in the works of Kant, Rawls, and Habermas, there are of course important differences among them. Some of these differences can be highlighted by briefly comparing several concepts that are centrally important to each theorist.

(1) First, and perhaps most importantly, there is the concept of autonomy and the way it is subsequently embodied in a description of the moral point of view. Kant himself described autonomy in a number of different ways: To act autonomously is to act from principles that reflect our noumenal selves. It can also be described as acting from laws that we give to ourselves or as acting on maxims that are not self-contradictory when universalized. Finally, autonomy is described as acting out of respect for the Moral Law or from duty for duty's sake. Although it may be possible to formulate a "detranscendentalized" version of autonomy through a selective reading of Kant's texts, the concept is generally understood to entail a rigid distinction between the noumenal and phenomenal self and thus to place reason in sharp opposition to empirical inclinations, needs, and desires.[12] Reason is associated with the absence or suppression of desires and passions; the noumenal self is rational, reflective, and (ultimately) free of moral conflicts. Moreover, the exercise of autonomy is generally viewed as a monological process in which the self single-handedly (and often against great odds) brings its passions and desires into conformity with the *a priori* Moral Law.

In Rawls's conception of autonomy, the opposition between reason and desire is less strong. Autonomy does not mean bringing maxims of the will into conformity with the *a priori* Moral Law, but acting from principles that reflect our conception of ourselves as free and equal moral persons. Although in selecting principles of justice the parties in the original position are deprived of the knowledge of their particular interests and desires, they still select the principles of justice in view of a list of primary social goods. In this sense, principles that express our autonomy are not necessarily ones that suppress or ignore all social and historical aspects of our selves. Further, in his description of the model-conceptions of the well-ordered society and the person, Rawls recognizes the social nature of persons more profoundly than Kant: The fact that who we are is greatly shaped by the social institutions in which we are raised is a major consideration for regarding the basic social structure as the primary subject of justice. However, it can also be argued that Rawls's description of the two fundamental moral powers of persons (e.g., the capacity to form, revise, and pursue a conception of the good and the capacity to have an effective sense of justice) still does not adequately capture the intersubjective dimension of moral autonomy. More importantly, Rawls's representation of the moral point of view in the original position clearly seems to downplay the importance of the intersubjective recognition of norms for their validity. The parties in the original position do not discuss their interests or the social norms that shape them; rather, the original position (as a description of the moral point of view) is constructed in such a way that the principles of justice are chosen in accordance with the (monological) maximin rule of choice under conditions of uncertainty.

For Habermas, by contrast, the concept of moral autonomy is linked from the outset to a notion of communicative reason and action. Autonomy is understood as the capacity to reflect critically upon one's desires, preferences, and maxims of action, the capacity to assess the consequences of pursuing them from the standpoint of those who might be affected, and the capacity to enter into discursive argument with others about the validity of contested norms or need interpretations. Autonomy is therefore not represented as the capacity to test norms monologically by means of an application of the categorical imperative or to make choices from within a hypothetical choice situation. Rather, it points to the idea of a dialogical process in which needs and interests are subject to communicative interpretation and discursive argumentation. Moreover, this model does not assume that a person's preferences or desires are pregiven or fixed, or that they are necessarily in opposition to reason (or indifferent to reason, since reason is merely instrumental). The idea is that of a procedure in which needs and preferences can be transformed in the process of rendering them "communicatively fluid."

(2) The notion of publicity also functions prominently, though differently, in the work of each of these authors. For Kant, the "principle of publicity" is introduced as a principle of practical reason that possesses a transcendental status.[13] It functions primarily as a criterion or standard for assessing the legislation and public policies of the political sovereign. To the extent that this principle actually attained an institutional foothold in early bourgeois society, it also designated a public sphere of discussion and debate among reasoning citizens. At the same time, however, the institutional realization of this principle was restricted in that the public sphere was for the most part accessible only to "active" citizens—that is, propertied males.

In Rawls's theory of justice, the notion of publicity is both more inclusive and has a wider scope.[14] It requires, for example, that society be regulated by principles of justice that are publicly known, that the justification of these principles be made with reference to a notion of "free public reason," and that, according to what Rawls calls the "full publicity condition," the principles and their justification be acceptable to each member of society.

> Publicity ensures, so far as the feasible design of institutions can allow, that free and equal persons are in a position to know and to accept the background social influences that shape their conception of themselves as persons, as well as their character and conception of their good. Being in this position is a precondition of freedom; it means that nothing is or need be hidden. (*KC*, 539)

The principle of publicity thus specifies the ideal of a non-ideological public acceptance of social norms and institutions. However, insofar as Rawls tends

to limit this notion of publicity to an informal argument for his two principles of justice and regards it primarily as a constraint on the choice of the
parties within the original position (see *TJ*, 175–182), he shies away from the
more radical implications of his own assumptions. Despite his remarks concerning the "full publicity condition," institutions of a distinct public sphere
(even in Kant's sense) are not specifically thematized as part of what Rawls
calls the "basic structure" of society.

For Habermas, by contrast, the principle of publicity is not limited to
use as a criterion or standard for determining the legitimacy of legal norms
or basic principles of justice but requires its own institutional embodiment.
Of course, the basic principle of Habermas's discourse ethics can also be
viewed as an intersubjective or "public" version of Kant's categorical imperative. But insofar as a discourse ethics requires that the validity of social
norms be tested in actual discourses rather than through monologically conducted thought experiments, his construal of the principle of publicity
emphasizes more strongly than either Kant or Rawls the need to encourage
and maintain a wide array of institutions that together constitute an active
and robust public sphere. The concept of publicity thus assumes a more
prominent role in the work of Habermas.

(3) These differences with respect to the concept of publicity also point
to differences in the status and function of the social contract (or idea of
agreement) in the theories of Kant, Rawls, and Habermas. In relation to the
earlier natural law tradition, the idea of the social contract already undergoes
revision in Kant's theory where, as an "idea of (practical) reason," it (like the
principle of publicity) functions primarily as a test for the legitimacy of legislation. In *A Theory of Justice*, the idea of the social contract (or agreement)
functions at a deeper level since it is now the principles of justice which are
to regulate the basic social structure that must be agreed to in the original
position. Rawls also argues that his two principles of justice are ones that
would be chosen or agreed to by all if they regard themselves from an appropriate perspective, namely, as free and equal moral persons.[15] Thus, as for
Kant, the notion of agreement in the social contract is closely tied to the
notion of practical reason (rather than instrumental reason or self-interested
rational choice). Finally, in Habermas's theory of communicative action, the
idea of agreement is extended in two ways. On the one hand, the idea of an
agreement based on mutual recognition is located from the outset in the
structure of communicative action and then subsequently represented, in a
more demanding form, in the basic principle of a discourse ethics: a norm is
valid only if it is one that could be agreed to by all concerned as participants
in a practical discourse. On the other hand, in contrast to the social contract
tradition, the idea of agreement must not remain wholly counterfactual.
Rather, a central task of critical social theory is to identify ways in which this

ideal can be institutionalized within an actually functioning public sphere.

(4) These differences in the conceptions of autonomy, publicity, and the social contract also give rise to differences in how each of these philosophers distinguish between the right and the good, or between what is a matter of justice to which all persons have a claim and what is a matter of one's individual pursuit of a particular conception of the good life within the limits of justice. For Kant, the "Universal Principle of Justice" confers upon each citizen the equal right to pursue his own ends compatible with a like liberty for all. The principles of justice or right must, however, be defined independently of (and prior to) particular conceptions of the good life. Kant attempts to uphold this distinction on *a priori* grounds with reference to a concept of pure practical reason and the distinction between our noumenal and phenomenal selves. Rawls also insists upon the priority of the right over the good, but since his two principles are derived from a hypothetical choice situation rather than "deduced" from the concept of pure practical reason, the distinction must be drawn in a different way.[16] The right is still defined with reference to a model-conception of the person (or conception of moral agency), but Rawls also introduces a determinate set of primary goods as general social conditions necessary for its effective realization. The distinction between the right and the good is thus not made on *a priori* grounds, but is relative to more "empirical" arguments about what social conditions are necessary for the exercise of moral autonomy. Finally, Habermas also insists upon a distinction between normative issues of justice and evaluative issues of the good life, although the question of when and how this distinction is to be made is one that must finally be settled within a practical discourse. The distinction is not based upon a basic natural right nor made with reference to a stipulated list of primary goods. Rather, within the process of communicative need interpretation and discursive argumentation, the satisfaction of those needs and interests whose validity is recognized by all concerned have priority over the pursuit of particular conceptions of the good life. At the same time, the general social conditions necessary for effective participation in practical discourses would also seem to be a matter of justice or right to which all individuals have a legitimate claim.

(5) Finally, the kind of justification offered for the normative grounds of social criticism differs for each of these theorists. For Kant, the validity of the Moral Law and the concept of autonomy ultimately rest upon a (nondemonstrable) "Fact of Reason." For Rawls, the process of "reflective equilibrium" replaces this idea as a method of justification. Not only the two principles of justice, but also the model-conceptions of the well-ordered society and the person and the way these are represented in the original position refer to ideas deeply embodied in our public culture that all would accept upon due reflection. Like Rawls, Habermas also rejects the possibility of

ultimate foundations; however, he attempts to avoid the relativistic interpretation to which Rawls is exposed by grounding the basic principle of a discourse ethics in a reconstruction of the unavoidable pragmatic presuppositions of speech and argumentation.[17]

This brief overview is offered only as an initial sketch of some of the similarities and differences found in the work of Kant, Rawls, and Habermas. It suggests that the idea of an agreement among free and equal persons, which already figures prominently within the liberal tradition of social contract theory and is then made even more explicit in Rawls's theory of justice and Habermas's theory of communicative action, constitutes the normative ground of social criticism.[18] For each theorist, the goal is to specify a procedure for critically assessing the legitimacy of social norms and institutions by reference to a normative conception of practical (or communicative) reason. However, with each successive theorist, or so I shall argue, this project is better able to withstand various criticisms and objections that have been raised against it. The remainder of this introduction will be devoted to a brief outline of the argument of each of the chapters.

Chapter 1 presents a reconstruction of Kant's theory of justice in order to reveal its connection with his notion of pure practical reason and demonstrate the unity of his practical philosophy. Like his moral theory generally, Kant's theory of justice (found primarily in the first part of the *Metaphysics of Morals*) presupposes the notion of autonomy (or positive freedom). In contrast to Hobbes, the legitimacy of the state and public law does not rest upon considerations of rational self-interest, but upon a notion of pure practical reason (or moral autonomy). As an analysis of his theory of property rights clearly reveals, however, an irresolvable paradox appears at the center of his theory of justice. On the one hand, property rights constitute a major part of the moral justification for the use of force in the creation of civil society; on the other hand, in the state of nature these rights remain merely provisional and are subject to the unanimous agreement of all in the social contract. Kant is at best only partially able to mitigate this paradox (as he is other paradoxes in his practical philosophy) through a teleological conception of history, that is, the view that nature will inevitably produce what individuals should but are unwilling to bring about.

Chapter 2 takes up Rawls's so-called "Kantian interpretation" of justice as fairness. I argue that it is mistaken to view *A Theory of Justice* as an attempt to derive substantive principles of justice from a neutral (or instrumental) notion of rationality. Rather, Rawls attempts to detranscendentalize Kant's notion of autonomy by providing a "procedural representation" of the categorical imperative in his construction of the original position. The specific features and constraints built into the original position are argued for in relation to certain moral ideals or "model-conceptions" of the person and the well-ordered society. This strategy is especially evident in his Dewey Lectures, "Kantian Constructivism in Moral Theory." At the same time, however, in some of his most recent writings Rawls seems to have retreated from other Kantian aspects of his theory of justice. In particular, he no longer claims that the justification of the two principles depends upon a philosophical argument for a specific conception of practical reason or moral autonomy, but suggests that, as part of a practical task of resolving matters of justice, the principles can be derived from a broad overlapping consensus that exits within our public culture. This position, I argue, threatens to undermine the critical potential he claims for his theory and makes it susceptible to a relativist interpretation, even if this goes against his own stated intention.

In chapter 3 I discuss Habermas's formulation and justification of discourse (or communicative) ethics. According to Habermas, these ethics can be viewed as an alternative attempt among philosophical theories of morality to provide a clarification and justification of the moral point of view. After clarifying what Habermas means by communicative action and responding to certain misinterpretations of it, I consider his claim that the principle of universalizability specified in discourse ethics can be derived from the pragmatic presuppositions of speech and argumentation. This requires a brief excursus on speech act theory and Habermas's pragmatic theory of meaning. I then argue that both his analysis of communicative action and his pragmatic theory of meaning are crucial for the defense of a discourse ethics.

Chapter 4 returns to the difficult question of the role of the concept of the person (or moral autonomy) in both Rawls and Habermas. On the one hand, I attempt to defend Rawls's conception of the person against several recent critical interpretations. On the other hand, I am sympathetic with those who criticize the way in which Rawls represents this ideal of moral autonomy in connection with the original position. After comparing the different characterizations of the moral point of view in Rawls, Kohlberg, and Habermas, I offer some reasons for prefering Habermas's characterization of moral autonomy in terms of a model of communicative competence and suggest how this conception of autonomy can provide a preliminary basis for distinguishing between questions of justice and questions of the good life (or the right and the good): The distinction would no longer be drawn *vis-à-vis* a private sphere defined by a substantive theory of natural rights, but in terms of the social conditions essential for the development of moral autonomy understood as communicative competence. The chapter concludes with a comparison of Rawls's notion of primary social goods and Habermas's notion of generalizable interests.

The final chapter attempts to bring together some of the conclusions reached in the previous chapters in order to develop the idea of normative social criticism. I begin with an internal criticism of Rawls's two principles of justice and a discussion of the ambiguous status of the principle of democratic participation within his theory. After briefly reviewing the major features of two prevalent models of democracy—pluralism and neocorporatism—I suggest that the model of "deliberative" democracy implicit in Habermas's writings presents a preferable alternative for realizing some of the normative ideals in Rawls's theory. The chapter concludes with a discussion of the role of the public sphere in Habermas's work and some more specific proposals about how institutions of the public sphere might contribute to this model of a deliberative democracy.

1

KANT'S THEORY OF JUSTICE

I. INTRODUCTION

This chapter explores the unity of Kant's practical philosophy by examining the relationship between politics and morality in his writings.[1] Kant's attempt to ground principles of justice (*Recht*) in a notion of pure practical reason, it will be argued, constitutes a distinctive feature of his liberalism that can be contrasted with attempts to ground such principles in a notion of instrumental reason and self-interest (Hobbes) or in a theory of natural rights (Locke). According to Kant, "A system of politics cannot take a single step without first paying tribute to morality."[2] This tribute consists of nothing less than the concept of autonomy (or positive freedom)—the capacity to act from laws that the agent gives to himself—serving as the cornerstone for his notion of a just political order:

> In fact, my external and rightful *freedom* should be defined as a warrant to obey no external laws except those to which I have been able to give my own consent. Similarly, external and rightful *equality* within a state is that relationship among citizens whereby no one can put anyone else under a legal obligation without submitting simultaneously to a law which requires that he can himself be put under the same kind of obligation by the other person.[3]

Of course, to maintain that the concept of autonomy provides the cornerstone for Kant's theory of justice is not to claim that citizens will in fact always act from laws that they could (rationally) give to themselves, either individually or collectively. Kant describes this ideal as the "kingdom of ends" or the "kingdom of God on earth" precisely to contrast it with the notion of a just political order. Rather, the claim is that his theory of justice

11

must assume that individuals are beings capable of acting in this way, if the project of grounding principles of justice in a notion of pure practical reason (in contrast to empirical practical reason) is to succeed.

This claim concerning the unity of Kant's practical philosophy may seem suspect to those already familiar with his political theory. After all, Kant not only drew a sharp distinction between the realm of legality and the realm of morality, he also claimed that progress in the former does not insure any improvement in the latter. Moral improvement consists in greater conformity of the agent's maxims to the categorical imperative, but no amount of coercive legislation can create a good will. Moreover, Kant believed that the task of creating a just political order could be solved by a "race of devils" as long as they possessed understanding—that is, *Verstand* in contrast to *Vernunft*. And, as commentators have been quick to note, if the task can be solved by devils it surely can also be settled by "Benthamites trying to maximize their utility function."[4] Such views would not seem to permit a great deal of unity in Kant's practical philosophy and, therefore, also seem to threaten the distinctiveness of his political liberalism.

The first reply that might be made to this objection would be to insist on the familiar Kantian distinction between validity and genesis. That is, while the validity of a just political order lies in its conformity to "laws of freedom" and, ultimately, the constraints of practical reason, its historical genesis need not (and generally does not) conform to these requirements. However, although this sort of reply is open to Kant, it does not get to the heart of the objection. The question is whether the principles agreed to by interest-maximizing Benthamites would be the same as those specified in relation to a normative concept of practical reason. If so (as the "race of devils" passage suggests), the distinctiveness of Kant's theory would be lost since practical reason would not provide a unique criterion for determining the legitimacy of the rules which define the political order.

A second reply might proceed as follows: As many commentators have noted, Kant is able to insist on the harmony between principles agreed to by a race of devils and principles grounded in practical reason only by assuming a teleological conception of history. The providential hand of nature insures that what individuals ought to create will be brought about despite their unwillingness. However, Kant's predictions about the course of historical events have not fared any better than Marx's. Nature has produced neither just political orders nor a condition of international perpetual peace. If Kant's teleological conception of history is unjustified (as I believe it is), what consequences does this have for his assumption about the unity of practical philosophy? Although Kant claimed that his assumptions about what nature would inevitably produce were secondary or subsidiary to the moral principles grounded in practical reason, my own view is that his teleological conception of history has influenced his substantive views on social justice.[5] I develop this objection in the conclusions to this chapter where I indicate a number of problems raised by Kant's two-world doctrine and the peculiar status he ascribes to property rights in his theory. However, rather than developing these criticisms here, let me indicate what I take to be some of the virtues of Kant's political theory.[6]

The distinctiveness of Kant's liberal political theory, I will argue, lies in his attempt to ground principles of justice in the notion of pure practical reason or, as I prefer to speak of it, a conception of the person as a free and equal moral being.[7] This project provides an alternative to the tradition of "possessive individualism," be it that of Hobbesian rational self-interest or that of Locke's natural law theory.[8] Kant does not begin with a natural right to private property (Locke) nor does his theory of the social contract rest upon considerations of rational self-interest (Hobbes). Rather, Kant's aim is to specify a set of basic rights and a criterion of political legitimacy (the social contract) with reference to a notion of practical reason that cannot be reduced to instrumental reason or self-interested rationality. At the same time he also rejects a more metaphysical conception of reason, such as can be found in the classical tradition of natural law.[9]

The attempt to ground principles of justice in a notion of practical reason also provides the basis for Kant's distinction between the right and the good, or questions of justice and questions of the good life. Whereas principles of justice are based on what all can agree to as free and equal moral beings, there exists a plurality of irreconcilable conceptions of the good. Kantian liberalism affirms a plurality of conceptions of the good within the limits of justice or right. Although this distinction is certainly controversial, it will be important to see how Kant defends it and where the strengths and weaknesses of his arguments lie.

Finally, a third distinct feature of Kant's liberalism concerns the status of property rights in his theory. They are based not upon a natural right to the objects of one's labor, nor upon considerations of social utility or efficiency. Rather, however problematic in the end, Kant develops a theory of property rights with reference to a conception of the person or moral autonomy. Further, property rights remain provisional and subject to the united agreement of all in the social contract and the realization of international peace among nations.

Several commentators have noted a tension between the theory of property rights (and justification of coercive legislation) developed in the *Metaphysics of Morals* and the idea of the social contract found primarily in Kant's "occasional" writings on politics and history.[10] I believe that this interpretation is mistaken, due in part to the failure to perceive the unique function of the "Universal Principle of Justice" (UPJ) in the *Metaphysics of Morals,* and the idea of the social contract in Kant's political theory. The UPJ is primarily introduced to provide a justification for the use of coercion, while the idea of the social contract provides a test for just legislation. However, both notions have their roots in the concept of autonomy or practical reason.

I should also add that the following exposition of Kant's practical philosophy differs from several recent studies with regard to its method of interpretation. Rather than relying primarily upon Kant's "occasional" writings, I take the *Metaphysics of Morals* to be his most important and systematic discussion of topics in political philosophy. The general neglect of this work is apparently due, at least in part, to the widespread conviction, voiced quite early by Schopenhauer, that Kant's philosophical abilities were well beyond their prime at the time of its publication (1797) and that, consequently, it should not be included among his "critical" works.[11] This conviction is often accompanied by the hope that such essays as "Theory and Practice" and "Perpetual Peace," or even the third *Critique,* will offer a better point of departure for reconstructing Kant's practical philosophy. Despite the many difficulties contained in the *Metaphysics of Morals,*[12] I believe its neglect is unjustified and that we must look to it for Kant's systematic views. This is not to suggest, however, that the occasional writings are unimportant. On the contrary, they often fill out and illuminate views that Kant formulates all too briefly in the *Metaphysics of Morals.*

II. JUSTICE AND MORALITY IN KANT

A. Autonomy and the Moral Law

In his introduction to the *Metaphysics of Morals,* Kant lists "moral personality" as one of the concepts common to both the *Rechtslehre* and the *Tugendlehre.* It is defined as "the freedom of a rational being under moral laws," and contains two aspects: the capacity to have a conception of the good, that is, to frame and pursue ends of our own choosing rather than simply to adopt ends given to us by nature (*MdS,* 392; *KU,* 427); and the capacity to act in accordance with, as well as out of respect for, the Moral Law or, derivatively, laws that express our freedom and autonomy (*MdS,* 223).[13] Moral personality can thus be defined as the capacity to act autonomously. Although the *Rechtslehre* does not assume individuals will in fact act autonomously, it does presuppose that individuals equally share this capacity. Similarly, the *Rechtslehre* presupposes the objective validity of the Moral Law (in Kant's sense). Kant refers twice to the conclusion reached in the second *Critique,* namely, that we become aware of our freedom or autonomy only through the Moral Law (*MdS*, 226, 239).[14] According to Kant, apart from the objective validity of the Moral Law, there would be no moral authority to compel others to form a civil society under public laws, or, more broadly, no moral basis for (coercively) enforcing claim-rights against others.[15] However, although the *Metaphysics of Morals* presupposes both the concept of autonomy and the objective validity of the Moral Law, it does not offer any arguments for either. For these we must turn, however briefly, to Kant's earlier writings on morality and, in particular, to the *Critique of Practical Reason.*

In a well-known footnote in the preface to the second *Critique,* Kant states that while freedom is the *ratio essendi* of the Moral Law, the Moral Law is the *ratio cognoscendi* of freedom, that is, the Moral Law requires freedom for its objective validity, yet we are able to assume our freedom only because we can first become conscious of the binding character of the Moral Law upon us (*KpV*, 4n). Kant develops this position (together with the related doctrine of the "Fact of Reason") as an alternative to the "vainly sought deduction" of freedom promised earlier in the *Groundwork* (*KpV*, 47).[16] And, even if Kant did express some dissatisfaction with this alternative at the end of his career, it must be considered his final position on the matter.[17] I cannot take up here the considerations that may have led Kant to abandon his efforts to provide a theoretical proof of freedom and replace it with the doctrine of the Fact of Reason. However, three remarks are relevant for our own "constructivist" interpretation of Kant's moral philosophy, and for a clarification of the dependence of the *Metaphysics of Morals* on the second *Critique,* particularly for the notion of autonomy and the objective validity of the Moral Law.

First, the Fact of Reason, or consciousness of the Moral Law, is not a rational insight into a moral order that can be grasped apart from or prior to the conception of ourselves as moral agents.[18] This is the interpretation argued for by Patrick Riley in opposition to constructivist views.[19] Kant, however, consistently opposed such intuitionism as dogmatic and a violation of human autonomy.[20] For Kant, the notion of moral personality entails that "a person is subject to no laws other than those that he (either alone or at least jointly with others) gives to himself" (*MdS*, 223), and Kant would have considered this a criticism of rational intuitionism, "divine command" theory, and other versions of moral realism.[21] Rather, the objective validity of the Moral Law is based on the fact that it is a law that the rational agent gives to himself in accordance with the structure of practical reasoning. According to Kant, it is also a law which the moral agent becomes conscious of in the process of constructing maxims of the will (*MdS*, 225; *KpV*, 28).[22] I will discuss the role of maxims for understanding the categorical imperative as a test procedure in section C; here I only wish to note its importance for understanding Kant's notion of consciousness of the Moral Law as a Fact of Reason: As moral agents we construct or adopt maxims or general rules of conduct. We are not simply beings who reason calculatively in light of pregiven ends. Rather, we are able to adopt various ends and pursue different courses of action. It is in the process of constructing maxims (or in reflection upon this process) that we become conscious of the binding character of the Moral Law. We experience guilt or shame when our conduct violates this capacity in others, and we experience admiration for others and respect for ourselves when we act upon maxims that acknowledge this capacity in others and in ourselves (see *KpV*, pt. 3).

Second, Kant's position in the second *Critique* is that the objective validity of the Moral Law is not known through something outside of, or independent of, reflection upon our moral experience. This may be Kant's most significant departure from the *Groundwork*.[23] The doctrine of the Fact of Reason is not an argument *from* an independent or more narrow conception of rationality (e.g., theoretical reason or rational self-interest) *to* the validity of the Moral Law. The claim is rather that the Moral Law is a principle that represents to us what is already present and effective in common moral experience.[24] (This explains, incidentally, why Kant did not consider it an objection when a critical review noted that the second *Critique* did not provide a new principle of morality, but only a new formula [*KpV*, 8 n. 5].) The Fact of Reason is, to use a juridical metaphor, a fact confirmed by the testimony of witnesses who attest to the binding character of the Moral Law upon them.[25] The achievement of the first *Critique* was to show that freedom (and hence the Moral Law) are at least theoretically possible, however, the objective validity of the Moral Law cannot be established by means of non-moral considerations. This interpretation also coincides with Kant's most developed position in the *Religion* where he argues that to act against the Moral Law does not mean that we act irrationally (in the narrower sense), although in so acting we deny our autonomy.[26]

Third, Kant's argument *from* the objective validity of the Moral Law *to* the notions of freedom and autonomy should only be viewed as a deduction in a "weak sense."[27] That is, it does not demonstrate whether we are free and autonomous, but *how* it is possible to regard ourselves as free and autonomous agents. The Fact of Reason, once it has been introduced into court as evidence, can be used as a "credential" for establishing our freedom and autonomy. It adds to the negative conclusion of the first *Critique*—that freedom is at least possible—the positive conclusion of how there can be "a reason which determines the will directly through the condition of a universal lawful form of the maxims of the will" (*KpV*, 48). The "positive concept of freedom" (the capacity of reason to be of itself practical) is revealed "through the subjection of the maxim of every action to the condition of its fitness to be a universal law" (*MdS*, 214). Thus, by virtue of our consciousness of the Moral Law as a Fact of Reason, we are entitled to view ourselves not only as part of a phenomenal world, but also as members of a noumenal realm. The notions of autonomy, the noumenal self, and the objective validity of the Moral Law are thus all presupposed in the *Metaphysics of Morals:*

> In the theory of duties, man can and should be represented from the point of view of the property of his capacity for freedom, which is completely supersensible, and so simply from the point of view of his humanity considered as a personality, independently of physical determinations (*homo noumenon*). (*MdS*, 239)

These preliminary (and controversial) remarks are no doubt insufficient given the complexity of Kant's views, but they must suffice for our own purposes and we can now turn to a closer examination of the *Metaphysics of Morals*. I will return to some further questions in Kant's moral philosophy (for example, the interpretation of the categorical imperative as a test procedure) when I consider the relation between the Moral Law and the Universal Principle of Justice.

B. The Moral Law and the Universal Principle of Justice

Contrary to many interpretations, and contrary even to some of Kant's own remarks, the *Metaphysics of Morals* does not divide neatly into a discussion of "duties of justice" in the *Rechtslehre* and "duties of virtue" in the *Tugendlehre*.[28] The central task of the *Rechtslehre* is not to define duties of justice, but rather to clarify the related, though different, distinction between "laws of justice" (*Rechtsgesetze*) and "ethical laws" (*Sittengesetze*) and the parallel distinction between "juridical legislation" and "ethical legislation."

According to Kant, all duties (both juridical and ethical) can be determined through an application of the categorical imperative as a test procedure to our maxims. To be sure, in the *Tugendlehre* Kant amends this procedure for determining duties of virtue by introducing a material doctrine of ends (*MdS*, 380–1), but for duties of justice he apparently accepts without alteration the formulations he has already provided in the *Groundwork* and the second *Critique*.[29] Rather than introducing a further criterion for determining duties of justice, the *Rechtslehre* takes up a topic not treated in these earlier writings, namely, the moral possibility of using coercion against others. This was a topic of discussion within the natural law tradition which Kant took over and attempted to solve within the context of his own moral philosophy.[30] The contrast between these two sets of problems (i.e., between determining duties and providing a moral justification for the use of force) is evident in the fact that someone's failure to act according to the requirements of justice (as determined by an application of the categorical imperative) does not by itself give someone else a moral permission to compel him or her to do (or to refrain from doing) those acts. Likewise, the moral obligation to perform an act (i.e., the fact that the contrary of its maxim is prohibited by an application of the categorical imperative) does not mean that an individual is morally justified in coercing someone else to observe that right. The task Kant sets for himself in the *Rechtslehre* is to specify the conditions under which it is morally permissible to use coercion against another.

Since, as we have seen, the principle of autonomy stands at the center of Kant's moral philosophy—we are morally subject only to those laws that we could give to ourselves—this task must appear highly suspect, if not entirely self-defeating. How can the principle of autonomy provide a moral justification for the use of force? Moreover, in contrast to some of his contemporaries, notably Fichte, Kant does not attempt to deduce or derive claim-rights (and, with these, the legitimate use of force) directly from the Moral Law. Rather, and this is crucial for a proper understanding of the structure of the *Rechtslehre,* Kant regards the use of force as a long-standing and unsolved political problem and he attempts to provide a solution for it by means of the categories of his moral theory.

The basis of Kant's solution to this problem can already be found in the Introduction to the *Metaphysics of Morals* in his distinction between the two forms of legislation (*Gesetzgebung*).

> All legislation (whether it prescribes internal or external actions, and whether these either *a priori* through mere reason or through another person's will) consists of two elements: firstly, a law that objectively represents the action to be done as necessary, that is, makes the action a duty; second, an incentive that subjectively links the ground determining the will to this action with the representation of the law. (*MdS,* 218)

As is even more clear from Kant's notes to the *Metaphysics,* he is here invoking a distinction between a principle of judgment (*Beurteilung; principium diiudicationis*) and a principle of execution (*Ausübung; principium executionis*).[31] The principle of judgment is the Moral Law which, through an application of the categorical imperative as a test procedure for maxims of action, specifies our duties. Insofar as it abstracts from consideration of the incentives to follow the law, "it is mere theoretical knowledge of the possible determinations of the will, that is, a knowledge of practical rules" (*MdS,* 218). The principle of execution, on the other hand, considers the mode of compliance or incentive through which an action is performed in accordance with the law.

> Therefore (even though one legislation may agree with another with regard to actions that are required as duties; for example, the actions might in all cases be external ones) all legislation can nevertheless be differentiated with regard to the incentives. (*MdS*, 218-9)

The distinction between ethical and juridical legislation is a distinction regarding the principle of execution or mode of compliance, not the principle of judgment: Ethical legislation (whether of duties of justice, such as fulfilling contractual obligations, or duties of virtue, such as promoting the happiness of others) makes duty itself the incentive, whereas juridical legislation (which, according to Kant, only applies to certain duties of justice) makes use of incentives other than the idea of duty itself. These other incentives to compliance are "pathological" in that they consist of sanctions that appeal to our inclinations and disinclinations. "Therefore, the *Rechtslehre* and *Tugendlehre* are distinguished not so much by their differing duties as by the difference in the legislation that combines one or the other incentive with the law" (*MdS*, 220). Thus, to restate Kant's problem more specifically, the task of the *Rechtslehre* is to specify the conditions under which it is morally permissible to employ external sanctions in order to bring about compliance with the specified duties of justice.

Corresponding to this distinction between ethical and juridical legislation is the distinction between ethical laws and juridical laws (*MdS*, 214). Ethical laws (and, again, these may be of virtue or of justice) are those in which duty or respect for the Moral Law becomes the determining ground of the will (or the motive for compliance), whereas juridical laws are directed only to external compliance (in abstraction from the agent's motivation). Both types of law are "laws of freedom," in contrast to laws of nature, and thus their validity (or principle of judgment) is found in their agreement with the Moral Law (as determined by the categorical imperative as a test procedure). Kant then adds:

> whether we consider freedom in the external or in the internal exercise of the will, its laws, being pure practical laws of reason governing the free will in general, must at the same time be internal grounds of determination of the will, *although these laws must not always be considered from this point of view.* (*MdS*, 214, my emphasis)

That is, although any morally legitimate law must be one that *could* be an ethical law (because all laws are determined by the same principle of judgment), juridical laws can also be viewed from another perspective, namely, their capacity to become laws whose compliance is insured through external sanctions.

Although Kant's distinction between ethical and juridical legislation (and ethical and juridical laws) is fairly clear, what still remains unclear is the way in which Kant provides a justification for the use of coercion. Kant's solution to this problem is found in a "practical law" that has a unique (if problematic) status in Kant's practical philosophy, the Universal Principle of Justice (or Right).[32]

> Every action is just (right) that in itself or in its maxim is such that the freedom of the will of each can coexist with the freedom of everyone in accordance with universal law. (*MdS*, 230)

A second formulation, which he calls "the law of justice," reads,

> act externally in such a way that the free use of your will is compatible with everyone according to a universal law. (*MdS*, 231)

The UPJ introduces Kant's notion of "strict justice," or right in a strong sense[33]—that is, it does not merely define a moral permission, obligation, or prohibition (as the categorical imperative does), but identifies the conditions under which an individual has "the moral capacity to bind others" (*MdS*, 237). That is, it states when coercion is morally justified, or when freedom can legitimately be restricted. Kant cites three conditions that must obtain if the UPJ is to apply, that is, if the use of coercion is to be justified: First, it refers only to *external action* insofar as these affect the freedom of others; second, it refers only to actions (or their maxims) that individuals can *universally will*—that is, it does not refer to the particular needs, wishes, or desires that an individual may have; and third, it refers to the formal character of an agent's maxim (not to its material end). (*MdS*, 230)

Although the UPJ seems quite straightforward, it is difficult to give it a clear interpretation and to locate its proper status in Kant's practical philosophy.[34] One reason for this confusion is to be found in the fact that the UPJ is frequently viewed as a principle for defining duties of justice, whereas it is primarily introduced by Kant in response to the question of the legitimate use of coercion. The UPJ states that a specific class of free actions may justifiably be restrained by force.

> If a certain use of freedom is itself a hindrance to freedom according to universal laws (that is, unjust), then the use of coercion to counteract it, inasmuch as it is the prevention of a hindrance to freedom, is consistent with freedom according to universal laws; in other words, this use of coercion is just. (*MdS*, 231)

However, whether an action falls under this category or not must itself be determined by the CI-procedure (see next section). What Kant lacks is an account of the just use of force, and it is this, I suggest, that the UPJ is intended to provide. After introducing the UPJ, Kant can go on to say that the concept of justice (that is, "strict justice") is not composed of two parts (i.e., a juridical obligation and the authorization to use coercion); rather, it "can be held to consist immediately of the possibility of the conjunction of universal reciprocal coercion with the freedom of others" (*MdS*, 232).

Strictly speaking, then, the UPJ is not another formulation of the categorical imperative. That is, it is not introduced by Kant as a test procedure for maxims in order to determine duties of justice. Rather, it has a quite different status and function in Kant's moral philosophy: It is introduced as a solution to the problem of the legitimate use of coercion. Further, unlike the various formulations of the categorical imperative, the UPJ is not directed to the incentives to action, but only to external actions themselves.

> Admittedly, this law imposes an obligation on me, but I am not at all expected, much less required, to restrict my freedom to these conditions for the sake of this obligation itself. Rather, reason says only that, in its very Idea, freedom is restricted in this way and may be so restricted by others in practice.... We may not and ought not to represent this law of justice as being itself an incentive. (*MdS*, 231)

On the other hand, as Kersting notes, the UPJ is also not a hypothetical imperative.[35] It imposes upon us an unconditional obligation whose source can only be derived from the Moral Law.

> Strict justice is admittedly founded on the consciousness of each person's obligation under the law; but, if it is to remain pure, this consciousness may not and cannot be invoked as an incentive in order to determine the will to act in accordance with it. (*MdS*, 232)

In light of these considerations it is perhaps best to assign the UPJ a unique status in Kant's practical philosophy. It is a practical law in a scientific doctrine (*doctrina scientiae*) of morals whose purpose is to specify the conditions under which the use of coercion is morally justified (see *MdS*, 375, 218). I will attempt to clarify the unique status of this principle in Kant's practical philosophy, and the relationship between justice and morality more generally, by contrasting my own interpretation with three others in the recent secondary literature.

C. Three Interpretations of Justice and Morality in Kant

The first interpretation of the relation between justice and morality I will call, following Kersting, the "independence thesis."[36] It asserts that

Kant's concept of justice, and the task of establishing a just political order in general, can be clarified without reference to the basic categories of Kant's moral philosophy, and in particular without reference to the notion of autonomy (or "positive freedom"). The thesis is expressed in the following quotation from Yovel's *Kant and the Philosophy of History:*

> Good citizenship is possible even in a kingdom of devils. It requires no ethical community (kingdom of ends) and presupposes none. It is something that can be imposed by coercion, while morality can be rooted only in the free or spontaneous will of individuals. Therefore, *even to the best of states cannot be attributed a moral value per se, and it is not in any political organization that the end of history is to be placed.*[37]

This passage contains several assertions that need to be sorted out. Yovel is certainly correct in claiming that, according to Kant, a just society does not entail that its citizens act on the basis of moral incentives and thus does not require the existence of an ethical community. Similarly, it is true that for Kant the highest good and "end of history" is not a just political order. Neither of these observations, however, warrant the conclusion that no "moral value per se" can be attributed to a political order founded on principles of justice. Further, in contrast to Yovel's interpretation of the "kingdom of devils" passage, I do not think that it can be understood to mean that the problem of creating a just political order can be solved on the basis of considerations of rational self-interest alone.[38] Since this passage from "Perpetual Peace" is central to Yovel's interpretation, I will cite it at length.

> As hard as it may sound, the problem of setting up a state can be solved even by a nation of devils (so long as they possess understanding). It may be stated as follows: "In order to organise a group of rational beings who together require universal laws for their survival, but of whom each separate individual is secretly inclined to exempt himself from them, the constitution must be so designed that, although the citizens are opposed to one another in their private attitudes, these opposing views may inhibit one another in such a way that the public conduct of the citizens will be the same as if they did not have such evil attitudes." (*KPW,* 112–13)

As I noted in my introduction, this passage is admittedly difficult to reconcile with Kant's position in the *Rechtslehre* and requires an interpretation of the relation between Kant's philosophy of history and his systematic theory of justice (for which Yovel's study would be indispensible). At this point I will only offer three considerations which weigh against Yovel's interpretation.

First, the claim that the problem of creating a just political order is merely a problem of "political technology" and can be solved on the basis of rational self-interest (that is, on the basis of *Verstand* rather than *praktische Vernunft*) conflicts with other claims made by Kant not only in other writings, but even within "Perpetual Peace": "A true system of politics cannot therefore take a single step without first paying tribute to morality.... For all politics must bend the knee before right, although politics may hope in return to arrive, however slowly, at a stage of lasting brilliance."[39]

Second, as Yovel is also aware, the "kingdom of devils" passage is closely connected to Kant's notion of a providentially guided nature or what Yovel calls "the cunning of nature." Thus it is not rational self-interest alone, but self-interest together with the providential guidance of nature, that is able to solve the problem of a just political order. If Kant's assumptions about the "mechanisms of nature" are wrong, or at least if these mechanisms do not yield the consequences he predicts, then we cannot look to rational self-interest alone to produce a just political order. In other words, the "critical turn" that Yovel finds in Kant's decision to restrict the "cunning of nature" to the production of a just state (and not the production of an ethical community) would have to be extended further.[40]

Third, two different readings of the "kingdom of devils" passage are possible, depending on what knowledge one wishes to attribute to the devils. If they know the Moral Law but choose not to act on it, in their rational calculations they may still devise a constitution that would be different from one in which their calculations were made without any knowledge of the Moral Law at all (that is, one that was based on rational self-interest alone).

In light of these considerations, we must give priority to Kant's systematic presentation of the concept of justice as it is contained in the *Rechtslehre*. As we have noted, the concept of moral personality or autonomy is a basic category for this work. Consequently, the only acceptable interpretation of the independence thesis is the formulation offered by Mary Gregor in her *Laws of Freedom*:

> Law is independent of ethics in the sense that it has no need of ethical obligation in determining its duties. But it cannot be independent of the supreme moral principle; for if its laws were not derived from the categorical imperative, then the constraint exercised in juridical legislation would not be legal obligation but mere arbitrary violence.[41]

A second interpretation of the relationship between justice and morality, more prevalent in the secondary literature than the independence thesis, is the teleological interpretation. Riley's *Kant's Political Philosophy* offers one of the most sustained defenses of this position.[42] I refer to this interpretation as teleological for two reasons. First, it is teleological in the sense that it is opposed to constructivist interpretations of Kant's moral philosophy. Rather than viewing Kant's moral theory as a construction based on a conception of the person as an autonomous moral agent, it maintains that Kant's moral theory depends upon a rational intuition of "objective ends" given to us.[43] Second, it is teleological in that it regards justice, and politics more generally, as something that exists "for the sake of" these objective ends. Thus, Riley writes,

> public legal justice is instrumentally (purposively) related to morality in two ways: in a *weaker sense,* it creates legal conditions for the exercise of a good will—it limits occasions for sin and creates occasions for morality; in a *stronger sense,* it legally enforces part of what ought to be, even where a good will is absent.[44]

We have already discussed the first aspect of a teleological reading in section A above: Kant rejects such a teleological conception because it violates the notion of human autonomy. Further, it runs counter to the basic principle of his critical philosophy, namely, that we cannot have knowledge beyond the bounds of sense experience. The second aspect of the teleological interpretation is more difficult to criticize since, like the independence thesis, it finds some support in Kant's writings, especially "Perpetual Peace" and "The Conflict of the Faculties." As before, the rule of interpretation must be to read these essays in light of Kant's more systematic presentations, and that means the *Rechtslehre* must be given priority. One reason for our earlier discussion of Kant's distinction between two forms of legislation and between the principle of judgment and the principle of execution was to show that the validity of juridical and ethical laws is the same, namely, their conformity to the Moral Law. To describe justice as existing "for the sake of" morality is thus to diminish the intrinsic value of political rights and duties, just as the independence thesis denies them moral worth altogether. Political rights and obligations, according to Kant, are unconditional commands of pure practical reason, whether they produce a greater degree of *internal* morality or not (although Kant was, I think, ultimately of the opinion that they would). In this regard it is also important to note that while Kant considered legality inferior to morality when it refers to the incentives upon which people act, this does not mean that a just political order is somehow inferior to and merely instrumental for the moral kingdom of ends.

A third, more promising interpretation of the relationship between morality and justice, and specifically the UPJ, is found in Onora Nell's *Acting on Principle.*[45] This is partly because Nell rejects a teleological interpretation of Kant's practical philosophy and argues for a constructivist interpretation. Further, her study offers a comprehensive interpretation of the categorical imperative as a test procedure that, in contrast to numerous other interpretations, attempts to preserve both the "formality" and the "fertility" of Kant's moral theory. Since I consider this interpretation the most plausible reconstruction of Kant's theory, and since it provides the background for her rendering of the UPJ as a "restricted version" of the categorical imperative, I will offer a brief summary of her interpretation.

A moral theory that, like Kant's, proposes a universality test of principles for determining the moral status of particular acts confronts what Nell calls "the problem of relevant act descriptions."[46] Since an act can be viewed under a number of different principles, and since different acts can be performed under the same principle, it is difficult to see how the moral status of an act can be determined by a universality test of principles. Kant's own solution to this problem, Nell argues, is that the agent's maxim provides the relevant act description or appropriate principle for assessing the moral status of an act.

Maxims, according to Kant, are "subjective principles," or general rules of conduct that underlie an agent's voluntary actions (*MdS*, 225). We need not assume that an agent is always conscious of the maxim upon which he or she acts, but, according to Kant, it must be possible for the agent to identify or supply a maxim upon reflection. Some examples of maxims that Kant offers in the *Groundwork* and second *Critique* are: to neglect developing my natural gifts if I find it convenient (*GMS*, 423), not to tolerate an unavenged offense (*KpV*, 19), and to increase my property by every safe means (*KpV*, 27). Accordingly, Nell proposes the following as a formal schema of a maxim: "To___if..." or "I will___if...," where "___" and "..." can be filled in with some act description and some agent description respectively (p. 35).

It is clear from these examples that maxims already involve a degree of generality and abstraction from a concrete context of action. They are not descriptions of intentions to carry out specific actions such as, "I will eat dinner with friends every Friday evening," or "I will drink beer at five o'clock," but more general descriptions of a course of life conduct under which the intentions to carry out more specific activities would fall.[47] Thus, Kant states that maxims are "general determinations of the will which have under them several practical rules" (*KpV*, 19). Kant offers no mechanical method for identifying maxims (or practical rules of sufficient generality for applying the CI-procedure) and seems to hold that this requires an element of judgment that comes only with age and experience.[48]

Further, Kant assumes that the maxims to which the CI-procedure can be applied (or better, the agents acting on those maxims) are rational in two senses: the agent is able, upon reflection, to order his or her maxims and more specific practical rules into a coherent and consistent scheme, and the agent is able fully to intend both the conditions required for the completion of the act and the consequences that can reasonably be predicted to follow from the act.[49] Both of these assumptions can be, more or less, inferred from Kant's Principle of Hypothetical Imperatives: "If I fully will the effect, I also will the action required for it" (*GMS*, 417). With this solution to the problem of relevant act descriptions in hand, we can turn to Nell's reconstruction of the CI-procedure as a test applied to an agent's maxims.

In its most basic form, the categorical imperative or "supreme principle of morality" reads, "Act only on that maxim which you can at the same time will that it should become a universal law" (*GMS*, 321). The first step in the CI-procedure is to formulate the intended maxim as a universal law. Thus, "I will break promises if it is advantageous" can be formulated as "Everyone is to break promises if it is advantageous," and the schema "To___if..." has the universalized counterpart, "Everyone to___if..."

Since nature, "in its most general sense," means a system of effects governed by universal law, Kant says that the categorical imperative may also be formulated, "Act as if the maxim of your action were to become through your will a universal law of nature" (*GMS*, 421). From Kant's more detailed description of this formula in the second *Critique*, it is clear that it is indispensable for understanding how to apply the CI-procedure. He states:

> The rule of judgment under laws of pure practical reason is: ask yourself whether, if the action you propose should take place by a law of nature of which you yourself were a part, you could regard it as possible through your own will. (*KpV*, 72)

The second step in the CI-procedure requires not only that we formulate the intended maxim as a universal law, but also that we regard it as a law of nature. We thus arrive at "Everyone will break promises if it is advantageous," and the corresponding schematization, "Everyone will___if..." (which Nell calls the "universalized typified counterpart"). To be sure, maxims, as rules that underlie voluntary actions, belong to the realm of freedom not nature, but Kant's point is that unless we can regard the universalized maxim as if it were a law of nature—that is, as a law that governs a normal and predictable set of events—it will not be possible to decide whether the intended maxim is in contradiction with it.

Kant elaborates upon this second step in the section of the second *Critique* entitled, "Of the Typic of Pure Practical Judgment," a section which is important for avoiding some common misunderstandings of the "law of nature" formula. In this passage Kant is quite specific about what we may and may not assume in viewing universalized maxims as laws of nature. On the one hand, in treating the universalized maxim as a law of nature, we are not making empirical assumptions about what might in fact happen if I were to act on the intended maxim. Because I choose to break promises if I consider it advantageous does not mean that others will also act in the same way. Rather, we make a fictive or counterfactual assumption about a system or order of things in which everyone acts in this way as if it were a law of nature. On the other hand, we are also not attributing a purposive or teleological plan to nature (as some interpretations have proposed).[50] The laws of nature serve as a *type* for practical laws.[51] What he means by this is that we should take no more from the world of sense than "the form of lawfulness" (*KpV,* 71–2), that is, the form of order or regularity in the production of an effect.[52]

However, and this brings us to the third step in the CI-procedure, it is still not clear how a contradiction might arise since it would seem that the maxim "I will break promises if it is advantageous," is only a particular instantiation of its universalized typified counterpart, "Everyone will break promises if it is advantageous." The answer is found in the phrase "at the same time," contained in the first formulation. We are asked to consider if it is possible without contradiction to will simultaneously the intended maxim (together with its necessary conditions and reasonably predictable consequences) and its universalized typified counterpart. Nell offers the following summary of the CI-procedure:

> It asks whether we can simultaneously intend to do 'x' (assuming that we must intend some set of conditions sufficient for the successful carrying out of our intentions and the normal and predictable results of such execution) and intend everyone else to do 'x' (assuming again that we must intend some conditions sufficient for the successful execution of their intentions and the normal and predictable results of such execution). (p. 73)

For example, we are to ask ourselves if we could simultaneously will to break promises if it is advantageous and will a system of nature, of which we are a part, in which everyone breaks promises if it is advantageous. Kant claims this is not possible since it would undermine the conditions necessary for such an intention.

There are a number of difficulties and further considerations that a full discussion of Nell's reconstruction of the CI-procedure would have to take up, but I must pass over these here.[53] The above summary is sufficient to enable us to see how Nell interprets the UPJ and how she views its relation to the Moral Law.

One of the stronger claims in her study (which has not yet been mentioned) is that the distinction between the two kinds of tests introduced by Kant in the *Groundwork* (the test for a contradiction-in-conception and the test for a contradiction-in-will) provides a criterion for distinguishing between duties of justice and duties of virtue.[54] Accordingly, the contrary of maxims that fail the contradiction-in-conception test (that is, maxims that cannot even be *conceived* as universal laws) define the class of duties of justice, while the contrary of maxims that may survive the contradiction-in-conception test but fail the contradiction-in-will test define the class of duties of virtue. Nell then suggests that the UPJ may be viewed as a variant on the contradiction-in-conception test. That is, "Act externally in such a way that the free use of your will is compatible with the freedom of everyone according to a universal law," is materially equivalent to (i.e., yields the same results as) the contradiction-in-conception test (which, according to Nell, itself only shows certain external acts to be forbidden).

There are several difficulties that this claim needs to address. I will briefly note two here. First, Kant introduced the two tests not as a way of distinguishing between duties of justice and duties of virtue (which he does not mention in the *Groundwork*), but as a way of distinguishing between perfect and imperfect duties. Moreover, in contrast to the traditional (natural law) distinction between perfect and imperfect duties, which *does* parallel Kant's later distinction (in the *MdS*) between duties of justice and virtue (i.e., those that may and those that may not be externally legislated), Kant's own distinction between imperfect and perfect duties in the *Groundwork* is based on a different criterion, namely, one that distinguishes between duties that allow for an exception in the interest of inclination and those that do not (*GMS*, 422n).[55]

Second, it is significant that in his later ethical writings Kant does not make use of this distinction between the two tests and, in particular, the *Metaphysics of Morals* does not distinguish between duties of justice and duties of virtue by means of this device. Rather, in the *Metaphysics of Morals* Kant introduces a material doctrine of ends to contrast duties of virtue with those of justice (*MdS*, 395).

What is more important for our own investigation, however, is Nell's further claim that the UPJ can be viewed as a "subsidiary formula" of the categorical imperative and thus that it is a test procedure for determining duties of justice (p. 39; see also p. 45). This interpretation of the principle conflicts with my own claim that Kant's major concern in the *Rechtslehre* is not to define duties of justice, but to provide an answer to the natural law question about the legitimate use of coercion. It also overlooks the unique status that the UPJ possesses in Kant's theory. Two considerations may be raised against Nell's interpretation. First, Kant does not use the UPJ as a test for maxims of action and, as we have seen, it is very difficult to read it in this way. The determination of duties of justice (as well as duties of virtue) is the task of ethics, not of the *Rechtslehre*. Second, such an interpretation of the UPJ makes it very difficult to understand the subsequent uses Kant makes of it, specifically with respect to the justification of property rights and the moral obligation (which can be coercively enforced) to enter into a civil society or social contract. These are applications of the UPJ that will be considered in the next chapter.

Let me briefly summarize the several points which this section has sought to establish concerning Kant's theory of justice: First, the *Rechtslehre* introduces the discussion of rights in connection with a conception of practical reason that cannot be reduced to a narrower notion of rational self-interest. (Rawls will later make essentially the same point in his own distinction between the Reasonable and the Rational.) The *Rechtslehre* thus presupposes the notion of moral personality or autonomy (positive freedom). To an extent yet to be considered, this may mean that Kant's theory of justice stands or falls with the success of his justification of the Moral Law as a Fact of Reason and of the related notion of transcendental freedom.

Second, Kant's theory of justice (and his practical philosophy in general) is constructivist, not teleological. A teleological interpretation of his theory undermines the fundamental principle of autonomy.

Third, one implication of his moral constructivism is that Kant does not view the question of political justice as less important or "merely for the sake of" his theory of morality. This claim was supported via a discussion of Kant's distinction between the two forms of legislation and the distinction between a principle of judgment and a principle of execution. Laws of justice have the same source of justification as do the laws of ethics, namely the Moral Law (or categorical imperative). The distinction between laws of justice and laws of virtue is a distinction within the principle of execution, that is, the incentive or motivation for compliance, and not within the principle of judgment. The UPJ provides a justification for the use of coercion with respect to a certain class of external actions, namely, duties of justice, but is not itself introduced as a test for determining or specifying those actions.

Finally, Kant's theory of justice is a theory about the legitimate use of force or coercion. However, unlike some of his contemporaries, notably Fichte, the use of force is not derived or deduced directly from a moral principle. Rather, Kant more or less simply appropriates this problem from existing discussions within the natural law tradition and proposes a solution that invokes the basic categories of his moral philosophy. Thus the UPJ is introduced primarily as a justification for the use of coercion.

III. PROPERTY RIGHTS AND THE SOCIAL CONTRACT

For all contract theorists, including Kant, political legitimacy is based upon the (counterfactual or hypothetical) consent of the governed. The differences among them begin to emerge when we inquire into the motivations and considerations which lead up to the agreement. For Kant, consent to the social contract is not based upon considerations of rational self-interest or prudence (Hobbes), nor upon a natural right to self-preservation and the guarantee of absolute property rights (Locke), but upon a moral obligation to institutionalize and make conclusive in a social contract property rights that in the state of nature have only a provisional character. Whether this approach ultimately makes the idea of a voluntary agreement superfluous is a question I will address below.[56] First, I would like to consider the unique status Kant assigns to property rights in his theory of the social contract. This status has for the most part not been observed in the secondary literature, and Kant has even been accused of falling behind the achievements of Locke and Rousseau by grounding property rights on an element of brute force.[57] However, since Kant himself espoused a labor theory of property rights in his earlier writings, it is important to consider carefully the basis for its later rejection in the *Rechtslehre*. Further, since Kant's theory of property rights constitutes an alternative to Locke (as well as to Hobbes and Rousseau), it may be possible to find within the contract tradition an alternative to the view of property rights found in some of its contemporary versions (e.g., Rawls, Nozick, or Buchanan).

In the natural law tradition (as well as in Kant) the right to private property implies an authorization on the part of the owner to prohibit others from its use by coercion.[58] For Kant, therefore, it is a matter of "strict justice," and falls under the "universal principle of justice."[59] Since, according to this tradition, the earth was originally given by God to all men in common, the central question for the theory of property rights is how such an obligation/authorization could arise. Furthermore, since rights entail a moral authority over others and since one cannot acquire an authority over others without their consent, Grotius and Pufendorf argued that property rights could only come about through an actual contract or agreement in which everyone relinquishes his common right to the use of the land and agrees to a principle for its individual or private distribution. For these theorists, the validity of private property rights presupposes that this unique and irrevocable contract actually took place at some point in the past. As is well known, Locke (and many others) rejected this notion of an original contract: "If such a consent as that was necessary, Man had starved, notwithstanding the Plenty God had given him."[60] According to Locke, individuals acquire a direct right to property, apart from the consent of others, simply by "mixing" their labor with it or by otherwise "joining" it to themselves. It is this direct and absolute right that then provides the basis for the social contract. Thus, to a certain degree, Kant's rejection of Locke's theory represents a return to the natural law conception that a person can acquire a right to an object—and hence the authority to prohibit others from its use—only on the basis of their consent. However, unlike natural law theorists, Kant does not assume that this consent actually took place in the past. Rather, he introduces the notion of a united agreement as an Idea of practical reason and identifies it with the social contract or formation of a civil society. In the state of nature, property rights have only a provisional status in lieu of their institutionalization or "self-positivization" (Kersting) in the social contract.[61] Further (and this is also important for Kant's break with a labor theory), property rights cannot be analytically derived from the one innate right to freedom (or independence from the constraint of another's will) (*MdS*, 237). An additional postulate of practical reason, introduced as a "permissive law," is required. As we shall see, this notion of a permissive law is important for Kant's criticism of Locke and for an understanding of the status property rights have in Kant's theory of the social contract.

A. Physical and Intelligible Possession

Possession, according to Kant, is the "subjective condition of the possibility of the use of an object" (*MdS*, 245). I have a right to possesssion only if I can claim that the use of an object by someone else, without my consent, constitutes an injury to me. By "injury" Kant means anything that diminishes my freedom (*MdS*, 250). Now it is clear that if someone wrests something from my hand or drags me off a piece of land on which I am camping, he injures me. Thus,

> A proposition about rights with respect to empirical possession is analytic, for it says no more than follows from the concept of empirical possession by the law of contradiction, namely, that if I am the holder of a thing (that is, physically connected to it), then anyone who touches it without my consent (for example, wrests an apple from my hand) affects and diminishes that which is internally mine (my freedom). Consequently, the maxim of his action stands in direct contradiction to the axiom of justice. (*MdS*, 250)

However, is it also possible to claim an injury in cases where I am not actually (physically) detaining an object? This question, according to Kant, points to an ambiguity in the concept of possession for if I can be injured by someone's use of an object that I am not in fact detaining, then we cannot be speaking merely about physical possession. "Intelligible possession" (*possessio noumenon*) means pure *de jure* possession, possession without detention, and the claim of a right to possession without detention is thus also the claim that intelligible possession is possible (*MdS*, 246). However, unlike physical (or empirical) possession, the right to (and possibility of) intelligible possession is not analytically contained in the concept of external freedom (*MdS*, 250). For while it may be self-evident that I am injured in my person if I am forcibly removed from a piece of land on which I am camping or if an apple is wrested from my hand, it is not self-evident that I am similarly injured by someone's use of a piece of land or an object not in my physical possession. According to Kant, the claim to a right to external possession without detention is a synthetic *a priori* proposition about rights: it is synthetic because such a right is not necessarily implied by the concept of external freedom; and it is *a priori* because, for Kant, the validity of any claim-right cannot be based on experience, but must be derived from pure practical reason.

Kant's denial that the right to external possession is analytically contained in the concept of external freedom marks a shift from his earlier views on property rights. In his *Bemerkungen zu den Beobachtungen über das Gefühl des Schönen und Erhaben,* written around 1765, Kant claimed that property rights were necessarily entailed by the concept of freedom or self-determination. An individual could extend his internal *suum* (or innate property, e.g., life, body, and limbs, as well as reputation and personal action) to encompass external objects by modifying them through his freedom (that is, by investing his labor in them).[62]

In the *Rechtslehre,* by contrast, Kant describes the right to external property as a synthetic *a priori* proposition about rights, and thus it stands in need of a "deduction." In an explicit analogy to the *Critique of Pure Reason,* Kant illustrates the need for such a deduction by means of an antinomy:[63]

> Thesis: It is possible to have something external as mine even though I do not have possession of it.

> Antithesis: It is not possible to have something external as mine if I do not have possession of it. (*MdS,* 255)

The apparent contradiction between these two assertions, Kant maintains, can be resolved by distinguishing between two notions of possession: in the thesis 'possession' refers to physical possession, while in the antithesis it refers to intelligible possession (*MdS,* 255). Consequently, the deduction that Kant must now provide is supposed to offer an answer to three related questions: how is it possible for something external to be mine or yours; how is intelligible possession possible; and how is a synthetic *a priori* proposition about rights possible (*MdS,* 249)?

B. The Postulate of Practical Reason as a Permissive Law

The "juridical postulate of practical reason" provides the key to Kant's deduction of property rights and reflects a reformulation of the antimony of practical reason sketched in his working notes to the *Metaphysics of Morals.* Kant offers two (roughly equivalent) formulations of the postulate:

It is possible to have any and every external object of my will as my property. (*MdS*, 246)

It is a duty of justice to act toward others so that external objects (useable objects) can also become someone's property. (*MdS*, 252)

It is clear from these formulations that this postulate amounts to the blunt assertion that external property rights (and, hence, intelligible possession) are possible. Therefore, the important question is what sort of justification Kant claims to have offered for its introduction, especially since he has claimed that these rights are not contained analytically in the concept of external freedom. Unfortunately, Ladd is misleading when he inserts into his translation of the text the phrase, "the reason for this postulate is as follows" (*MdS*, 246; Ladd, 52). What follows is not a justification of the postulate, but at best a sort of "indirect proof" (Lehmann) by way of a demonstration that the contrary of the postulate constitutes a contradiction of external freedom. However, the impossibility of its contrary is not sufficient to establish the necessity of the postulate. If this were the case, it would amount to the claim that the postulate is analytically contained in the concept of external freedom—something that Kant explicitly denies (*MdS*, 247, 255). The justification, I would like to suggest, lies in Kant's description of the postulate as a permissive law (*lex permissiva*) (*MdS*, 247). The view that property rights are established through a permissive law constitutes Kant's alternative to his earlier position that they could be derived directly from the law of external freedom. Therefore, we must determine more precisely what Kant means by a permissive law.

In the section in the *Rechtslehre* on the postulate (par. 2), Kant states that as a permissive law the postulate confers on us an authorization to impose an obligation upon others that they otherwise would not have had, namely, the obligation to "refrain from using certain objects of our will because we were the first to take possession of them" (*MdS*, 247). Mary Gregor, in her discussion of this passage, offers the following general definition of a permissive law:

> A permissive law states the conditions under which a general prohibition does not apply, and the permission to prohibit others from interfering with our exclusive use of an object is a limitation upon the prohibition, contained in the inherent right of freedom, against interfering with the freedom of activity of others.[64]

The concept of a permissive law was a topic of discussion in jurisprudence or natural right theory in Kant's time. Josef Niklas, the Imperial Count of Windischgrätz, even announced a contest in which scholars were invited to compete in clarifying the use of the concept with respect to legal contracts.[65]

In his essay on "Perpetual Peace," Kant mentions this contest, expresses his dissatisfaction with the contributions, and offers his own definition of a permissive law.[66] Although the immediate context of Kant's own treatment of permissive law in this essay concerns the question of how much latitude should be permitted in applying the various articles (or laws) he introduced for the realization of perpetual peace between nations, the more general problem he finds with earlier attempts to clarify the concept is that the introduction of permissive clauses appeared arbitrary and based on external contingencies.[67] Kant's hope is to provide such a "definite principle," and locate the proper place for the concept of permissive law "within the systematic divisions of reason." In this passage, Kant describes a permissive law as one that creates "a compulsion to do something one cannot be compelled to do," and from the context it is clear that it involves the *temporary* suspension of a general prohibition in anticipation of the creation of a more just state of affairs.

In a detailed study of the concept of permissive law in Kant's philosophy, Reinhard Brandt points out that Kant's remarks on permissive law were framed in response to contemporary discussions about the effects of the French Revolution and the possibility of constitutional reform "from above" in Prussia and Austria.[68] The French Revolution established (at least for a time) a republican constitution, but did so, according to Kant, by immoral means. Still Kant argued that the revolution could receive our moral sympathy (if not provide a moral example) and that the royalists were not justified in seeking to reestablish the monarchy.[69] Though itself an unjust action, the effects of the revolution could rightfully continue by a "permissive law" provided that gradual progress was made toward the cessation of all war and a true condition of perpetual peace. Similarly, with regard to the demand for constitutional reforms in Austria and Prussia, Kant argues that there is a "permissive law of reason" to allow unjust conditions to continue within a state (in contrast to attempts to remove them through "premature" reforms). "until all is ripe for a complete revolution or has been prepared for it by peaceful means. For any *legal* constitution, even if it is only in small measure *lawful,* is better than none at all, and the fate of a premature reform would be anarchy."[70] In both cases a condition of injustice (or one brought about through an unjust act) is allowed to remain on the assumption that the unjust elements will gradually be removed and that the present condition constitutes a greater degree of justice than would otherwise have existed. I will return to the further point that Kant's notion of a permissive law implicitly relies upon the fact that reform (and even revolution) can equally, and even preferably, be achieved by nature rather than by self-conscious political (or revolutionary) action.

In light of these reflections on the concept of a permissive law in Kant, we can return to the question of its role in the justification of the postulate in his theory of property rights. The postulate of practical reason, as a permissive law, allows an individual to prohibit others from making use of an object of his will because he was the first to take possession of it and thus it limits the freedom of others (*MdS*, 247). It imposes a restriction upon the law of freedom and creates an obligation upon others that otherwise would not have existed. The justification—to the extent that there is one—is that this restriction upon the general prohibition not to limit the freedom of others itself occasions a degree of freedom that would otherwise not have been possible. Without such a permission to restrict liberty, Kant claims, there would be no moral basis for leaving the state of nature and entering into a civil society (*MdS*, 256), and thus no basis for leaving a condition of injustice and establishing a society under law. However, in the state of nature property rights remain provisional; they are only made conclusive within a civil society, that is, with the united agreement of all (*MdS*, 256).

Finally, with this introduction of the postulate as a permissive law, Kant also claims that the deduction of the right to intelligible possession is complete and that the possibility of a synthetic *a priori* proposition about rights is demonstrated. "For if it is necessary to act according to this principle of right and justice, then the intelligible condition (of a mere *de jure* possession) must also be possible" (*MdS*, 252).

C. The Right of Original Acquisition and Kant's Critique of Locke

The deduction of the concept of intelligible possession attempts to show how the possession of external objects is possible. It constitutes Kant's reformulation of, and solution to, the question within the natural law tradition of how it is morally possible to extend the right of possession beyond one's internal *suum* to encompass external objects. As we have seen, according to Kant the one innate right is the right to freedom and one's internal *suum* (or innate property) is the right to be one's own master and to be treated equally by others (*MdS*, 237–8). The right to external property cannot be inferred directly from this innate right but requires an additional postulate of practical reason as a permissive law. However, since, by definition, external property is not innately mine, it can only be acquired. This presents Kant with a further problem that is not settled in the deduction of the concept of intelligible possession and that Kant describes as "the most difficult to solve" (*MdS*, 266), namely, the problem of the right of original acquisition. Kant's solution to this problem has been viewed by many as wholly unsatisfactory and as a thinly veiled justification for the use of force.[71] Thus we must look more closely at the reasons for Kant's change in order to judge the soundness of these criticisms.

The right of original acquisition fulfills a specific function in the natural law tradition (as well as in the works of Locke and Kant). It is not simply an ideological justification of the existing inequalities in the distribution of wealth. Rather, the right of original acquisition is a right restricted to the state of nature as a "condition of abundance," and is offered to explain how private property rights could legitimately come about in the first place, given that the land is originally in the common possession of all. Kant offers a clear formulation of the problem: Acquisition can only take place as a unilateral act of the will, that is, as taking possession of an object (the land); yet (at least for Kant), a unilateral act of the will can never create an obligation on the part of another nor can it provide an authorization to the inhabitor to use coercion: *Omnis obligatio est contracta*. Obligations can only arise through an agreement, and thus the obligation of everyone else to refrain from the use of an object can only come about through the agreement of all. While this view does indicate something of a return to natural law theory, as we shall see, Kant alters the content of this tradition within the context of his own theory. In contrast to both Locke and earlier natural law theorists, in the state of nature there are no absolute property rights, even the right of original acquisition remains provisional prior to the unanimous agreement of all, that is, prior to the formation of civil society. It is only the united agreement of all (as an *a priori* idea) that can transform physical possession (as a unilateral act of detention) into intelligible possession (*MdS*, 259).

Kant formulates the principle of external acquisition as follows:

> Mine is whatever I (according to the law of external freedom) bring within my possession, and what I (according to the postulate of practical reason) have the capacity to use as an object of my will and, finally what I will should be mine (in accordance with the idea of a possibly united will). (*MdS*, 258)

As this passage indicates, Kant distinguishes three aspects or moments within this principle: the apprehension or taking possession of a piece of land as a unilateral act of the will; a declaration or signification to others of this apprehension; and the appropriation of the land as an act of an external universal legislative will (*MdS*, 258–9). The first two moments constitute only an "empirical title" to possession and do not yield a "rational title" (*MdS*, 264). Although a unilateral act of occupation and its declaration to others are both necessary, they must be accompanied by a third moment to constitute a "rational title"—the united agreement of all (*MdS*, 264).

Kant describes this third moment as the *conditio sine qua non* of the right of acquisition (*MdS*, 264). This right cannot be based on a unilateral act of the will, but additionally requires the united agreement (or possible agreement) of all (*MdS*, 264; see also 258, 263, 268–9). In other words, according to Kant, the obligation to refrain from the use of a piece of land because someone else was the first to occupy it can only be incurred through the *a priori* united will or agreement of all who can enter into a practical relation with one another (*MdS*, 263).[72]

Corresponding to and complementing the idea of the *a priori* united agreement of all is the notion of an original common possession of the land (*communio possessionis originaria*) or community of common ownership (*communio fundi originaria*) (*MdS*, 250).

> All people are originally (that is, before all juridical acts of the will) in legitimate possession of the land, that is, they have a right to be where Nature or chance (without their choice) has placed them. (*MdS*, 262; see also 250–1)

The notion of an original common possession is also found in the earlier natural law tradition, as well as in Locke, but, again, Kant provides it with a new meaning and it assumes a different systematic role in his theory. Kant distinguishes this notion of an original community of common ownership from the notion of a primeval community (*communio primeava*) found in earlier natural law theory (*MdS*, 251, 258, 262). The latter notion assumes that such a community could only come about through an actual contract or agreement whereby each renounced his private possessions, thereby transforming them into a common possession. Kant rejects this notion as a "fiction" and contrasts it to the original community of common ownership as an Idea of practical reason (*MdS*, 251). Original common ownership cannot be based on a prior agreement or contract since that would presuppose that individuals already possessed private property rights and had already entered into a juridical or civil society. Rather, for Kant, the notion of common ownership serves as a presupposition or condition for the social contract and must itself be viewed as part of the original or innate right which all have simply by virtue of being born on the earth.[73]

The reason for Kant's introduction of this notion and its systematic status should now be clear: Rights and obligations can only arise through agreement, but a united agreement to recognize the right for original acquisition could not take place unless everyone already possessed a prior claim to the land. Nor, of course, could this prior claim itself be based on a still earlier agreement. For similar reasons, Kant also rejects the notion of an ownerless object (*res nullius*) as a contradiction (*MdS*, 246). Since property rights are based on agreements between persons, not relations between persons and things, if the land were not originally owned by someone no property rights could ever arise. The conclusion drawn from both of these considerations is that the notion of an original, noncontractual common ownership is a necessary presupposition for the possibility of property rights; without it no obligations regarding property could arise, including the most basic obligation to enter into a civil society. For this reason Kant calls the notion of an original community of common ownership "an Idea that has objective (juridical-practical) reality" (*MdS*, 251).

Thus, for Kant, the right of original acquisition ultimately depends upon the *a priori* Idea of the united agreement of all.

> But the state of a legislative, universal and truly united will *is* the civil state. Therefore, something external can be originally acquired only in conformity with the idea of a civil state, that is, in reference to it and its realization, though *before* its reality (since otherwise the acquisition occurs only in the civil state). (*MdS*, 264, 267)

However, as a permissive law this provisional right also creates a moral obligation for all to form a social contract and enter into civil society (*MdS*, 267). Before turning to Kant's notion of the social contract, I would like to indicate more specifically some of the differences between Kant and Locke, as well as some of the criticisms that have been raised against Kant's theory of property rights.

As we saw above, in his earlier writings Kant espoused a labor theory of property rights:

> A product of freedom is a product of nature which is modified through my freedom with respect to its form, for example, a tree which I have trimmed.... Apprehension is not every use of a thing, but rather where the form of a thing is modified through freedom.... If someone first discovers a land, raises a flag there and takes possession, still he does not have a right to it. But if he works the land, and applies his energies to the land, then he has apprehended it.[74]

In view of our reconstruction of Kant's theory, it is now possible to see the motivation for Kant's change. What Kant came to reject is the notion that a person could acquire a right to external objects exclusively on the basis of his relationship to those objects and apart from the possible agreement of those who might be affected by it. This is essentially the position advocated by Locke and it is within this context that Kant's critique of the labor theory must be understood: Since rights and obligations are relations between persons—not between persons and things—working the land does not in itself grant a person moral authority over another unless the other has also given his consent. What Kant returns to in the *Rechtslehre*—and what has fallen out of

Locke's theory altogether—is the earlier natural law conception of a *facultas moralis*, the notion that one can acquire a moral authority over another only on the basis of consent.[75] The right of acquisition is a right to exclude others from the use of an object and would thus violate their freedom unless they could consent to such a restriction. To be sure, Kant redefines the notion of a *facultas moralis* in terms of his own moral theory and the principle of autonomy: the only innate right is the right to freedom as this is known through the Moral Law, and the only laws to which a person is subject are those that she could prescribe to herself. There is no notion of an internal *suum* given by God to all and defined in connection with an independent order of being, as is the case with Grotius and Pufendorf. Further, the required consent is not viewed as a contract that took place at some point in the past, rather it is transformed by Kant into an idea of reason and identified with the notion of the original social contract as the founding principle of civil society.

Kant's identification of the united agreement with the notion of the social contract and formation of civil society points to another difference with Locke. According to Locke, in the state of nature property rights are absolute and the sole end of government is to protect and preserve these natural rights.[76] For Kant, by contrast, property rights remain provisional until the formation of a civil society and, strictly speaking, until the creation of a federal league of nations and the realization of international peace on earth (*MdS*, 350, 266). Property rights are not based upon an innate right to self-preservation nor upon the command of God to subdue and enjoy the earth; they rest ultimately upon the possibly united agreement of all. Despite some of the difficulties contained in this notion of a rational and universal agreement (see below), it is clear that Kant offers a justification and foundation for property rights that is quite different than Locke's. It should also be clear from our reconstruction that to accuse Kant of "a regression not only behind Rousseau, but also behind Leibniz and Locke"[77] is misdirected if it means that Kant's critique of the labor theory indicates a return to mere occupation or detention as a sufficient title to property rights. On the contrary, Kant's critique of the labor theory represents a much deeper rejection of Locke's conception of the basis for property rights.

There is one further difference with Locke that I have not yet mentioned but which is central to the criticism made by those who defend a labor theory. Toward the end of his discussion of the right of original acquisition, Kant poses the following question and answer:

How far does the authority to take possession of the land extend? So far as (there is) the capacity to have it within one's power, that is, so far as whoever wants to appropriate it can defend it, just as if the land were to say: 'If you cannot protect me, then you cannot command me.' (*MdS*, 265)

This view has been contrasted with Locke and Rousseau who limit the right of acquisition to what a person needs or can use.[78] Locke adds further that to take possession of more than one can use or to let something spoil is to offend against the common Law of Nature. However, these arguments which appeal to a notion of need and/or a concept of teleology are not open to Kant and he himself confessed that "the indeterminacy with respect to the quantity as well as the quality of acquired objects makes the task (of original acquisition) the most difficult to solve" (*MdS*, 266). Still, this passage does not permit the interpretation that at this point Kant allows a dimension of force to enter into his theory of property rights. As we have seen, the right of acquisition does not reside in the unilateral act of occupation, but in the possibility of the united agreement of all. The capacity to defend a piece of land does not grant a "rational title" to it, although it may be a condition for its original acquisition in the state of nature. Finally, the passage refers only to the right of original acquisition, which for Kant (as well as for Locke) applied only to the (conceptual) beginning of societies, when conditions of scarcity did not obtain. In fact, for Locke, with the introduction of money and the emergence of conditions of scarcity, the requirement that one can only possess what one can use falls away and there are (arguably) no further restrictions on the degree of wealth that a person can acquire.[79] For Kant, by contrast, the right of external acquisition remains provisional until the formation of civil society at which time other restrictions on the degree of inequalities in wealth come into play.[80]

D. The Social Contract as an Idea of Practical Reason

The close relationship between Kant's theory of property rights and his notion of the social contract should by now be clear. On the one hand, the right to private property, introduced as a permissive law, creates a moral obligation upon all to enter into civil society, that is, to form a social contract:

> If there were not even provisional property in the state of nature, there would be no duties of justice in respect to them, and consequently, there would be no command to quit the state of nature. (*MdS*, 313)

On the other hand, property rights cannot be analytically derived from the concept of external freedom; nor can the innate right to internal *suum* be extended to include external objects simply by mixing one's labor with them. Property rights require the united agreement of all as this is represented in the idea of the social contract. The questions I would like to address here are, first, whether Kant's notion of an original social contract is internally coherent and, second, whether it is rendered obsolete or superfluous by his attempt to provide an independent moral justification for property rights. To anticipate my conclusion, while there are certainly internal difficulties in Kant's theory (for example, his introduction of the distinction between active and passive citizens), I believe that Kant offers a theory of the social contract that is not only distinct from other contract theorists, but one which more strongly emphasizes the idea of a (counterfactual) agreement between free and equal moral persons.[81] However, the critical potential of Kant's notion of the social contract is in the end jeopardized by its dependence upon an uncritical philosophy of history in which social change and revolution are attributed to the hand of providence or forces of nature.[82]

For Kant, the original contract is qualitatively distinct from all other (voluntary) agreements.[83] Whereas voluntary agreements and associations within a society presuppose that the parties share certain goals or ends arbitrarily (or by choice), the original social contract contains "an end in itself which they all *ought to share*," namely, the formation of a state or civil society regulated by coercive public laws.[84] The end or goal of the social contract is one that all citizens share by virtue of their conception of themselves as free and equal moral persons. Since the social contract defines the basic institutions and social structures within which other voluntary transactions and associations take place, the considerations and motivations that lead to it differ from those that lead to the formation of "private" agreements.

Kant identifies three basic features or "juridical attributes" that characterize the parties who form the original social contract: freedom, equality, and independence.[85] They are free in that they are subject to no other laws than those to which they can give their consent (*MdS, 314*) and in that each is regarded as having her own conception of the good:

> No one can compel me to be happy in accordance with his conception of the welfare of others, for each may seek his happiness in whatever way he sees fit, so long as he does not infringe upon the freedom of others to pursue a similar end which can be reconciled with everyone else within a workable general law.[86]

The agreement made in the original contract is not based upon a particular conception of the good; but upon a conception of the person as an agent capable of framing, revising, and pursuing various conceptions of the good.

Second, the parties are regarded as equal in the sense that each views the other as free in the above sense, and hence no one has a greater right than another to decide upon the principles that are to regulate the basic structure (*MdS, 314*). Although this notion of formal equality in determining principles of justice does not mean that there must be strict equality in the distribution of social wealth, it does require that no laws be enacted that arbitrarily bestow privileges upon some.[87] It stipulates an equality of opportunity in which all are equally free to develop their talents and advance their own conception of the good.

Finally, the parties to the original contract must be independent. A person must be "his own master," which for Kant means that he must not be dependent upon another for his income or livelihood.[88] If such a person could vote, Kant argues, it would unduly advantage those on whom the parties depend. However, with this qualification (and the related distinction between active and passive citizens) Kant slips into one of the deeper paradoxes of his theory. On the one hand, it is in the social contract that property rights are to be secured; yet, the condition of independence excludes all but property holders from taking part in the agreement establishing property rights.[89] Unanimity is insured by excluding nonproperty holders from voting. This paradox is at best only partially mitigated by the fact that no legislation can be enacted that would prohibit dependent or passive citizens from raising themselves up to the status of active citizens.[90]

In a familiar passage, Kant states that the original social contract is not something that actually took place in history:

> It is in fact merely an *idea* of reason, which nonetheless has undoubted practical reality; for it can oblige every legislator to frame his laws in such a way that they could have been produced by the united will of a whole nation, and to regard each subject, in so far as he can claim citizenship, as if he had consented within the general will.[91]

However, what is also evident in this passage is that Kant sees the idea of the social contract as analogous to the categorical imperative It is a standard or test for legislation in the same way that the categorical imperative is a test for the maxims of individual action. If the analogy is pushed a bit further, it could even be said that the social contract does not provide an account of the origin or genesis of legislation; rather, it is a test to be applied to possible (or existing) legislation. Furthermore, it is also clear from this passage that for Kant the test is primarily intended for use by the legislator or monarch, rather than his subjects.[92] In this connection Kant's distinction between "forms of sovereignty" (or rule) and "forms of government" should also be noted: For Kant, it is more important that the monarch govern in a republican manner, than that the form of sovereignty be democratic.[93]

The distinctive features of Kant's theory of the social contract will become more clear if we contrast it with the views of some of his predecessors. Despite its obvious indebtedness to Hobbes and Rousseau, Kant's theory attempts to overcome difficulties in both and even achieve a sort of "reconciliation" between them.

Although Kant's references to Hobbes are generally critical—for example, the section on political rights in "Theory and Practice" is subtitled, "Against Hobbes"—he accepts Hobbes's transformation of the classical doctrine of politics in the claim that the state owes its legitimacy to the consent of the governed.[94] Kant also adopts much of Hobbes's conceptual apparatus, though often supplying it with a different content. Thus, the "state of nature" is a state of war not bliss (Rousseau), but what Kant emphasizes is its lack of an established public authority to adjudicate conflicting claims.

> A state of nature need not be a condition of injustice (*injustus*) in which men treat one another solely according to the amount of power they possess; it is, however, still a state of society in which justice is absent (*status justitiae vacuus*) and one in which, when there is a controversy concerning rights (*jus controversum*), no competent judge can be found to render a decision having the force of law.[95]

However, Kant differs importantly from Hobbes on the reason or motivation for leaving the state of nature. Whereas for Hobbes this motivation is based on rational self-interest or even the fear of death, for Kant it is based on a principle of right (*MdS*, 307). This basic disagreement leads to other differences in their respective views of the social contract. Perhaps the most significant is that, for Kant, the individual does not surrender all his rights to an absolute sovereign. Rather, Kant is closer to Rousseau in regarding the contract as marking a transition from a state of "wild, lawless freedom," to a state in which the individual finds "his whole freedom again undiminished in a lawful dependency" (*MdS*, 316). If Kant retreated from what he took to be the revolutionary implications of Rousseau's idea of the contract and (closer to Hobbes) argued that any public authority is preferable to the state of nature, the contract is still not a justification for absolutism, but a norm for testing the legitimacy of legislation. Thus, in the end, Kant's theory of the social contract has a critical function not possible for Hobbes.[96]

Kant's indebtedness to Rousseau's political ideas is of course much greater than to those of Hobbes and, consequently, the differences are more difficult to discern.[97] This indebtedness reaches to the core of Kant's notion of autonomy and the claim that "a person is subject to no laws other than those that he (either alone or at least jointly with others) gives to himself."[98] This echoes Rousseau's definition of freedom as "obedience to the law one has prescribed for oneself."[99] Similarly, Rousseau's formulation of the "fundamental problem" that the social contract is intended to solve applies equally to Kant: "Find a form of association that defends and protects the person and goods of each associate with all the common force, and by means of which each one, uniting with all, nevertheless obeys only himself and remains as free as before."[100] Finally, Rousseau's distinction between the general will and the will of all—together with its problems—is mirrored in Kant's distinction between *Wille* and *Willkür* and between the idea of an *a priori* united agreement of all and the notion of an (empirical) majority.[101]

Despite these deep affinities, several differences are still evident. The most important of these, I want to suggest, is reflected in Kant's liberal commitment to the distinction between the right and the good. For Rousseau, the passage from the state of nature to civil society produces a "remarkable change in man, by substituting justice for instinct in his behavior and giving his actions the morality they previously lacked."[102] This transformation is so great that Rousseau is apparently able to assume that within a good state private interests will largely disappear and be replaced by the general will or common good. Thus he can say, "In a well-run City, everyone rushes to assemblies."[103] For Kant, by contrast, the passage from a state of nature to civil society does not presuppose such a radical transformation, nor does he assume that a citizen's private interests or conception of the good will be replaced by a general devotion to the common good. It is only necessary that these private interests be limited by principles of right or justice. Thus Kant is able to affirm a plurality of conceptions of the good in a way not open to Rousseau.[104]

Kant's distinction between the right and the good is also reflected in the different attitude he has concerning representative forms of government. According to Rousseau, "As soon as public service ceases to be the main business of citizens, and they prefer to serve with their own pocketbooks rather than with their persons, the state is already close to its ruin."[105] On the other hand, for Kant, as we saw, "every true republic is and can be nothing else than a representative system of the people if it is to protect the rights of citizens in the name of the people" (*MdS*, 341). According to Kant, direct democracy as a form of government leads to despotism because it is unable to maintain the separation of powers necessary for a republican constitution.[106] More generally, I think it is fair to say that for Rousseau the idea of the social contract was to serve as a principle for the political organization of the state, while, to repeat, for Kant it represents the norm or standard against which the constitution and legislation are to be judged. Consequently, Rousseau's theory is utopian in ways that Kant's is not.

By way of a conclusion to this section I would like to comment briefly on three questions that have been raised in connection with Kant's theory of the social contract. First, there is the question of whether Kant's theory of justice, based upon *a priori* postulates of practical reason, does not make the notion of a voluntary agreement or contract superfluous. In his excellent study of social contract theory, J. W. Gough concludes:

> For Kant, indeed, it [the social contract] was altogether superfluous, since political obligation could quite well be founded directly, without any interpolation of a contract, on the moral obligations which he already recognized as universally binding. Kant, in fact, brings us within sight of the end of the history of the contract theory.[107]

This view, however, fails to see the transformed status Kant assigns the idea of the contract in his theory. As I have argued, it is not introduced to provide a basis for political obligation, but as a test for the legitimacy of legislation. If this status is kept in mind, it does not conflict with the moral obligation to quit the state of nature, since both ideas have their deeper origin in Kant's notion of practical reason and autonomy. While Kant no longer bases the grounds of political legitimacy on an actual agreement, the test for valid legislation remains the (now counterfactual) ideal of that to which free and equal moral persons could agree.

Second, in view of their obvious similarity, there is the question of the systematic relationship between the idea of the social contract and what Kant calls "the transcendental principle of public right": "All actions affecting the rights of other human beings are wrong if their maxim is not compatible with their being made public."[108] My suggestion is that the principle of publicity is, so to speak, the citizens' counterpart to what is, strictly speaking, a standard or criterion for the legislator. This interpretation is suggested by Kant's example of taxation: Whereas the legislator, before introducing a war tax, is to ask himself if all citizens could agree to it (e.g., the idea of the social contract), citizens may appeal to a principle of publicity in voicing their opposition to a proposed tax.[109] Both notions refer back to the idea of the general will or united agreement, but whereas the former is primarily intended as a test for the legislator, the latter points to the public sphere as a realm of discussion and debate among reasoning citizens.[110]

Kant's idiosyncratic use of the notion of "public reason" in "What is Enlightenment?" should also be mentioned at this point.[111] In contrast to the more customary usage, it does not refer to the institutions of government and its civil servants, but to a civil and political sphere of public expression and debate among private citizens. The public use of reason thus stands over against the state and, for Kant, is the most important instrument for its criticism and gradual reform.

Finally, several commentators have pointed to a possible conflict between Kant's idea of the social contract and his rejection of a right to rebellion.[112] Despite his sympathy for the ideals embodied in the French Revolution, Kant rejected the view that a people had coercive rights against the monarch for at least two reasons: First, he suggests that a constitution

would be in contradiction with itself if it included a right to its own abnega-
tion; and second, a right to revolt would violate the principle of publicity.[113]
But, as Beck points out, both of these arguments rely on an excessive literal-
ism and formalism. Furthermore, Kant is only partially able to mitigate this
tension in his appeal to a teleological conception of history: What individual
citizens are not entitled to do (i.e., revolt), "nature" will inevitably bring
about of its own accord if the monarch fails to heed its call.[114] This response,
which is one of the clearest instances of Kant's two-world metaphysics influencing his substantive political views, will no doubt be unsatisfactory to
those with a different assessment of the natural course of social history. It is
at least arguable, for example, whether the development of the market and
foreign trade has produced such political reforms that citizens are deprived
of any higher "appeal to heaven" (to borrow Locke's euphemism).[115] Despite
Kant's claim that what we can practically assume nature will produce must
remain secondary and subsidiary to what morality requires, his teleological
conception of history had an effect upon his normative political theory.

IV. CONCLUSION: PROBLEMS AND PROSPECTS

This reconstruction of Kant's theory of justice has sought to establish a
number of points. First, it has suggested that the so-called Copernican Revolution in Kant's practical philosophy implies a rejection of the attempt to find a
normative ground for the justification or criticism of political institutions in
anything other than a concept of practical reason or conception of the person
as a free and equal moral being. The attempt to construct principles of justice
on the basis of such a conception of practical reason also marks the beginning
of a more egalitarian liberalism than that found among his predecessors and
stands in contrast to a natural right theory (such as Locke's) and attempts to
ground principles of justice in a notion of rational self-interest (such as
Hobbes's). Moreover, I argued that Kant's theory of property rights and the
idea of the social contract also have their roots in a notion of practical reason
and thus are not in such strong opposition to one another as is sometimes supposed. Kant's rejection of Locke's labor theory indicates his view that a specific set of property rights is legitimate only if it could receive the united
agreement of all in a social contract. Finally, I have noted the basis of Kant's
distinction between the right (or justice) and the good. Justice, in its most general sense, refers to what all can claim a right to on the basis of a conception of
themselves as free and equal moral beings. Within the limits of justice, however, Kant affirms a diverse plurality of conceptions of the good life.

On the other hand, in the course of this reconstruction I have also indicated a number of difficulties in Kant's theory, many of which can be traced back to his two-world doctrine. By way of a conclusion I would like to formulate some of these problems more specifically so that they can serve as a framework for approaching the ideas of Rawls and Habermas in the subsequent chapters.

First, the novelty of Kant's theory of justice—the attempt to ground principles of justice in a noninstrumental conception of practical reason—also seems to be its nemesis. As we saw, Kant's notion of autonomy or positive freedom presupposes the two-world thesis and concept of transcendental freedom (e.g., a spontaneous or uncaused action). Only if the moral agent is a citizen of two worlds, a noumenal and a phenomenal self, is he or she capable of autonomous action. However, the strong opposition Kant thereby establishes between the noumenal and phenomenal self generates a number of paradoxes in his political theory. Kant repeats Rousseau's juxtaposition of the general will to the will of the majority in his own distinction between *Wille* and *Willkür* and in his distinction between the united *a priori* agreement of all and the empirical will of the people. This opposition is at least partially responsible for Kant's belief that the monarch can legislate against the actual will of the people and that a constitutional monarchy represents a better form of government than a democracy. Similarly, the notion of a noumenal self provides the basis for Kant's distinction between the right and the good. It does so, however, in a way that coordinates this distinction with a strict separation between the public and the private sphere on the basis of specific "negative" rights and liberties. If one wishes to preserve something of Kant's notion of a noninstrumental conception of practical reason as a normative ground for principles of justice, the question that needs to be addressed is how the distinction between the public and the private sphere is to be made once Kant's metaphysical assumptions have been abandoned.

A second set of problems centers around Kant's opposition of practical reason to history, while at the same time embracing a teleological conception of the latter. Kant held the paradoxical view that the "highest political good" (an international federation of states) is both a command of pure practical reason *and* the inevitable product of natural forces. I have attempted to show that, if it expresses more than a debatable optimism about the "natural" course of social events, this view threatens the distinctiveness of the attempt to ground principles of justice in a notion of practical reason. That is, if the political order Kant envisions is one that could equally well be based upon calculations of rational self-interest guided by the "mechanisms of nature," the distinctiveness of the moral requirements that issue from a concept of practical reason is diminished, and Kant's vision of a just society could equally be realized by a "race of devils." Further, the teleological conception at work in his philosophy of history contributes to Kant's paradoxical views about revolution and to the peculiar status of property rights in his social contract theory. The provisional right to private ownership lies suspended between the idea of an original common ownership and a future condition of perpetual peace when this right is finally made peremptory. This "permissive law" enabling some to hinder the freedom of others without their (actual) agreement thus implicitly relies upon a teleological conception of history. (It, of course, also implicitly assumes the distinction between the noumenal and phenomenal self.) Although I have argued that Kant's theory of property rights marks an advance over his predecessors, the nature or form of property rights never actually becomes subject to public debate and agreement. In this sense, Kant's views contrast sharply with those of Rawls and Habermas.

Finally, the justification of Kant's conception of practical reason ultimately relies upon the problematic notion of a "Fact of Reason." This notion has been criticized for failing to take seriously the historical genesis and evolution of our moral concepts, as well as for failing to provide a justification that is convincing to at least a moderate skeptic. The attempt to preserve some form of a Kantian conception of practical reason must therefore address the problem of justification anew. In subsequent chapters I will explore this problem by examining Rawls's notion of reflective equilibrium and Habermas's attempt to derive the basic principle of a discourse ethics from an analysis of the pragmatic presuppositions of speech and argumentation.

2

JUSTICE AS FAIRNESS: RAWLS'S KANTIAN INTERPRETATION

I. INTRODUCTION

Much of the recent discussion of Rawls's theory of justice has revolved around the question of its Kantian roots.[1] Critics have charged both that it is too Kantian and that it is not Kantian enough. Moreover, in the essays since *A Theory of Justice,* Rawls has emphasized certain Kantian aspects of his theory, while at the same time retreating from others.[2] The purpose of this chapter is to clarify some of the issues in this debate and, hopefully, to strengthen a possible Kantian interpretation of Rawls's theory.

Critics who charge that Rawls's theory is not Kantian enough argue that his attempt to develop a nonmetaphysical or de-transcendentalized interpretation of Kant's practical philosophy runs aground at several points: In describing the initial choice situation (or the original position) as one based upon the parties' rational desire for the greatest amount of primary social goods rather than with reference to the notion of pure practical reason, the objection goes, Rawls admits a dimension of heteronomy excluded by Kant.[3] Further, the notion of primary goods itself relies upon various empirical features of human psychology and thus the Kantian claim to necessity and universality for the principles, of justice must be relinquished.[4] As a result, the principles of justice chosen in the original position have merely a hypothetical (as opposed to categorical) status and, as such, they are unsuitable as moral principles that obligate unconditionally.[5] The underlying assumption in all of these criticisms is that Rawls operates with a more narrow (or instrumental) conception of rationality and thus cannot possibly arrive at the more normative conclusions entailed by Kant's notion of pure practical reason.

Critics who charge that Rawls's theory is too Kantian also focus on the notion of practical reason. However, their criticisms move in the opposite

49

direction, that is, they claim that Rawls's attempt to ground substantive principles of justice in a notion of practical reason leads to an abstract and empty formalism. Michael Sandel, for example, describes Rawls's project as "deontology with a Humean face," and Bernard Williams and Charles Taylor both argue that Rawls's Kantian notion of practical reason distorts the characterization of the moral domain.[6] In general, these critics claim that Rawls's Kantianism makes him susceptible to many of the same objections that Hegel raised against Kant.

Both sets of criticisms, then, focus particularly upon Rawls's attempt to develop a nonmetaphysical interpretation of Kant's notion of practical reason or autonomy, that is, one that does not depend upon his two-world metaphysics. It is therefore not surprising that many of Rawls's essays since *A Theory of Justice* have also been devoted to clarifying the Kantian aspects of his theory and, in particular, to the status and function of his model-conception of the person (or moral agency). Rawls has been faced with the difficult task of defending a Kantian interpretation of his theory on two fronts: on the one hand, he has had to argue that his theory does not represent the attempt to ground substantive normative principles in a neutral or instrumental conception of rationality, and that the Kantian ideal of autonomy is adequately represented in his theory. On the other hand, he has also had to argue that his Kantian interpretation can be sustained against the recent wave of neo-Hegelian and neo-Aristotelian objections.[7] This has primarily involved clarifying his own distinction between the right and the good (or questions of justice and questions of the good life) and attempting to develop a conception of the person (or moral agency) that is not unduly individualistic or abstract ("disembodied"), but that nonetheless provides a nonsectarian basis for developing principles of justice.

I believe that Rawls has been at best only partially successful in this task, and this conviction is reflected in my own attempt to both strengthen and modify his project in connection with the work of Habermas. On the other hand, as I shall argue, many of the criticisms directed against Rawls have either misunderstood or misinterpreted his arguments (by confusing, for example, the important distinction between his model-conception of the person and his description of the parties in the original position) or abandoned important features of his Kantian interpretation that ought to be retained (for example, the distinction between the right and the good, or his effort to develop a notion of constructivism as an alternative to utilitarianism). I will develop some of my own criticisms of his conception of the person (or notion of autonomy) in chapter 4, after introducing Habermas's model of discourse ethics. In this chapter my aim is more constructive: to provide a systematic interpretation of *A Theory of Justice* that defends the Kantian interpretation. In attempting this, I will also draw upon his more recent essays where the Kantian roots of his theory have become more explicit. I will first try to clarify the structure of Rawls's argument in order to show why many criticisms have been misdirected or based on a misunderstanding (section II); then I will draw attention to some of the specific (and desirable) Kantian aspects of Rawls's theory (section III); and finally, I offer an interpretation and criticism of Rawls's notion of reflective equilibrium as a method of justification in moral theory (section IV).

II. THE ORIGINAL POSITION AS A "PROCEDURAL REPRESENTATION" OF THE CATEGORICAL IMPERATIVE

Rawls suggests that his theory of justice can be usefully divided into two main parts: "(1) an interpretation of the initial situation and the problem of choice posed there, and (2) a set of principles which, it is argued, would be agreed to" (*TJ*, 15, 54). The task of the first part is the description and defense of what he calls the "original position" as the "philosophically favored" interpretation of the initial choice situation (*TJ*, 122); the task of the second part is an elaboration and defense of the two principles of justice that Rawls believes would be chosen (from a limited set of possibilities) by the parties in the original position. Rawls also suggests that someone might accept the first part of the theory but reject the second, or vice versa (*TJ*, 15). This scenario is extremely unlikely, however, since Rawls also claims that the original position is defined so as to insure that his own two principles of justice will be chosen (*TJ*, 121). At most, one might generally accept the contractualist strategy of the first part, but then argue that the situation of initial choice should be characterized differently than Rawls has characterized it.[8] I mention this distinction here because it closely parallels one that I will introduce later between a principle or procedure of legitimation (for example, Rawls's original position or Habermas's ideal speech situation) and substantive proposals for principles of social justice (for example, Rawls's two principles or Marx's "to each according to his need"). Unfortunately, however, Rawls is unable to insist too strongly upon such a distinction since he designs the original position in such a way that only his two substantive principles of justice would be chosen in it.

This observation immediately leads to an important question concerning the status of the original position in Rawls's theory. If it is introduced to provide a neutral justification, based on a relatively uncontroversial notion of rational choice—the one found in game or decision theory—then it seems to be caught between two horns of a dilemma: If the description of the original position is really neutral and based only upon a narrow conception of rationality, then it will not be able to yield the substantive principles Rawls claims. If, on the other hand, it does yield substantive principles, then it must have stronger normative assumptions already built into it.[9] However, as I will attempt to show, this objection misunderstands the status and function of the original position. Rawls does not introduce it to provide a neutral or independent justification of substantive moral principles, but rather to serve as a device that represents to us certain moral ideals that we already accept, or at least would accept after due reflection (*TJ*, 21). On this interpretation, an analogy can be drawn between the Moral Law and the various formulations of the categorical imperative in Kant, and the relation between certain moral ideals (the model-conception of the person, for example) and the description of the original position in Rawls. Kant refers to the various formulations of the categorical imperative as attempts to bring the Moral Law "nearer to intuition" (*GMS*, 103). The justification of the Moral Law, however, is provided by the "Fact of Reason," even if the application of the categorical imperative to our maxims helps to make this Fact more vivid to us. Similarly, for Rawls the original position is a "procedural representation" of Kant's notion of autonomy (and the categorical imperative) (*TJ*, 256); but its justification (and hence the justification of the two principles) depends upon whether it adequately represents our "considered moral judgments," as these are established in a process of "reflective equilibrium" (see section IV, below).

Rawls's description of the original position as a "procedural representation" of the categorical imperative and Kant's notion of autonomy brings us back to the first set of criticisms mentioned above. Rawls claims that the principles chosen in the original position are ones that express an individual's full autonomy or ones that reflect Kant's conception of the person as a free and equal member of a Kingdom of Ends: "The description of the original position interprets the point of view of noumenal selves, of what it means to be a free and equal rational being" (*TJ*, 255–56). However, these claims do not seem to hold up when one examines the particular features of the original position. For example, the parties in the original position are "not bound by moral ties to each other" (*TJ*, 128). Rather, they are described as mutually disinterested calculators whose sole interest is to secure the greatest amount of primary goods possible for themselves (*TJ*, 144). Further, they are deprived of any particular conception of the good. A "veil of ignorance" is imposed that denies them much of what is often regarded as morally relevant information (such as their personal commitments, familial and religious ties, and the like) (*TJ*, 136f). In short, the original position is designed to be a situation of rational choice under conditions of uncertainty and, in a description reminiscent of Kant's own "race of devils" passage in "Perpetual Peace," Rawls states that the principles chosen there are "those a person would choose for the design of a society in which his enemy is to assign him his place" (*TJ*, 152). Surely, this is a long way from Kant's notion of principles of justice whose validity is found in the idea of pure practical reason! This description substitutes principles of heteronomy—principles based on a set of desires and empirical assumptions—for Kant's principle of autonomy. It is thus difficult to see how principles chosen in such a situation could be said to bind categorically.

A proper response to these considerations requires a closer look at the arguments Rawls offers for including the various features in the construction of the original position. Again, whether or not Rawls's arguments are ultimately convincing, I think it can be shown that at least some, if not most, of these criticisms are misdirected. They result primarily from a confusion of the description of the parties in the original position with Rawls's description of fully autonomous citizens in the well-ordered society. As Rawls has more recently stated: "The intent of justice as fairness is badly misunderstood if the deliberations of the parties and their rational autonomy are confused with full autonomy. Full autonomy is a moral ideal and part of the more comprehensive ideal of a well-ordered society. Rational autonomy (which characterizes the parties in the original position) is not, as such, an ideal at all, but a device of representation used to connect the conception of the person with definite principles of justice" (*KC*, 533–4). The parties in the original position are not free and equal moral persons; they do not alone represent Kant's notion of the noumenal self. Rather, Rawls's claim is that the principles chosen from the original position are equivalent to principles that would be chosen by autonomous citizens in Kant's Kingdom of Ends. And this is because the original position *taken as a whole*—not just the description of the rationality of the parties—represents, in a procedural device, Kant's notion of autonomy.

This interpretation of the status of the original position becomes clearer for the first time in Rawls's Dewey Lectures, "Kantian Constructivism in Moral Theory," where he explicitly discusses the crucial distinction between the "three points of view" in *A Theory of Justice*: "that of the parties in the original position; that of citizens in a well-ordered society; and, finally, that of ourselves—you and me who are examining justice as fairness as a basis for a conception of justice that may yield a suitable understanding of freedom and equality" (*KC*, 533; see Figure 2-1). The first two points of view occur within the theory of justice itself: on the one hand, there is the ideal of the well-ordered society and, as part of this ideal, the model-conception of the person as a free and equal moral being; on the other hand, there is what Rawls calls the "mediating conception" of the original position: it is a "device of representation" that mediates between the ideals contained in the description of the well-ordered society and the definition of the principles of justice. Roughly stated, for the characterization of the original position we look primarily to the ideal of the well-ordered society; at the same time, it

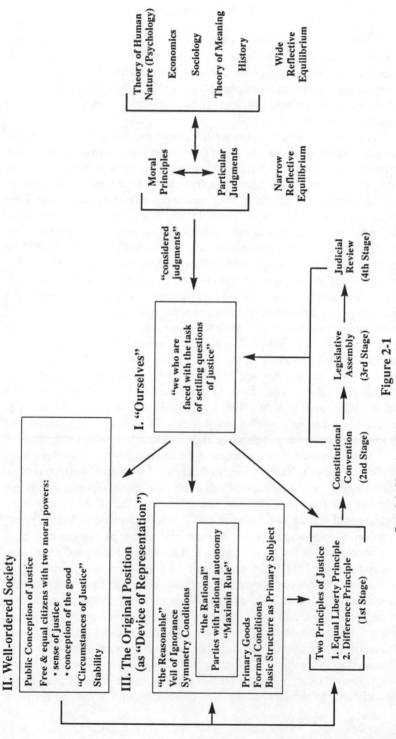

I. "Ourselves"

"we who are faced with the task of settling questions of justice"

Judicial Review (4th Stage)

Legislative Assembly (3rd Stage)

Constitutional Convention (2nd Stage)

"considered judgments"

Moral Principles ↔ Particular Judgments

Narrow Reflective Equilibrium

Theory of Human Nature (Psychology)
Economics
Sociology
Theory of Meaning
History

Wide Reflective Equilibrium

II. Well-ordered Society

Public Conception of Justice

Free & equal citizens with two moral powers:
• sense of justice
• conception of the good

"Circumstances of Justice"

Stability

III. The Original Position (as "Device of Representation")

"the Reasonable"
Veil of Ignorance
Symmetry Conditions

"the Rational"
Parties with rational autonomy
"Maximin Rule"

Primary Goods
Formal Conditions
Basic Structure as Primary Subject

Two Principles of Justice
1. Equal Liberty Principle
2. Difference Principle
(1st Stage)

Figure 2-1

Rawls's Kantian Constructivism and the Three Points of View

helps to make vivid to us why the ideals contained in the well-ordered society, when combined in a suitable way, yield the two principles of justice. Finally, there is the position of ourselves who have the task of finding principles of justice for our society (KC, 518, 533). To anticipate a bit, the description of the well-ordered society (together with its model-conception of the person) and the characterization of the original position, as well as the specific principles of justice, must all correspond to "our considered judgments upon due reflection," that is, they must all agree with those judgments at which we would arrive as a result of carrying out the process of reflective equilibrium. The entire procedure is constructivist or nonfoundationalist in that it does not accept any intuitions as indubitable and does not begin with the assumption that there are first principles in moral theory. Rather, the principles of justice are the result of a process of construction: first, from the point of view of ourselves to the clarification of the ideals in the well-ordered society; then from these ideals to the construction of the original position as the "philosophically favored" situation of initial choice; and, lastly, from the deliberation of the parties in the original position to the selection of the two principles themselves. Finally, each of these "points of view" can serve as a corrective to considerations and features introduced in the other; no one perspective is taken as fixed or absolute, although, at the end, the results must be acceptable to us as citizens faced with the task of finding principles of justice.[10] For the moment, I will leave aside the position of ourselves and the notion of reflective equilibrium. I will begin instead with Rawls's model-conceptions of the well-ordered society and the person, note how they reflect Kant's notion of autonomy, and show how these are used to construct the original position. This should hopefully make clear why the original position may be described as a procedural representation of the categorical imperative and why it should not be viewed simply as an attempt to ground substantive principles in a neutral theory of rational choice.

Rawls cites four distinct features that combine to make up the model-conception of the well-ordered society as a self-sufficient system of social cooperation for mutual advantage.[11] First, a well-ordered society is one that is "effectively regulated by a public conception of justice" (TJ, 453; KC, 537). This means (a) that each citizen accepts, and knows that others accept, the same conception of justice (whatever it turns out to be); (b) that the basic institutions of the society satisfy this conception of justice and are with good reason believed by everyone to satisfy it; and (c) that this public conception of justice is based upon reasonable beliefs established by widely accepted methods of inquiry (i.e., it does not presuppose controversial metaphysical or religious doctrines) (TJ, 454; KC, 537). Thus, this feature of the well-ordered society excludes conceptions of justice that cannot be publicly affirmed or that rely upon ideological deception (such as Plato's Noble Lie) or controversial worldviews for their maintenance. It closely resembles Kant's "transcendental principle of publicity" discussed in the previous chapter.

Second, the citizens in a well-ordered society are, and recognize themselves as being, free and equal moral persons (*TJ*, 505; *KC*, 525). Rawls calls this feature the "model-conception of the person." Although it is found in *A Theory of Justice,* there is no doubt that it has become more prominent in his later writings, especially to counter those interpretations that view the earlier work as an attempt to ground principles of justice in a neutral conception of rational choice.[12] Since this model-conception is so central to my own interpretation of Rawls, I will discuss it in some detail.

(a) The citizens in the well-ordered society are characterized as having *"two highest order moral powers"*: the capacity for a sense of justice, that is, "the capacity to understand, to apply, and to act from (and not merely in accordance with) the principles of justice"; and "the capacity to form, to revise, and rationally to pursue a conception of the good" (*KC*, 525; *TJ*, 505). In ascribing the first moral power to citizens in the well-ordered society, it is assumed that whatever the appropriate conception of justice turns out to be, citizens are capable of being effectively motivated by it. The requirement that the principles of justice be ones that are stable also appeals to this capacity: their public affirmation must be capable of reproducing and sustaining this capacity among citizens. The second moral power suggests that citizens have their own conceptions of the good that motivate them and give them a sense of purpose or worth in life. However, they are not viewed as being permanently attached to any one conception of the good; rather, citizens are free to change their ends and ideals at various points during the course of their lives, and the recognition of this capacity to revise their conception of the good is an important feature of their characterization as moral persons.

(b) The citizens are *equal* in that "they each have, and view themselves as having, a right to equal respect and consideration in determining the principles by which the basic arrangements of their society are to be regulated."[13] This notion of the equality of citizens in determining the principles of justice is more fundamental than (and the basis for) the ideals of equality that are institutionalized in the basic structure of society (e.g., formal equality before the law, equality of opportunity with respect to powers and offices defined by the social structure, etc.). It is based on their common status as moral beings.

(c) Citizens in the well-ordered society are *free* and recognize each others' freedom, in several respects. First, each is viewed as having the capacity to form, revise, and pursue a conception of the good (*TJ*, 505; *KC*, 544). This repeats the second moral power noted above. It also reflects Rawls's liberal commitment to a plurality of conceptions of the good and his belief that principles of justice should not rely upon any particular conception of the good, but upon a conception of the person (as a free and equal moral being). Thus, it also reflects Kant's attempt to distinguish between the moral agent and the ends to which she might be attached at any given time. Second, citizens are free in that they are, and recognize one another as being, "self-originating sources of valid claims" (*KC,* 543). This follows directly from the view that there is a plurality of conceptions of the good, all of which are permissible so long as they are pursued within the limits of justice. Finally, citizens are free in that they recognize one another as being responsible for their ends or conceptions of the good. Persons are not merely the subjective bearers of preferences that, so to speak, assail them from without. This implies, among other things, that a utility function defined solely according to the strength or intensity of preferences or desires does not provide an acceptable criterion for the interpersonal comparison of levels of well-being, since it does not consider the way in which persons have come to have those preferences.[14]

The third and fourth features of the model-conception of the well-ordered society primarily refer to the background conditions and arrangement of its institutions. Rawls assumes that even in a well-ordered society the "circumstances of justice" will obtain (*TJ,* 126; *KC,* 525).[15] Following Hume, he notes both a subjective and objective side to these: while the well-ordered society does not imply a zero-sum game, moderate scarcity exists in the sense that it cannot be assumed there are enough natural and social resources to satisfy all legitimate demands. This is partly due to the subjective circumstance that in a well-ordered society there will still be a plurality of conflicting conceptions of the good within the limits of justice. Thus, unlike Marx's "association of free producers," the well-ordered society is not a society "beyond justice." To make such an assumption, Marx had to presuppose either the capacity of science and technology to renew infinitely the sources of social wealth (on a more scientistic reading of his texts) or that in a fully communist society citizens share a comprehensive and unified conception of the good, thereby eliminating the source of conflicting claims (on a more Aristotelian or Hegelian interpretation). Finally, a well-ordered society is said to be stable with respect to its conception of justice (*TJ,* 454; *KC,* 522). "This means that, viewing the society as an ongoing concern, its members acquire as they grow up a sufficiently strong and effective sense of justice, one that usually overcomes the temptations and stresses of social life."[16]

In "Kantian Constructivism," Rawls suggests that these four features of the well-ordered society can be united under "the Reasonable" and "the Rational" terms of social cooperation. (These two notions correspond closely to Kant's distinction between *Vernunft* and *Verstand.*) Social cooperation is Reasonable since it incorporates the ideals of mutuality and reciprocity (*KC,* 528): All who cooperate reasonably share in the benefits and burdens as established by principles agreed to from an appropriate perspective, namely, the perspective of citizens regarded as free and equal moral persons. The notion of the Reasonable is also connected to the notion of a citizen as fully autonomous, that is, as having the capacity to act from a sense of justice, and his right to equal consideration in determining principles for the regulation of the basic structure. The terms of social cooperation are "Rational" since they allow for "each participant's rational advantage, what, as individuals, they are trying to advance" (*KC*, 528). This is reflected in the person's highest-order moral power, the capacity to form, revise and pursue a conception of the good, as well as the commitment to a plurality of such conceptions within the limits of justice. In a rather elegant passage, Rawls clarifies the relationship between the Reasonable and the Rational in a well-ordered society:

> The Reasonable presupposes and subordinates the Rational. It defines the fair terms of cooperation acceptable to all within some group of separately identifiable persons, each of whom possesses and can exercise the two moral powers. All have a conception of their good which defines their rational advantage, and everyone has a normally effective sense of justice; a capacity to honor the fair terms of cooperation. The Reasonable presupposes the Rational, because, without conceptions of the good that move members of the group, there is no point to social cooperation nor to notions of right and justice, even though such cooperation realizes values that go beyond what conceptions of the good specify taken alone. The Reasonable subordinates the Rational because its principles limit, and in a Kantian doctrine limit absolutely, the final ends that can be pursued. (*KC*, 530)

We are now in a position to consider how these features of the well-ordered society are represented in the original position. Recall that the idea is to make these features more plausible or intuitive so that their relation to the two principles of justice can be more easily seen. It is in this sense that the original position is a "mediating conception" and a "device of representation." I will begin with a brief summary of the aspects of the original position (see Figure 2–1). These can be roughly broken down into two groups: those that represent "the Reasonable" features of the well-ordered society (the formal constraints imposed on the principles of justice; the veil of ignorance; the symmetry of the parties; the list of primary goods; and the designation of the basic structure as the primary subject of justice) and those that represent "the Rational" features of the well-ordered society (primarily the rationality of the parties and the fact that they seek for themselves the greatest amount of primary goods possible). However, this grouping is not hard and fast, and the various features of the well-ordered society are represented in the original position in numerous ways.

(1) Rawls introduces five formal constraints or conditions to which any

acceptable conception of justice must conform. Although I do not believe he can be right about this (see below), he suggests that they are "suitably weak" and perhaps exclude only various forms of egoism (*TJ*, 131). These constraints must apply to any principles of justice chosen by the parties in the original position. They include the condition of generality ("it must be possible to formulate them without the use of what would be intuitively recognized as proper names, or rigid definite descriptions" [*TJ*, 131]); the condition of universality ("they must hold for everyone in virtue of their being moral persons" [*TJ*, 132]); the condition of publicity (the principles are to serve as a public conception of justice which everyone could acknowledge as if it were the result of an agreement); a principle of ordering of conflicting claims (*TJ*, 134); and the condition of finality—"The parties are to assess the system of principles as the final court of appeal in practical reasoning. There are no higher standards to which arguments in support of claims can be addressed; reasoning successfully from these principles is conclusive" (*TJ*, 135). The idea is that the introduction of each of these constraints upon principles chosen in the original position is itself to be argued for in terms of the various features of the well-ordered society (in view of our considered judgments in reflective equilibrium). Thus, the conditions of generality and publicity each represent aspects of the criterion of publicity operative in the well-ordered society. Similarly, the conditions of universality and finality represent aspects of the model-conception of the person—for example, the condition of finality reflects the view of the person as autonomous and a self-originating source of valid claims. There is no further appeal to religious or metaphysical doctrines and, assuming that we accept the constraints imposed on the original position as a representation of this model-conception, we cannot ask to vote again because we are not satisfied with the outcome (*TJ*, 135).

(2) The introduction of the "veil of ignorance" is also argued for by reference to features of the well-ordered society. By excluding morally irrelevant information from the initial choice situation, it is intended to insure that the principles chosen reflect the conception of ourselves as free and equal moral beings (*TJ*, 252; *KC*, 523). Further, by permitting only general facts about human society, it is intended to represent the fact that the principles are to serve as a public conception of justice, for example, that they are based upon reasonable beliefs established through widely accepted methods of inquiry. "The parties are not to be influenced by any particular information that is not part of their representation as free and equal moral persons with a determinate (but unknown) conception of the good, unless this information is necessasry for a rational agreement to be reached" (*KC*, 549). This distinction between the two tasks of the veil of ignorance—excluding morally irrelevant information and permitting only enough information to insure a rational choice—is the basis for Rawls's distinction between the "thin" and

the "thick" veils of ignorance.[17] Although the motive for their introduction is clear and, I believe, relatively unobjectionable, other aspects of this strategy are not. Most importantly, there is the question of who decides what is suitably general or morally irrelevant information.[18] Two replies are open to Rawls: He could argue that "we" who must find principles of justice for the basic structure must decide among ourselves, in a suitable manner, what is general and what is morally irrelevant information. On this interpretation the information provided to the parties in the original position might vary from society to society and, in turn, affect the choice of the principles. This would move the notion of the original position more in the direction of Habermas's notion of discourse, where it is left up to the participants themselves to determine what interests are generalizable. The other interpretation—the one, I think, that is closer to Rawls's position in *A Theory of Justice*—is that deciding what information should be given to the parties is relatively uncontroversial and can be done by the philosopher alone.

(3) It is much easier to account for the symmetry of the parties in the original position since this follows from the description of the citizens in the well-ordered society as equal moral beings. "We simply describe all the parties in the same way and situate them equally, that is, symmetrically with respect to one another. Everyone has the same rights and powers in the procedure for reaching agreement. Now it is essential to justice as fairness that the original position be fair between equal moral persons so that this fairness can transfer to the principles adopted" (*KC*, 550). The reason for the symmetry of the parties is thus also tied to Rawls's notion of pure procedural justice.

(4) The rationality of the parties, on the other hand, refers back to the Rational aspect of the well-ordered society, that is, the capacity of the person to form, revise, and pursue a conception of the good. However, the rationality Rawls attributes to the parties in the original position is the notion of rational choice found in game or decision theory. The parties are simply trying to advance their own conception of the good (whatever it happens to be) and they do this by trying to secure for themselves the greatest amount of primary goods possible. Given certain other features of the original position (notably, the veil of ignorance), Rawls argues that the "maximin rule" is the most reasonable rule of choice for the parties to employ (*TJ*, 154): Since the parties have no knowledge of what their social position will be once the veil of ignorance is lifted and since, given the list from which they must choose, there is reason for them to believe that the worst outcome is not so bad and the best is not so much better, it is reasonable for them to choose that principle or set of principles in which they will fare best if they turn out to be in the position of the worst off.[19] However, it should also be clear from this brief review that the rational autonomy of the parties is not the same as the

full autonomy of the citizens in the well-ordered society. Rather, the parties represent only limited aspects of the model-conception outlined above.

(5), (6) I will discuss the notion of primary social goods and the basic structure as the primary subject of justice in more detail at a later point. I mention them here simply to note that they too are argued for by reference to the features of the well-ordered society. The primary social goods are described as "necessary conditions for realising the powers of moral personality"; and the basic structure is specified as the subject of justice because in so doing it insures that each citizen is accorded equal concern and respect as a moral person.

This brief review of the features of the original position should indicate how they are related to the model-conception of the well-ordered society. It is undisputed that the original position presupposes a conception of the person. However, the model-conception that it presupposes cannot be directly read from the description of the rationality of the parties. It is not their capacity for rational deliberation alone, but rather the entire set of features built into the original position, that is intended to provide a "procedural representation" of Kant's notion of moral autonomy and noumenal selves. This reconstruction of Rawls's strategy should also indicate that the real burden of justification rests with the notion of reflective equilibrium, as this is appealed to in arguing for the ideals contained in the well-ordered society. This is the topic of the final section. First, however, I want to review briefly some of the other Kantian aspects of Rawls's theory.

III. OTHER KANTIAN ASPECTS OF
RAWLS'S THEORY OF JUSTICE

In addition to the model-conception of the person and the description of the original position as a procedural representation of the categorical imperative, there are other specific features of Rawls's theory that warrant its comparison with Kant. I will sketch several of these here in order to strengthen the claim that Rawls's theory belongs to a distinctively Kantian tradition in liberal political theory.

A. The Basic Structure as the Subject of Justice

One of the unique features of *A Theory of Justice* is that it treats the basic structure as the primary subject of justice (*TJ*, 7; *BS*). However, the importance of this for distinguishing Rawls's theory from others within the contract tradition has not been widely noticed.[20] The deeper intuition behind this idea is that our notions of what justice is may vary according to the subject matter to which the notions apply. Thus, our sense of what it means to deal justly with others in personal relations may be different from our notion of justice when it applies to basic social institutions. For this reason it is important to be clear about the appropriate subject of justice, and to offer reasons why one subject is preferred over another. Although Kant did not state that the proper subject of justice is the basic social structure, in drawing attention to the unique status of the original social contract he was aware that the principles arising from it are of a different nature than those intended to regulate private transactions between individuals (e.g., that contracts be voluntary and nonfraudulent). To this extent, I believe that Rawls's focus on the basic structure can be considered Kantian. A further Kantian element is reflected in Rawls's rejection of natural rights. The basic structure defines the rights and duties of individuals. Apart from the basic right to equal concern and respect as free and equal moral persons, as arrived at in the process of reflective equilibrium, there are no individual "natural" rights.[21] In this section I will consider Rawls's definition of the basic structure and some of the advantages in taking it as the primary subject of justice. (In chapter 5, section III, I will offer several criticisms of it.)

Rawls defines the basic structure as "the way in which major social institutions fit together into one system, and how they assign fundamental rights and duties and shape the division of advantages that arises through social cooperation" (*BS*, 47). Not all institutions within a society belong to the basic structure, but (apparently) only those that have a significant influence upon the life expectations of its (representative) members. Private clubs and associations, for example, do not belong to the basic structure (and thus the principles of justice chosen in the original position do not apply to them). Further, the principles of justice do not apply to each institution individually but to the way that they fit together into one scheme. Only in view of this restriction can one see, for example, why Rawls does not apply the Difference Principle to the nuclear family (see *TJ*, 511). Presumably, inequalities in life expectations that arise from it are corrected for in other ways (educational opportunities, tax policies, etc.). This, too, suggests that there is a wide degree of flexibility in deciding how the principles of justice chosen in the original position can best be applied to any particular basic structure.

Among the social institutions included in the basic structure, Rawls lists the following: The political constitution (*TJ*, 7, 304–9), the nuclear family (*TJ*, 7, 300, 511), the competitive market (*TJ*, 7, 304–9), an autonomous legal system—"the rule of law" (*TJ*, 235), and an interventionist welfare state (*TJ*, 275). Obviously, this list is greatly influenced by historical tradition, and there seems to be no clear criterion for determining what institutions should be included within it. Why, for example, should the family be included and religious institutions and other voluntary associations excluded? In chapter 5 I will argue that nonstate institutions of the public sphere also constitute a conspicuous omission. Rawls's rule of thumb seems to be that only those institutions that exercise significant influence over the life expectations of representative members within a society are to be included (*TJ*, 259), but it can always be disputed what social institutions this rule will single out. A further difficulty (to which I will also return in chapter 5) arises from Rawls's division of the basic structure into two fundamental parts, roughly corresponding to the traditional distinction between the public (state) and private (market) sphere. (He then argues that each of the two principles of justice primarily apply to one part: the Equal Liberty Principle to the public sphere and the Difference Principle to the private sphere.)

However, despite some of the difficulties in deciding which institutions belong to the basic structure, there are several advantages in regarding it as the primary subject of justice. First, if we begin with the more traditional idea that justice refers to transactions between individuals (e.g., they must be voluntary and without fraud), we are immediately confronted with the task of determining what social background conditions must be obtained for these transactions to be fair. Further, even if a series of transactions between consenting adults is fair, there is no guarantee that its resulting affect upon the social system over a period of time will maintain fair background conditions. In both cases we must look beyond the transactions themselves to the social institutions of the basic structure.[22] Only if these are regulated by appropriate principles of justice is the system as a whole just or fair.

Second, Rawls claims that by treating the basic structure as the primary subject of justice the "social nature of persons"—that is, the extent to which who we are is shaped by social and historical factors over which individually we have no control—is taken more seriously (*BS*, 55f.). This claim and Rawls's related claim that the distribution of natural talents and abilities is to be regarded as a "common asset" (*TJ*, 101, 179) has led to a number of misunderstandings that need to be rectified. The point is not that Rawls views the person as an "essentially unencumbered subject of possession" (Sandel), but that there is no way to distinguish between what individuals, on the basis of their natural talents and abilities, can acquire within society and what they might have acquired outside society, say, in a state of nature (*BS*, 61).[23] An individual's talents and abilities acquire whatever value they have only within a specific system of social cooperation. Further, since these talents and abilities are the result of natural contingencies, they would seem to have no moral relevance in settling questions of social justice (see chapter 4, section II, for further discussion of this point). It is on the basis of considerations such as these that Rawls believes we should take the basic structure as the subject of justice. These institutions "shape the division of advantages that arises through social cooperation," and thus it is for these institutions that we must find the appropriate principles of justice. The distribution of natural abilities are considered a "common asset" in the following sense: it is reasonable that the benefits resulting from them be regulated according to principles of justice that all could agree to when viewed from an appropriate perspective, namely, from the perspective of citizens as free and equal moral persons as this is represented in the original position.

Finally, like Kant, Rawls draws a sharp distinction between the agreement underlying the original social contract and agreements and voluntary associations that take place within society (*BS*, 59–61). The agreement constituting the original contract is not voluntary in any ordinary sense of the term; nor is it possible to know what we would otherwise have been like "outside" our own society. Finally, unlike voluntary associations, there are no shared "ends" for whose purpose we commonly unite. For these reasons, the agreement behind the social contract must be evaluated differently than we might evaluate agreements of private associations. There are no independent ends in terms of which it can easily be judged if some of us find it unacceptable. Restricting choice in the original position to the basic structure draws attention to the uniqueness of this agreement.

B. Rawls's Contractualism

According to Rawls, *A Theory of Justice* belongs to the contractualist tradition of political philosophy: The basic structure of a society is just if it is regulated by principles that could be agreed to by all (*TJ*, 16). However, this claim has been challenged on several different levels.

One objection is similar to one we have already discussed in relation to Kant. If the description of the choice situation (here, the original position) relies too heavily upon a prior set of moral constraints, the force of the contractarian element is lost. The work of justifying principles of justice is performed by the moral constraints and not by the voluntary character of the agreement.[24] As our discussion of the basic structure already has indicated, there is an element of truth to this charge. Not any agreement is justified simply because it is entered into voluntarily and without fraud. We also need an account of the background structure in which such agreements take place. However, unless one accepts only libertarian versions of contract theory, this objection does not apply. As with Kant, the moral constraints are built into the description of the initial choice situation. Only agreements between free and equal moral persons are fair, thus the description of the contract situation must in some way exhibit these features of the contracting parties.

A second, more forceful objection is made by those critics who charge that the particular features Rawls attributes to the original position deprive it of its contractualist character. For example, the imposition of the veil of ignorance would seem to transform the original position from a situation of agreement between separate persons into a situation of rational choice by one subject.[25] Some view this as an advantage to Rawls's theory and argue that Rawls's contract language should be dropped (Alexander), others consider it its demise. Sandel argues that the veil of ignorance prohibits the original position from being one of voluntary choice that occurs between two or more persons, two conditions that are necessary for a contract: "What goes on in the original position is not a contract after all, but the coming to awareness of an intersubjective being."[26]

However, in response to both lines of this objection, Rawls has continued to insist on the appropriateness of contract terminology in describing his theory of justice. Against Alexander's charge that it would be better to drop the contract language in favor of rational choice, Rawls has argued that rational choices are not the same as unanimous agreements.[27] Unanimous agreement of the parties must be public, that is, the parties mutually know that the principles are to serve as a public conception of justice, and this fact influences the principles chosen (*TJ*, 177). Similarly, the principles chosen in the original position must offer a stable conception of justice, that is, it must be one that the parties believe can be sustained over a long period of time and is capable of reproducing an effective sense of justice among the citizens of a well-ordered society (*TJ*, 145). The description of the original position as a contract situation and a situation of rational choice only seems redundant because the conditions of publicity and stability are built into the choice situation from the outset.[28]

Rawls's reply to Sandel takes a different course. Although Rawls believes the original position *can* be viewed as a situation of a single rational choice (as long as these other conditions are kept in mind), Sandel takes the description of the original position too literally when he discovers in it not a plurality of selves, but one "intersubjective being." It is true that the original position presupposes a conception of the person, but, to repeat, this conception cannot be directly gleaned from the description of the parties. The conception of the person, as a fundamental intuitive idea implicit in our public culture, is part of the model-conception of the well-ordered society and is then represented in the original position as a whole. Of course, whether the conception of the person in the well-ordered society is acceptable, and whether it is adequately represented in the original position are two further (and important) questions. But Sandel does not discuss either of these questions, and his own reconstruction of the argument in *A Theory of Justice* distorts Rawls's actual position.[29]

There is, however, a further dimension to the charge that the contract is transformed into a single rational choice. This is connected with the claim that Rawls's model is monological not dialogical.[30] With the imposition of the veil of ignorance in both its thin and thick forms, the parties all have exactly the same knowledge and what they know are only those general facts about society necessary for arriving at a rational decision. Rawls believes these restrictions are necessary in order to insure that a unanimous decision is made; but for the same reason this unanimous decision amounts to a single rational choice. I suggested above that what knowledge is considered general or morally relevant is not something that the parties in the original position themselves decide. On the best interpretation it is decided by "us" in public debate; on the interpretation most likely intended by Rawls, it is decided by the philosopher. One consequence of the second interpretation is that these important and controversial questions do not themselves become the subject matter of debate. Although Kant's distinction between the noumenal and phenomenal self is detranscendentalized in this procedural representation, the task of identifying those features of the person relevant for achieving an impartial solution to the question of social justice (as well as what knowledge is to be attributed to the person) remains the privileged activity of the philosopher.

C. Rawls's Distinction Between the Right and the Good

According to Rawls, the distinction between the right and the good (or questions of justice and questions of the good life) is virtually synonomous with a deontological moral theory (*TJ*, 30).[31] This is because in teleological theories (whether perfectionist or consequentialist) the notion of the right depends upon and is part of a more comprehensive idea of the good, while in Kantianism the right is defined prior to and independently of notions of the good (by means of a notion of pure practical reason). As we saw in chapter 1, Kant drew the distinction by means of an application of the categorical imperative: the good is plural and consists in the class of all permissible actions (all actions whose maxim is not contradicted in the application of the categorical imperative); principles of justice, on the other hand, are obligatory and derive from our conception of ourselves as free and equal moral persons.

Rawls's basis for this distinction is similar:

> In Kant's terms, empirical practical reason is represented by the rational deliberations of the parties; pure practical reason is represented by the constraints within which these deliberations take place. The unity of practical reason is expressed by defining the Reasonable to frame the Rational and to subordinate it absolutely; that is, the principles of justice that are agreed to are lexically prior in their application in a

well-ordered society to claims of the good.... This priority of the right over the good is characteristic of Kantian constructivism. (*KC*, 532)

The idea is that, in a society marked by a plurality of competing conceptions of the good, principles designed to regulate the social order must not rely crucially upon any one conception since that would violate a principle of toleration or liberal neutrality.

However, this distinction between the right and the good has recently come under considerable attack. Charles Taylor, for example, argues that, rather than reversing the relation between the right and the good in utilitarianism as Rawls suggests, liberalism merely advances its own alternative conception of the good life.[32] According to Taylor, we cannot resolve questions of right or justice by adopting a neutral stance toward the goods humans value; rather, we must enter into the thicket of the "language of qualitative contrasts" in order to make unavoidable, if difficult, choices from among the diversity of goods.[33] Similarly, in contrasting his own notion of "complex equality" to what he calls the "simple equality" of Rawls, Michael Walzer claims that arguments about rights and distributive principles must take into account the shared meanings of various social goods. Rights cannot be defined prior to the good since the nature and scope of distributive principles will vary with respect to different social goods.[34]

In reply, Rawls concedes that principles of justice cannot be specified apart from any conception of the good. Even in *A Theory of Justice,* the articulation of the principles of justice relies upon a "thin theory" of the good that includes minimal assumptions about an individual's rational life plan and the value of social cooperation. As he now puts it, his aim is rather to avoid relying upon "comprehensive religious, philosophical or moral doctrines" that must inevitably remain controversial in a public culture characterized by the "fact of pluralism." Toward this end, he suggests that a "common ground" (which includes an account of the political virtues and good of political community) can be found if we abstract from our more or less comprehensive worldviews and restrict ourselves to the practical (or political) task of finding a basis for agreement in the "overlapping consensus" contained in the public culture of a democratic society.[35]

While this response may not be convincing to his more ardent "communitarian" critics, it is difficult not to concede that Rawls is pointing to a distinction that will be central in any liberal democratic regime. Priority is accorded to various liberal rights not simply because they happen to be valued more than other goods or ideals, but because of their fundamental role in securing equally the capacity of individuals to form and pursue their own conception of the good and thus to shape their own identity within mutually defined and recognized constraints (see *BL,* 50). According to Rawls, however, this conception of a citizen's autonomy, or the conception of the self as a free and equal moral person, and the related political virtues must be distinguished from conceptions of the good that constitute "comprehensive" doctrines.

On the other hand, although I believe Rawls is correct to insist upon the distinction between the right and the good, I am not convinced that he has worked it out in a satisfactory manner. The distinction should not rest solely upon ideals or "fundamental intuitive ideas" that just happen to be implicit in our public culture, but should be determined by arguments about the social conditions that are necessary for the realization of a political community based on mutual recognition among free and equal persons. In this sense, the distinction must always remain flexible and open to further argument. At the same time, however, it will be necessary for the social critic, in his or her advocacy role, to propose such a distinction hypothetically and tentatively. Issues of justice or "the right" relate to the guarantee and provision of those basic rights and resources necessary for securing the equal autonomy of citizens within a political community. I attempt to develop and defend such a basis for the distinction between the right and the good in chapter 4.

IV. REFLECTIVE EQUILIBRIUM AND THE PROBLEM OF JUSTIFICATION

It is now time to consider the third "point of view" indicated in Figure 2-1: the point of view of ourselves—"You and me who are examining justice as fairness as a basis for a conception of justice that may yield a suitable understanding of freedom and equality" (*KC*, 533). It is in connection with this point of view that Rawls's notion of reflective equilibrium as a method of justification comes into play: we must decide whether or not the model-conceptions of the well-ordered society and the person, their representation in the original position, and, finally, the formulation of the two principles chosen there, reflect our considered convictions upon due reflection (*KC*, 534). This characterization of Rawls's strategy should draw attention to the importance of reflective equilibrium for the justification of the two principles. It is not enough to argue that they would be chosen in Rawls's philosophically favored interpretation of the initial choice situation; we also need an argument for why this interpretation should be accepted. This, we have seen, is partially supplied by the claim that the original position duly represents features of the model-conceptions of the well-ordered society and the person. But then the question becomes, Why should we accept these model-conceptions? Rawls's reply is that they reflect ideals embedded in our public culture that all citizens would affirm upon due reflection (*KC*, 518). The process of reflective equilibrium, and not the description of the original position as a situation of neutral rational choice, thus bears the major weight in Rawls's justificatory strategy.[36]

Rawls introduces the notion of reflective equilibrium as a method of justification that represents an alternative to rational intuitionism (or the attempt to ground moral theory upon self-evident first principles), naturalism (or the attempt to analyze basic moral concepts in terms of nonmoral concepts), and moral skepticism or relativism.[37] For this reason, the method of reflective equilibrium may be regarded as one attempt among others to outline a method of justification that is fallibilistic and antifoundationalist, while at the same time not giving up a claim to objectivity within moral discourse. In the following I will outline Rawls's method and consider some of the objections raised against it.

At an initial level, reflective equilibrium refers to a condition in which an individual's concrete moral judgments have been brought into harmony with her higher-order moral principles. In seeking to achieve such a harmony, an individual may provisionally take certain judgments or principles as fixed, but in the process of organizing them into a coherent whole nothing is immune to revision. The idea is that by moving back and forth between concrete judgments (say, the belief that a certain policy or action is wrong) and moral principles of varying degrees of generality (for example, "be true to yourself," "treat others as you would have them treat you," "maximize happiness") a person can arrive at a coherent set of moral beliefs or, as Rawls later puts it, at least coherent enough for the practical task of settling questions of justice within the basic structure. Rawls calls this condition "narrow reflective equilibrium," and it is clear that by itself it constitutes a fairly conservative method, at most insuring that an individual's prejudices are coherently organized.[38]

The process of justification has not been completed, however, when one has reached a condition of narrow reflective equilibrium. Rather, Rawls also outlines a further step that he calls "wide reflective equilibrium."[39] A condition of wide reflective equilibrium exists when an individual's coherent set of concrete moral judgments and moral principles have also been corrected by and brought into harmony with a broader set of theories (theories of psychology, sociology, meaning, etc.) and various formal "conditions of rationality" (such as the conditions of generality, publicity, and universality noted above).[40] Norman Daniels offers the following summary of the condition of wide reflective equilibrium:

> A wide reflective equilibrium is a coherent ordered triple of sets of beliefs held by a particular person, namely, a set of considered moral judgments (a); a set of moral principles (b); and a set of relevant background theories (c). We collect the person's initial moral judgments and

filter them to include only those of which he is relatively confident and which have been made under conditions generally conducive to avoiding errors of judgment. We propose alternative sets of moral principles which have varying degrees of "fit" with the moral judgments. Rather than settling immediately for the "best fit" of principles with judgments, which would give us only a *narrow equilibrium,* we advance philosophical arguments which reveal the strengths and weaknesses of the competing sets of principles (i.e., competing moral conceptions).[41]

Of course, if the theories and considerations appealed to in the process of wide reflective equilibrium are to provide further credibility to the moral principles arrived at in narrow equilibrium, they must be sufficiently independent of those moral principles.[42] The theories of human nature, sociology, and economics that might be appealed to must have independent credibility; we then examine ways in which these theories tend to support or call into question alternative moral conceptions. For example, Rawls argues that some moral conceptions are not as suitable for fostering a sense of justice and social stability or that some moral conceptions are not as capable of being publicly affirmed as others. One could also inquire into the extent to which empirical research in moral psychology (say, Kohlberg's developmental theory or social learning theory) support various normative views. There is thus no claim of conclusively justifying moral principles on the basis of nonmoral considerations; nor is there any claim that the theories appealed to in a wide reflective equilibrium are "value neutral." The point is rather to submit various moral conceptions to the widest array of philosophical argumentation and theoretical scrutiny. Justification is a multifaceted and many-layered process in which beliefs are exposed to critical reflection at various levels and from a variety of perspectives (see *TJ,* 21, 579).

As a method of justification in ethics, reflective equilibrium has met with two sorts of objections. Some critics have questioned the extent to which it differs from more traditional forms of intuitionism, while others have questioned whether it can avoid the charge of relativism—and thus whether it really represents a form of justification at all. While I believe Rawls can defend his position reasonably well against the first criticism, reflective equilibrium can adequately respond to the second only by moving in the direction of a discourse ethics.

Earlier I suggested that for Kantian constructivism the notion of a rational intuition of first principles is a form of heteronomy (*KC,* 559). Rawls's theory is thus not intuitionist in that it denies that there is a moral order prior to, and independent of, the public conception of ourselves as free and equal moral beings. However, it has been argued that Rawls's theory is still intuitionist in that "there is a definite if limited class of facts against

which conjectured principles can be checked, namely, our considered judgments in reflective equilibrium" (*TJ*, 51).[43] Like intuitionism, Rawls's
method thus begins with a number of "fixed points."

Two responses seem to be available to Rawls: First, while it is true that
he begins with everyday moral conceptions, the important question is what
sort of limitations are imposed upon the construction of a conception of justice by beginning with these intuitions? According to Rawls, none of these
intuitions are immune to revision. For the intuitionist, on the other hand,
some intuitions are taken as fixed and unchangeable.[44] Second, intuitionist
theories tend to claim that there is always a correct answer to a moral question. For Rawls, however, there is no moral "fact of the matter" (*KC*, 564):

> Apart from the procedure of constructing the principles of justice, there
> are no moral facts. Whether certain facts are to be recognized as rea-
> sons of justice, or how much they are to count, can be ascertained only
> from within the constructive procedure. (*KC*, 519)

Reflective equilibrium is thus part of a distinctively constructivist approach
in moral theory. There is no stronger claim that there must be a right answer
to every moral question, or that his particular conception corresponds to a
deeper moral reality, that is, a reality independent of the agreement reached
by free and equal persons.

The second criticism moves in another direction and raises the spectre
of relativism. Since he abandons (or at least brackets) a stronger notion of
moral objectivity, Rawls has been criticized for not having a sufficiently critical method of justification.[45] Rawls has himself been somewhat ambiguous
in responding to this sort of criticism. In *A Theory of Justice*, for instance, he
apparently sought to distance himself from the threat of relativism by con-
ceiving the task of moral theory as analogous to the analysis of linguistic
competence (*TJ*, 47). The basic idea seems to have been that, like linguistic
competence, the capacity to form considered moral judgments may rest upon
a deeper structure of rules and principles that can only be captured in a sufficiently general theory of which the agent is not necessarily cognizant. While
ordinary moral judgments and precepts may provide a point of departure,
there is no guarantee that a hermeneutic interpretation of them will result in a
coherent set of moral principles or that they themselves will not have to be
fundamentally revised.

> There is no reason to assume that our sense of justice can be adequately
> characterized by familiar common sense precepts, or derived from the
> more obvious learning principles. A correct account of moral capacities
> will certainly involve principles and theoretical constructions which go

much beyond the norms and standards cited in everyday life; it may eventually require fairly sophisticated mathematics as well. (*TJ*, 47)

The idea that seems to be expressed in this passage (and elsewhere) is that a moral theorist has the task of identifying the deep structure rules that would explain an individual's capacity for moral judgment even though these rules are not immediately evident to the morally competent agent. A critical purchase on our everyday moral beliefs and judgments could then be attained through the theorist's clarification of their underlying structure.[46]

However, Rawls has not pursued this project in his later writings. Rather, in his more recent essays, Rawls has apparently retreated from the stronger model of justification suggested by this interpretation of reflective equilibrium and prefers instead to speak of the practical (or "political") task of justification.[47] He now claims that his model-conception of the person with its two highest-order moral powers simply articulates a "fundamental intuitive idea" contained in the public culture of democratic regimes.[48] According to Rawls, the further defense of a conception of moral agency as part of a comprehensive moral theory or metaphysical/philosophical conception of the person violates a "principle of tolerance" that must be observed in the attempt to justify principles of justice within a democratic society. Although I too would agree that any acceptable principles of justice must be ones that could be publicly acknowledged by all members of a society, this sort of retreat from philosophical argument ultimately reflects an untenable division of labor between philosophy and the more mundane interpretation of everyday beliefs and practices. It also seems to make the method of reflective equilibrium even more susceptible to the charge of relativism.

As we have already seen, the kind of justification that Rawls pursues is not foundationalist in the sense that it seeks to ground principles of justice in a morally neutral conception of rational choice.[49] On the other hand, Rawls now further argues that the defenses of liberalism found, for example, in Kant and in Mill are inappropriate in a democratic order since they rely on "comprehensive moral views"—a notion of autonomy in the first case, utilitarianism in the second—which will inevitably be controversial in a society characterized by the "fact of pluralism."[50] Between the Scylla of foundationalism and the Charybdis of a comprehensive moral doctrine, Rawls would seem to have little room to navigate.

The strategy Rawls now adopts for his constructivist approach is to argue from ideas that are assumed to be widely shared in the public political culture of modern democracies. "Justification," he claims, "is addressed to others who disagree with us, and therefore it must always proceed from premises that we and others publicly recognize as true.... It goes without saying that this agreement must be informed and uncoerced, and reached by citizens in ways consistent with their being viewed as free and equal persons."[51] Thus, while there may not be a morally neutral ground, Rawls claims that there is nevertheless a common ground and one which does not entail controversial philosophical assumptions. However, at this point Rawls is confronted by what I shall refer to as the "paradox of democratic justification": In a democratic forum, claims about rights or principles of justice are legitimate only if they are ones free and equal citizens would publicly accept; but if a meaningful distinction is to be maintained between *de facto* and *de jure* legitimacy, we need some criteria for determining whether an agreement reached is indeed between free and equal persons. In his earlier critique of Nozick, Rawls argued that in order to determine whether an agreement is voluntary, we need to know whether the background framework or "basic structure" of the society in which the agreement takes place is just (*BS*, 54). This requirement now returns to haunt him: Since his theory of justice is designed to assess whether the basic structure of our society is just, Rawls cannot appeal *directly* to a common ground or an overlapping public consensus for the justification of his principles.

Rawls might reply that he does not make such a direct appeal to a public consensus and that to assume so is to misconstrue the important role of reflective equilibrium in his constructivism.[52] As we have just seen, although the process of reflective equilibrium provisionally takes certain judgments and ideas as fixed, nothing is immune to criticism and revision. The principles of justice are therefore not justified by a direct appeal to just any set of widely shared views, but by an appeal to views that have been critically refined and adjusted in a process of reflective deliberation.

This interpretation of Rawlsian constructivism would also help to clarify the heuristic or "expository" role performed by the original position in his argument: "As a device of representation the original position serves as a means of public reflection and self-clarification. We can use it to help us work out what we now think, once we are able to take a clear and uncluttered view of what justice requires when society is conceived as a scheme of cooperation between free and equal persons...."[53] The original position does not introduce any further moral assumptions than those already provided by the model-conceptions of the person and the well-ordered society; but neither does it shift the context of argument to a morally neutral framework of rational choice. Rather, it is part of an exercise to help clarify ideas that you and I who have been asked to find principles of justice already recognize, or at least would recognize upon due reflection. It is an argumentative device that Rawls introduces in a public dialogue quite literally with us. It thus becomes less important (and is not surprising) that the parties in the original position unanimously choose the two principles—after all, they were constructed to select them. What matters is whether we as free and equal citizens (unanimously?) acknowledge the ideas employed in the construction of the original position as well as in its particular design. The reasoning that goes on inside the original position is part of a more general argument that we should accept the principles that would be chosen there, and it is this more general argument that appeals to the presence of an overlapping consensus in our public culture.

But while these qualifications suggest once more how Rawlsian constructivism differs from various forms of intuitionism and moral realism, they do not adequately deal with the threat of relativism or paradox of democratic justification.[54] Why should we regard the principles as justified unless it is our beliefs that have been brought into a condition of reflective equilibrium as a result of a process in which we have participated? And unless we have actually participated in the process, what reasons are there for preferring Rawls's characterization of impartiality in terms of the original position over other characterizations?[55] At this point, I think it is possible to push Rawlsian constructivism in either of two directions. Both have the advantage of seeing the justification of political ideals (or, more specifically, rights and distributive principles) within the context of a public dialogue. The first alternative, which can also be found in the work of Bruce Ackerman and Charles Larmore, construes the public dialogue as a *modus vivendi*.[56] The second alternative pushes Rawlsian constructivism in the direction of Habermas's discourse ethics. Although his recent writings suggest that Rawls might be inclined more toward the first interpretation, I will offer some considerations in support of the second.

On the first interpretation of Rawlsian constructivism, the justification of principles for regulating the basic structure is the result of a public discussion or, as Rawls puts it, the use of "free public reason."[57] The principles must finally be ones that would be accepted by us, or at least, ones that it would be unreasonable for us to reject.[58] However, on this interpretation, not any argument or consideration may appropriately be introduced into the public discussion. In view of what Rawls calls "the fact of pluralism," we cannot hope to reach an agreement about principles if appeal is made to what Rawls calls "general and comprehensive moral doctrines." Such a general and comprehensive doctrine, according to him, includes not only religious worldviews and substantive moral theories (such as natural law, utilitarianism, or Kantian autonomy), but also philosophical arguments and (non-common sense) theoretical assumptions from the social sciences.[59] His claim is that in a liberal democracy philosophical and social-scientific theories will also be controversial and thus cannot appropriately serve as a basis for agreement. Rather, the search for a consensus on the basis of which principles can be justified should only draw upon "fundamental intuitive ideas regarded as latent in the public political culture."[60] The search employs what Rawls elsewhere describes as a "method of avoidance" where the guiding question becomes: "What is the least that must be asserted; and if it must be asserted, what is its least controversial form?"[61]

This interpretation is close to the model of "conversational constraint" proposed by Ackerman and to the model of discursive legitimation offered by Larmore.[62] The idea is to remove from public discussion certain controversial claims, claims which finally come down to "a bare confrontation between incompatible personal points of view," so that a common basis for reaching agreement about principles can be established.[63] Rawls's particular strategy runs as follows: While it would be wrong to justify political principles by appeal to the notion that persons are free and equal moral beings on, say, Kantian or theological grounds, we are nevertheless entitled to appeal to this notion since it is widely shared in our public culture (even if on a more personal level this turns out to be so for a variety of different reasons). If such a strategy is to be at all successful, Rawls must be able to draw a reasonably clear distinction between such comprehensive doctrines and the common sense or mundane beliefs latent in the public culture. Toward this end he suggests that there is "lots of slippage" between the beliefs that individuals hold and comprehensive doctrines so that it becomes possible to appeal to the former in a public debate without invoking the latter.[64] Among these intuitive beliefs, Rawls includes a "commonsense political sociology" (which includes a belief in the fact of pluralism and its persistence in a democratic society), and a "reasonable moral psychology" (which presumably includes the model-conception of the person characterized by the two highest-order powers).[65]

However, it can certainly be argued that this strategy implies a moral epistemology of its own. It assumes, for example, that individuals have the capacity to distinguish between mundane beliefs and comprehensive doctrines, as well as between a public and nonpublic conception of their own self-identity. It also assumes that for the purpose of justifying political principles individuals are able and willing to set aside those comprehensive doctrines and personal points of view.[66] That is, it seems to presuppose a conception of the self or moral agency contained in a (detranscendentalized) interpretation of Kantian autonomy (see chapter 4).

Furthermore, Rawls must assume that the facts he cites are ones that would be acknowledged by all in a public discussion. Otherwise, they would not provide a suitable basis for establishing a broad overlapping consensus. Equally as important, "the guidelines of inquiry and publicly recognized rules of assessing evidence" used in identifying the facts must also be subject to public debate and discussion.[67] To be sure, such a debate could not consider such rules and guidelines all at once or *in toto*, but in principle the facts that help to define an overlapping consensus as well as the standards of rationality for determining those facts are also subject to public discursive justification. The public use of reason implies that present agreements are in principle always open to future discursive vindication.

These two considerations push Rawlsian constructivism in the direction of Habermas's discourse ethics. As with the first interpretation, the justification of principles regulating the basic structure is tied to the idea of a public discussion among free and equal persons. But on this interpretation, no prior constraints are imposed on the subject matter that can be introduced into the discussion. Rather, each participant is free to introduce any argument or consideration she believes relevant. The interpretation of specific needs and preferences (or conceptions of the good, more generally) cannot be excluded in advance by fiat; rather, the question is whether there are good reasons—reasons that could not reasonably be rejected by any of the participants—for excluding some preferences or conceptions of the good from affecting the selection of principles of justice. Such an interpretation of the public justification of political principles reflects the basic idea of a discourse ethics, namely, that a norm is justified only if it could be agreed to by all concerned as participants in a practical discourse where no force but that of the better argument prevails. The clarification and defense of this moral theory is the topic of the next chapter. What I have sought to show here is that Rawls's method of reflective equilibrium can succeed in avoiding some of the weaknesses noted above only if it is pushed in the direction of this alternative moral theory.[68]

3

COMMUNICATIVE ACTION AND
FORMAL PRAGMATICS: HABERMAS'S
DEFENSE OF A DISCOURSE ETHICS

I. INTRODUCTION

In the preceding chapter I argued that Rawls's attempt to provide a justification for his "philosophically favored" interpretation of the original position is deficient in several respects. If this argument is correct, we need to look elsewhere for a philosophical clarification and defense of the normative grounds of social criticism. In this chapter I will argue that Jürgen Habermas's theory of communicative action presents one possible alternative. As an heir to the early Frankfurt school of critical social theory, Habermas has long argued that the idea of critique found in Marx and the tradition of Western Marxism is in need of a renewed normative grounding. Since his own "linguistic turn" in the early 1970s, Habermas has attempted to provide such a grounding with the aid of insights from contemporary social theory and an analytic philosophy of language.[1] An important part of this project has been the development of what he (together with Karl-Otto Apel) calls "discourse" or "communicative ethics" in which Kant's categorical imperative is reformulated in terms of a discursive procedure for moral argumentation.[2] The basic idea of discourse ethics is thus that "only those norms can claim to be valid that meet (or could meet) with the approval of all affected in their capacity *as participants in a practical discourse*" (*DE*, 66). In defining what he means by a practical discourse, Habermas introduces his own "principle of universalizability" (U) as a constitutive rule of argumentation:

> Every valid norm has to fulfill the following condition: (U) *All* affected can accept the consequences and the side effects its *general* observance can be anticipated to have for the satisfaction of *everyone's* interests

(and these consequences are preferred to those of known alternative possibilities for regulation). (*DE*, 65)

His further claim, which will also be examined in this chapter, is that this principle can be derived from the "pragmatic presuppositions of argumentation" when these presuppositions are combined with a (relatively weak) notion of what it means to justify a norm of action—a notion implicit in the idea of communicative action. The clarification of these "pragmatic presuppositions" is the task of a theory of formal pragmatics. Thus, as I will argue, both the theory of communicative action *and* the theory of formal pragmatics are crucial to Habermas's attempt to justify a discourse ethics.

This attempt to specify a principle of universalizability in connection with a theory of speech acts initially invites a comparison with R. M. Hare's moral theory.[3] The similarity, however, is only apparent. Apart from the fact that his theory is Kantian (in a sense to be explained) and not utilitarian, Habermas is also not interested in demonstrating the existence of a "logic of imperatives" that imposes certain constraints (prescriptivity and universalizability) on their use. Further, even if Hare could show that his principle of universalizability can generate morally substantive requirements, he will still not have shown why we ought to adopt a logic of imperatives or why we should consider it an analysis of "our" moral language.[4] Habermas's strategy is to argue that the understanding of any basic speech act (whether an indicative or an imperative) is essentially connected to a set of validity claims and to the possibility of the hearer taking a rationally motivated "Yes/No" position toward those claims. The specific validity claim thematized in a practical discourse may vary from that of descriptive utterances (the claim to normative rightness rather than truth becomes the central focus), but a whole range of basic validity claims are implicitly raised in any literal speech act. In this sense, there is no possibility of opting out of the (quasi-transcendental) obligation to justify a norm of action short of opting out of communicative action entirely. Moreover, if the validity of a norm is contested, it (no less than the validity of a factual assertion) must be redeemed through good reasons and, if necessary, by entering into a "discourse" in which nothing but the force of the better argument prevails.

Habermas's project more closely resembles other neo-Kantian attempts to derive normative principles from a notion of practical reason (or rational agency), perhaps most notably that of Alan Gewirth. After introducing Habermas's notion of communicative action in the next section, I will therefore compare his proposal to Gewirth's. This will make it possible to underscore the importance of beginning with a notion of communicative, in contrast to purposive-rational, action. Despite the strong justificatory claims Habermas wishes to defend, unlike Gewirth he is not interested in showing that it is prudentially rational to act morally. In fact, Habermas considers such arguments to contain a category mistake and thus, in this respect too, he is more in keeping with the Kantian conception of the connection between reason and morality defended in the previous chapters. It suffices if a philosophical theory of morality can show that there exist nondesire-based reasons—that is, reasons based upon the general features of moral agency rather than upon the agent's more specific and concrete aims and attachments—that can be regarded as the ground of moral obligation and thus seriously considered as a source of moral motivation.[5]

Finally, according to Habermas, the task of moral theory is quite limited. Its aim is to provide a clarification and justification of the moral point of view. It does not promise a decision-procedure for resolving all ethical conflicts.[6] For some, such a conception is reason to forego a formalistic ethics altogether (Williams), for others, it signals a failure to do what moral theory ought to do (Hare). Habermas's position, as I understand it, falls between these two extremes. Some moral/ethical conflicts may in fact be irresolvable. A formal theory will be of little use; moral judgments and difficult choices must be made that cannot easily be described as the only ones that are right. A moral philosopher can write about such conflicts in an attempt to clarify issues, but only as one who also struggles with them. On the other hand, not all conflicts are of this character and some, falsely posed in terms of equally legitimate but irreconcilable interests, function ideologically within a society. In response to moral conflict generally, a formalistic moral theory may still be able to supply general criteria by means of which the individuals involved can determine whether or not the conflicts are in fact rationally irresolvable or whether they embody concealed generalizable interests. It is this more limited task of moral theory that Habermas adopts in his attempt to provide a clarification and justification of a discourse ethics.

II. COMMUNICATIVE ACTION AND MORAL THEORY

The importance of the concept of communicative action to Habermas's work scarcely needs mention. The evolution and basic categories of his social theory can be approached in terms of it: consider, for example, his remarks on the theme of labor and interaction in Hegel's Jena writings, his reconstruction of Marx's distinction between the material base and ideological superstructure of societies, his own distinction between the "institutional framework" of society and its purposive-rational subsystems in his essay on Marcuse, or his recent (and controversial) distinction between social integration and systems integration. I do not intend to trace the development of the concept of communicative action here; nor can I address all of the criticisms that have been raised against it.[7] Rather, in this section, I want to argue that a distinction between communicative and strategic action can be made intuitively plausible, and that it must be made plausible if his justification of a discourse ethics is to meet with any success. I begin with a discussion of his basic concepts of social action, and attempt to clarify several misunderstandings concerning them. Habermas's strategy, as I understand it, is to show that once the concept of communicative action has been made intuitively plausible, it can be further strengthened and clarified with insights from a theory of formal pragmatics.[8] However, unless this order is maintained it will not become clear why, for example, Habermas proposes a reclassification of Searle's taxonomy of basic illocutionary acts—a question Searle has put to him on a number of occasions.[9]

Habermas's basic distinction is between "consent-oriented" (or communicative) and "success-oriented" (or purposive-rational) actions; within the latter class he distinguishes further between strategic and instrumental action.[10] Instrumental actions are goal-oriented interventions in the physical world. They can be appraised from the standpoint of efficiency and described as the following of technical rules.[11] Strategic action, by contrast, is action that aims at influencing others for the purpose of achieving some end. It too can be appraised in terms of its efficiency and described with the tools of game theory and theories of rational choice.[12] Many instrumental actions can also be strategic, and some forms of strategic action may be instrumental. Communicative action, however, constitutes an independent and distinct type of social action. The goal or "telos" of communicative action is not expressed or realized in an attempt to influence others, but in the attempt to reach an agreement or mutual understanding (*Verständigung*) with one or more actors about something in the world. Thus, while all action is teleological or goal-oriented in a broad sense (*TCA* 1: 101), in the case of communicative action any further ends the agent may have are subordinated to the goal of achieving a mutually shared definition of the agent's life worldly situation through a cooperative process of interpretation.[13] In acting communicatively, individuals more or less naively accept as valid the various claims raised with their utterance or action and mutually suppose that they each are prepared to provide reasons for them should the validity of those claims be questioned. It is because of this intimate connection between validity, reasons, and action that communicative action must also be initially approached from the internal perspective of the participant. Communicative action is connected to domains of validity that can only be understood "from the inside," that is, by those who as (virtual) participants are able to give and assess the reasons for an action.[14] Habermas's claim is that any subject capable of speech and action is able, at least intuitively, to distinguish between what it means to seek agreement or understanding with someone on the basis of the exchange of reasons and what it means to try to influence someone for some further end (*TCA* 1: 286).

In a slightly more technical (and controversial) sense, and one that is tied more specifically to modern structures of rationality, Habermas also holds that individuals who act communicatively self-reflectively aim at reaching understanding about something in the world by relating their interpretations to three general types of validity claims which are constitutive for three basic types of speech acts: a claim to truth raised in constative speech acts, a claim to normative rightness raised in regulative speech acts, and a claim to truthfulness raised in expressive speech acts (*TCA* 1: 319f.). I will take up Habermas's defense of this "stronger" (distinctively modern) characterization of communicative action below.[15]

What Habermas understands by communicative action can be further clarified with reference to two related questions: How is social action possible, and how is social order possible?[16] In response to the first question, Habermas's claim is that a strong notion of mutual or common knowledge is a condition of possibility for social action as we know it. In their social interactions, individuals draw upon mutually shared interpretations of their lifeworldly situation. These interpretations embody a variety of claims whose validity depends, however counterfactually, upon the ideas of uncoerced consent and mutual reciprocity. Any competently speaking and acting subject is aware, at least implicitly, of what it means to justify his or her beliefs or actions to another with reasons and is prepared to provide such a justification should the mutually supposed claims be contested. It is this rationally binding force at work in our everyday communicative practices that is constitutive for communicative action and is a condition of possibility for social action in general. Thus, in a broader sense (since it refers not only to direct acts of reaching understanding, but to all social interaction coordinated on the basis of them) Habermas sometimes refers to communicative action as any social interaction in which the coordinating mechanism is action oriented to reaching understanding or agreement. Social action is possible in general by virtue of the rationally binding force that results from the actors' readiness, however counterfactual, to make good the claims raised in their actions.[17]

In response to the second question, "How is social order possible?" Habermas's appeal to the notion of communicative action reflects his agreement with sociologists such as Durkheim, Weber, and Parsons who maintain that societies can neither be created nor sustained through force or strategic action alone. In his dispute with Niklas Luhmann, Habermas defended the position that social order and collective identities rely upon a mutual recognition of norms and values, and at least their *de facto* legitimacy.[18] At the same time, however, the notion of communicative action also indicates a break with Parson's conception of norms in that it points to the active and ongoing interpretive accomplishments of social actors in contrast to a more or less passive process of socialization.[19]

In clarifying this model of communicative action, Habermas introduces as its complement the important notion of the sociocultural lifeworld—"the culturally transmitted and linguistically organized stock of interpretive patterns":

> Subjects acting communicatively always come to an understanding in the horizon of a lifeworld. Their lifeworld is formed from more or less diffuse, always unproblematic, background convictions. This lifeworld background serves as a source of situation definitions that are presupposed by participants as unproblematic. (*TCA* 1: 70)

Thus, in their social interactions, individuals draw upon the lifeworld as a resource in the forms of cultural knowledge, legitimate social orders, and acquired individual competencies; at the same time, however, the symbolic reproduction and maintenance of the lifeworld depends upon the interpretive accomplishments of its members within each of these broad institutional domains (e.g., culture, society, and personality).

> I call *culture* the store of knowledge from which those engaged in communicative action draw interpretations susceptible of consensus as they come to an understanding about something in the world. I call *society* (in the narrower sense of a component of the lifeworld) the legitimate orders from which those engaged in communicative action gather a solidarity, based on belonging to groups, as they enter into interpersonal relationships with one another. *Personality* serves as a term of art for acquired competences that render a subject capable of speech and action and hence able to participate in processes of mutual understanding in a given context and to maintain his own identity in the shifting contexts of interaction.[20]

By so correlating the concept of the lifeworld with the concept of communicative action, Habermas is able to highlight a distinction that is only implicit in comparable phenomenological analyses. On the one hand, as a *resource* that is drawn upon in communicative action, the lifeworld remains in the background as implicit knowledge. On the other hand, as a *topic* about which communicative actors seek to reach agreement, segments of the lifeworld are selectively thematized as problems.[21] In their efforts to reach agreement about something in the world, social actors draw upon resources within the lifeworld, but they also make use of a reference system (or "scaffolding") of formal world-concepts that is implicit in the structure of communicative action. Habermas frequently distinguishes these two dimensions of the lifeworld by means of a contrast between lifeworld (resource) and world (topic) and in connection with a spatial metaphor:

> While the segment of the lifeworld relevant to the situation encounters the actor as a problem which he has to solve as something standing as it were in front of him, he is supported in the rear by the background of his lifeworld. Coping with situations is a circular process in which the actor is two things at the same time: the *initiator* of actions that can be attributed to him and the *product* of traditions in which he stands as well as of group solidarities to which he belongs and processes of socialization and learning to which he is subjected.[22]

In *The Philosophical Discourse of Modernity,* Habermas warns that this description of a circular process should be accepted with caution: Actors are not products of the lifeworld in the sense that the latter can be viewed as a self-generating process that has a life of its own. Rather, individuals (and groups) reproduce the lifeworld through their communicative action and with reference to the formal world-concepts, and the lifeworld as resource is "saddled *on*" the interpretive accomplishments of its members.[23] While Habermas thus rejects conceptualizing the lifeworld as the noematic correlate of an act of (transcendental) consciousness, he also resists reifying it in ways that obscure its roots in the interpretive achievements of concrete individuals and groups.

With this rough outline of the notion of communicative action in view, I would like to take up several misunderstandings and/or criticisms of it. Ernst Tugendhat and others have pointed to ambiguities in Habermas's characterization of communicative action and questioned whether it forms an exclusive type over against strategic action.[24] On the one hand, Tugendhat suggests that all human action is teleological (or purposive-rational); thus Habermas's contrast between consent-oriented and success-oriented action (or actions which are means toward ends) does not seem to be a distinction between two types of action. Few people (if any) communicate solely for the sake of communication; rather, we communicate in order to achieve other ends. On the other hand, Habermas's suggestion that communicative action is more basic or "originary" than strategic action seems to be either false or merely the trivial observation that one of the most effective ways of influencing others is through language. In general, I cannot influence someone by my words unless she can understand what I say.

However, apart from the fact that Habermas is not always entirely clear in his formulation, it is difficult to see precisely what Tugendhat's disagreement is. At one point he acknowledges that Habermas describes the communicative/strategic distinction not as a distinction between nonteleological and teleological action, but, within the general category of teleological action, as a distinction between action-oriented toward success and action-oriented without reservation toward reaching understanding, and this is undoubtedly Habermas's preferred description.[25] Further, Habermas's claim is not that we communicate as an end in itself, but rather that in communicative action all other goals and purposes are subordinated to that of reaching agreement. It is in this sense that reaching understanding is "constitutive" of communicative action and can be a "mechanism" for coordinating social interaction.

Tugendhat is correct, however, in noting that Habermas too hastily identifies strategic action with the customary definition of a perlocutionary act.[26] Many perlocutionary acts can be openly pursued (such as trying to convince or persuade) and others (such as implying, hinting, or suggesting) do not easily fit into Habermas's definition of strategic action. Acts of communication (or speech acts) can become strategic, however, if someone is unwilling to acknowledge his perlocutionary aims or, more importantly, if someone is unwilling or (logically) unable to subordinate them to the process of reaching understanding itself. Tugendhat is thus also correct in pointing out that it is initially the attitude of the actor that is crucial for distinguishing between communicative and strategic action. Habermas's position, however, is that this attitude is not solely a subjective property of the actor, but is "structurally required" for an action of the respective type:[27] Strategic action generally relies upon the internal structure of communicative action for its success. At the same time, its structure differs from that of communicative action since it involves aims or purposes that cannot be openly acknowledged without jeopardizing the validity bases on which it rests. As we shall see, it is a clarification of the internal structure of communicative action that Habermas hopes to provide through an analysis of illocutionary acts.[28]

A related misunderstanding results from confusing communicative action with acts of communication (or speech acts).[29] On the one hand, not every speech act is "action oriented to reaching understanding"; speech acts can also be used strategically to attain individual goals or to influence others. Other speech acts (many perlocutionary acts, for example), while not strategic, are still not essential for reaching understanding. (My statement that I found your lost book may make you happy, but that effect is neither essential to an understanding of my utterance, nor is it readily classifiable as strategic action.) On the other hand, communicative action is not limited to linguistic acts. As I have suggested, communicative action refers to all modes of social interaction that are coordinated on the basis of mutual understanding (*Verständigung*). Communicative action and speech acts are thus two overlapping but analytically distinct aspects of social reality.[30] To summarize the claim to be pursued in the next section, communicative action can be analyzed in connection with linguistic acts of a certain sort, namely illocutionary acts. It is "distinguished from strategic action by the fact that all participants pursue illocutionary aims without reservation in order to arrive at an agreement that will provide the basis for a consensual coordination of individually pursued plans of action."[31] Social interactions that rely upon the coordinating potential of illocutionary acts are rational to the extent that this potential can itself be traced back to the Yes/No position hearers can adopt with respect to the claims or offers made with illocutionary acts.

A third, potentially more substantive criticism has been leveled against Habermas's view of the relation between communicative action and power.[32] The criticism has both a strong and weak version: First, one could (like Foucault) deny that there are any power-free interactions and insist that all social relations occur within a body politic constituted by power strategies and technologies of control.[33] To make good on this claim, one would have to maintain not only that (contrary to a certain naive understanding) communicative action does not exist, but also that the proposed alternative model of social action is both internally coherent and useful for social analysis. However, as many critics have pointed out, it is difficult (if not impossible) for a Foucaultian to do this without lapsing into some sort of a performative contradiction.[34] The weaker version of this criticism, on the other hand, need not be committed to the view that all social interaction is strategic, but could nevertheless argue that Habermas's distinction between communicative and strategic action prohibits him from being able to analyze certain social phenomena because, for example, it suggests that some domains of the lifeworld are power-free while others seem to function on the basis of strategic action alone.[35] Here the burden of proof is thrown back on Habermas: He must be able to show that his model of communicative action does not commit him to such an interpretation of social reality, but rather that it provides a basic criterion for identifying the effects of the illegitimate distribution of power in whatever ways it may be manifested. While I believe that Habermas is able to provide such a response to this criticism, I will not pursue it here. The outline for such a response should be evident, however, in chapter 5.[36]

Finally, before turning to Habermas's theory of formal pragmatics and his analysis of the "rationally binding force" contained in certain basic illocutionary acts, I would like to indicate the importance of his notion of communicative action for the justification of his discourse ethics. I will pursue this, first, by briefly contrasting his project to Gewirth's and, second, by indicating how the notion of communicative action may be useful both for delineating the range or scope of moral phenomena as well as for explaining the *Sollgeltung* or morally binding force of norms (or, to use Kant's term, their categorical character).

Alan Gewirth has offered a derivation of a "supreme moral principle" from a notion of purposive-rational action.[37] Since the strategy bears a strong resemblance to Habermas's, I will review Gewirth's argument and indicate what I take to be its central weakness. To state my criticism at the outset, Gewirth's attempt to derive a moral principle from prudential reason alone cannot succeed because the notion of a claim-right already moves beyond the framework allowed by purposive-rational action. The notion of a claim-right already presupposes a norm of reciprocity or mutual recognition in a way that cannot be conceptually clarified solely with reference to a notion of purposive-rational action.[38] In making this criticism I thus also hope to underscore the importance of beginning with a concept of communicative action as Habermas does.

Gewirth proposes to begin with an analysis of a general concept of purposive-rational action. This is appropriate, he believes, because it is a concept found within most moral theories, secular and religious, and so does not unduly prejudice any one perspective. The two "generic features" yielded by his analysis of action are freedom (or voluntariness) and purposiveness (or intentionality). His claim is that a "supreme moral principle," what he calls the "Principle of Generic Consistency," can be derived from this concept of action simply by applying a principle of formal consistency to claims that anyone who acts in accordance with these generic features of action must make. That is, individual claims can be scrutinized by means of a "dialectically necessary method": Beginning with statements the agent would accept from her own first-person perspective, conclusions are reached that she is logically required to accept. The derivation proceeds as follows:

Any agent A who freely and intentionally does X for some end or purpose E must think (1) "I do X for end or purpose E" and (2) "E is good" (where 'good' is not understood in a moral sense nor as an objective description, but simply in the sense that A values E). If A values E, she must also value those generic means necessary for attaining E, generally her freedom and well-being. Thus A must also think (3) "I must have freedom and well-being" (where 'must' again does not imply a moral obligation, but a "practical-prescriptive requirement"). Given the notion of a (prudential) claim-right, this thought can also be formulated as (4) "I have a right to freedom and well-being" since a denial of that claim-right is a denial of the claim (from A's own prudential perspective) that others ought not to interfere with A's freedom and well-being and hence also a denial of (3). Thus, from (1) we arrive at the generic rights stated in (4) that A is logically required to accept. However, Gewirth notes, so far we have only prudential generic rights, not moral generic rights. The transition from the prudential to the moral is achieved in two further steps. From the above considerations A must also think (5) "I have rights to freedom and well-being because I am a prospective purposive agent." That is, A has the generic rights of freedom and well-being not because she has some arbitrary feature R, but by virtue of the generic feature of voluntariness and purposiveness. But by the mere formal principle of consistency anyone who thinks (5) must also think (6) "All prospective purposive agents have rights to freedom and well-being." Thus if A is to be logically consistent with regard to her own generic rights, she must also accept as a principle for her action (7) "Act in accord with the generic rights of your recipients as well as yourself." And (7) is Gewirth's Principle of Generic Consistency.[39]

Gewirth's derivation of the Principle of Generic Consistency has been subject to a number of criticisms and he has, in turn, offered several replies.[40] Much of the discussion focuses on Gewirth's transition from the prudential to the moral, that is, on his attempt to derive an "ought" from an "is." However, if one accepts his premises, especially his definition of a prudential claim-right, the argument seems to go through rather smoothly.[41] The crucial question thus seems to be whether this notion of a claim-right makes sense from within the framework of purposive-rational (or prudential) action. Contrary to Gewirth's position it would seem that, just as a solipsist can only carry on a conversation with himself, a purposive-rational agent cannot intelligibly make claims, moral or otherwise. A claim-right entails a minimal recognition of another to whom a correlative duty or obligation applies. But purposive-rational action need not (perhaps even cannot) presuppose a recognition of other subjects or agents, and thus cannot serve as a basis for elucidating the concept of a claim-right. I do not mean to suggest that everyone who has a duty must already be conceived as a subject with rights. Slaves have duties, not rights. But, as Hegel argued in his treatment of the dialectic of the master-slave relation, the master's need for recognition by the slave is ultimately responsible for the transformation of their relationship. My own, less dramatic claim is that in granting a claim-right to a prudential agent, Gewirth already moves outside the framework of purposive-rational action toward a notion of action that implies a minimal degree of reciprocity or communication. To have duties is to be at least a *potential* right-bearer: Slaves may have only duties, but trees are not even capable of having these!

I do not thereby mean to suggest that all claim-rights are also moral rights—many clearly are not.[42] My claim is, rather, that the notion of a claim-right only makes sense if the prudential agent already recognizes that there are others capable of having duties, and that just this sort of recognition implies a notion of action other than merely purposive-rational. A purposive-rational agent need not see the world as anything more than objects to be conquered or goals to be overcome; there need not be anyone to whom claims can apply, so there might not be any real sense to a "prudential claim-right."

There are many other questions that could be asked in connection with Gewirth's notion of generic rights, particularly with respect to their more substantive implications. However, I need not pursue these here. If my argument is correct, I have shown that Gewirth's transition from the prudential to the moral is not successful, and this takes much of the wind out of his sails. Gewirth, it seems, is only able to arrive at a moral principle of universalizability if he already presupposes a normative conception of rationality. If so, then we would do better to turn to someone who explicitly begins with a notion of communicative action that entails such a normative model. Habermas does not view his project as an attempt to derive moral principles from prudential or purposive-rational action. Rather, the notion of communicative action points toward a quite different account of the source of moral obligation, or what Kant calls its categorical character.

III. THEORIES OF MEANING AND FORMAL PRAGMATICS

In his 1969 inaugural address at Oxford, P. F. Strawson identified two broad approaches toward developing a theory of sentence-meaning for a natural language.[43] Theorists of formal (or truth-conditional) semantics argue that a theory of meaning is best pursued by way of a theory of truth: To understand the meaning of a sentence in a language is to know the conditions under which it would be true. Davidson's attempt to extend Tarski's truth-definition for formal languages into a recursive theory of meaning for a natural language is the most ambitious and well-known example of this approach. Convention T (s is true in L if and only if p) offers a procedure by means of which someone can assign a meaning to a sentence by specifying its truth-conditions. Moreover, Davidson claims it can do this without making essential use of any semantic terms other than a very general notion of truth.[44] By contrast, theorists of communication-intention, including Strawson, argue that a complete theory of sentence-meaning must also include an account of what speakers characteristically do with sentences and that this can best be achieved with reference to the communicative or audience-directed intentions of speakers.[45] An analysis of (at least) indicative sentences in terms of truth-conditions may be fine as far as it goes, but an account of the general notion of truth (required for a theory of truth-conditions) is still needed, and this can only be provided through an analysis of speech acts such as stating and asserting.

> And here the theorist of communication-intention sees his chance. There is no hope, he says, of elucidating the notion of the content of such speech acts without paying some attention to the notions of those speech acts themselves.... And we cannot, the theorist maintains, elucidate the notion of stating or asserting except in terms of audience-

directed intention. For the fundamental case of stating or asserting, in terms of which all variants must be understood, is that of uttering a sentence with a certain intention...which can be incompletely described as that of letting an audience know, or getting it to think, that the speaker has a certain belief....[46]

The meaning of a sentence is (at least in part) dependent upon the (conventional) rules governing the use a speaker makes of a sentence of that type, and these rules are themselves determined by what a speaker standardly intends to do with such sentences. Thus, Strawson concludes, truth-conditional semantics, "so far from being an alternative to a communication theory of meaning, leads us straight into such a theory of meaning."[47]

The path leading from semantics to pragmatics is, however, apparently not as straight as Strawson would have it. Most truth-conditional theorists, even those who are sympathetic with the attempt to supplement a theory of meaning with a theory of force, have not seen the problem in quite this way.[48] The more frequent response has been to argue just the reverse: Far from providing an account of sentence-meaning, theories of communication-intention must presuppose the identity of sentence-meaning in order to be able to specify the appropriate or "crucial" (Davidson) communicative intention. Thus, if what Davidson calls the "autonomy of meaning" is to be preserved, if a theory of meaning is not to become grossly circular, an account of sentence-meaning (and presumably also truth) must be provided that makes no essential reference to communicative intentions or the conventional rules defined by them.[49]

At this point in the debate the issues become quite complex, and it is not clear that there is even any agreement on precisely what a theory of meaning is supposed to accomplish.[50] According to one view held by many truth-conditional (or formal) semanticists, the task of a theory of meaning is to provide a theoretical account of what someone who does not already know a given language needs to know in order to be able to assign a meaning to (or provide a translation of) sentences in that language. This is the formulation of the task that underlies the problem of radical translation made famous by Quine's description of the jungle translator.[51] It also seems to be the motivation behind Davidson's call for the "autonomy of meaning."[52] The goal of a theory of meaning on this view is to provide an "objectivistic" account of sentence-meaning that does not refer to the speaker's knowledge or beliefs and makes no reference to other semantic notions. On a second view, advocated by theorists of communication-intention, the goal of a theory of meaning is to provide a theoretical reconstruction of a practical ability possessed by competent speakers of a language.[53] There is no further assumption that the theory be "objectivistic" in the sense that it absolve itself of any reference to the speaker's knowledge or beliefs and make no reference to other semantic terms. Rather, as John McDowell puts it, the task is to provide a "perspicuous mapping of the interrelations between concepts which...can be taken to be already perfectly well understood."[54]

As I understand his position, Habermas is closest to theorists of communication-intention. A theory of meaning should provide a theoretical reconstruction of what it is that a competent speaker implicitly knows (in addition to the relevant background knowledge) when he or she understands the utterance of a sentence in her language.[55] A central part of such a theory will therefore include an account of the (pragmatic) rules that govern the standard employment of utterances of that type. On the other hand, Habermas rejects at least one version of communication-intention semantics (known as meaning-nominalism) that describes linguistic meaning as the "fossilized conventions" of prelinguistic intentions.[56] Like some truth-conditional theorists, Habermas also argues that this attempt to develop a theory of meaning exclusively with reference to the (prelinguistic) intentions and beliefs of individuals is ultimately circular.[57]

In the following section I will review the project of meaning-nominalism and certain criticisms of it. Then I will consider a second version of communicative-intention theories found in the work of Austin and Searle and pursued further in Habermas's theory of formal pragmatics. The claim Habermas wants to defend is that understanding the meaning of a sentence requires understanding the acceptability conditions that are constitutive for the different types of speech acts speakers can perform. These acceptability conditions are themselves analyzed in terms of the different validity claims speakers make with their utterances and toward which the hearer can take a rationally motivated "Yes/No" position. Finally, this analysis of the rationally motivated binding force of basic illocutionary acts can provide the basis for a pragmatic justification of a discourse ethics (section IV).

In "Meaning," H. P. Grice introduces a distinction between natural and nonnatural meaning as part of a broader attempt to explain how a speaker (S) can nonnaturally mean something by her utterance.[58] In contrast to something that has a (natural) meaning because it is a symptom of something else (in the sense that clouds "mean" rain or red spots "mean" measles), a sign, action, or utterance can nonnaturally mean something because it is intended by someone to produce an effect in an audience (A). Thus S may draw a picture or make an utterance with the intention of getting A to believe something. However, not every action in which S intends to get A to believe something can be described as a case of S meaning something by her action. For example, in opening a window S may intend to produce in A the belief that it is raining, but it would not be appropriate to say that by opening the window S means that it is raining. Only those cases in which S intends to get

A to believe something by means of A's recognition of S's intention can be described as cases of S meaning something. Thus, to contrast the examples mentioned above, in the first case A may look out the window and, as a result, come to believe that it is raining without ever recognizing S's intention to produce that belief. However, in the case of drawing the picture, unless A recognizes S's intention in drawing the picture it is unlikely that A will come to believe what S intends by the action.

Grice's problem (and his solution) can be made clearer in terms of what has been called the "one-off predicament."[59] S wants to get A to believe that P. However, since S cannot make use of a commonly shared language or other convention—that is what Grice wants to explain—S is forced to come up with some other means. Apart from a few extreme and perhaps limited options (such as brainwashing), one possibility is the use of a "Gricean mechanism": S does X (or utters U) with the intention of producing in A the belief that P by means of A's recognition of that intention. Grice then offers the following definition of nonnatural meaning:[60]

S means that P by X =
   (a) S intends (i–1) to produce in A the belief that P by X
   (b) S intends (i–2) that A recognize i–1
   (c) S intends (i–3) that A's recognition of i–1 be part of the
       reason for A coming to believe that P.

The second stage in the meaning-nominalist strategy concerns the transition from speaker-meaning to sentence meaning. This is accomplished by means of the definition of 'convention' introduced by David Lewis in connection with problems of coordination found in game theory.[61] According to Lewis, a convention is a mutually known regularity in behavior, sustained by a set of preferences and expectations, for which there exists a possible alternative.[62] Driving on the right-hand side of the road is an obvious example: We do so, and prefer to do so, because we expect others to do so, and know that they share these same preferences and expectations. The attraction of this definition, especially for the meaning-nominalist strategy, is that it provides an account of how conventions can arise and be maintained even in the absence of an explicit agreement between the parties involved (remember the "one-off predicament").

One crucial aspect of this definition of a convention, however, is that the regularity in behavior, as well as the system of preferences and expectations sustaining it, must be mutually known by all (or at least most) of the parties involved. According to Lewis's definition, mutual knowledge requires not only that A knows that P and B knows that P, etc., but also that A knows that B knows that P, and B knows that A knows that P, and that A knows that

B knows that A knows that P, etc.[63] This requirement is necessary to distinguish between conventions and regularities in behavior that are based on mere coincidence or mistaken beliefs. Further, eliminating the possibility of mistaken or false belief is especially important for problems of coordination in game theory. If A falsely believes something about B this may shape his preferences, and if he does not have reason to believe certain things about B, he will have no basis upon which to frame his own expectations. If the convention in question is to be sustained not by an explicit agreement—an unlikely possibility in the case of language, and one that is excluded in coordination problems in game theory—but by a rational set of individual preferences and expectations, then the parties involved must have reasons to act upon certain preferences and these reasons must be mutually known.[64] I will return to some problems with this requirement in the criticisms below.

An extension of Lewis's notion of convention to the analysis of sentence meaning has been made by Bennett and by Schiffer. Bennett offers the following account:[65]

> Let us say that there is a convention whereby utterance-type S means that P within a given tribesman's idiolect, if (a) in the past he has uttered S only when he meant that P, and (b) this fact is mutually known to him and his hearers, and (c) because of the mutual knowledge mentioned in (b) it continues to be the case that when he utters S he means and is understood to mean that P.

The twofold strategy behind meaning-nominalism is thus (1) to offer a definition of speaker-meaning in terms of a "Gricean mechanism," and (2) to regard sentence meaning (or utterance-type meaning) as a "fossilization" or conventionalization (in Lewis's sense) of speaker-meaning.[66] The proposal is offered not as an historical account of how language arose, but rather as a theoretical analysis and reconstruction of how linguistic meaning is possible. A hearer understands a sentence because she recognizes it as a token of a conventional utterance-type of a Gricean mechanism—that is, she has reason to believe that what the utterance-type conventionally means is what the speaker presently intends and, similarly, the speaker has reason to believe that she (the hearer) will so understand it. Conventional sentence meaning, once established, is then sustained by the network of preferences and expectations of the sort described by Lewis.

A number of criticisms have been raised against this version of communication-intention semantics. Since the meaning-nominalist strategy has been laid out in two stages, the criticisms can also be presented in two stages: those that focus on the Gricean mechanism, and those that address the notion of convention.

A number of critics, including Strawson, have raised questions about the sufficiency of Grice's definition of nonnatural meaning. Strawson, Schiffer, and Searle have all introduced counterexamples that meet all of Grice's criteria, but do not seem to be cases of what we would ordinarily describe as S meaning that P. Imagine the following situation where A is watching S, S knows that A is watching, but A does not know that S knows. S arranges papers on her desk with the intention of producing in A the belief that he has been at work on a new manuscript. S intends that A see her doing this and that A recognizes in the action S's intention to produce that belief. Finally, S intends that the recognition of this intention be at least part of the reason for A acquiring the belief. All of Grice's criteria have been met, yet, Strawson argues, because of the "sneaky" or hidden intention involved (A does not know that S knows that A is watching), we would not normally say that S's action means that she has been working on a new manuscript (at least not at all in the way S would mean it if she simply told A). "It seems a minimum further condition of his trying to do this that he should not only intend A to recognize his intention to get A to think that p, but that he should also intend A to recognize his intention to get A to recognize his intention to get A to think that p."[67] As Strawson noted, however, further examples could also be introduced indicating the insufficiency of his own criteria and leading eventually to the need for still higher-order intentions. Strawson's point is that a complete communicative-intention, that is a version of a Gricean mechanism, must be "wholly overt." Others have therefore suggested that Strawson's revision be seen as introducing the further condition that none of the intentions listed in Grice's definition (i–1, i–2, and i–3) be in principle concealed, or, what amounts to the same thing, that all the intentions be essentially avowable. In his more recent writing on meaning, Grice has accepted this condition.[68]

A second, related criticism has been made by Searle. In *Speech Acts,* Searle charges that Grice has confused illocutionary with perlocutionary acts and attempts to provide an account of the former by means of the latter. Habermas has developed the same point in the claim that Grice and Bennett attempt to explain acts of direct understanding on the basis of indirect understanding or "giving something to be understood."[69] I will discuss the distinction between illocutionary and perlocutionary acts in more detail below, but it must be briefly introduced here to clarify Searle's criticism. Illocutionary acts, according to Searle, are acts aimed at "securing uptake" (Austin) or "reaching understanding" (Habermas), whereas perlocutionary acts are acts that produce an effect other than, or in addition to, understanding. Thus, according to Searle, when Grice describes meaning as "intending to produce a belief," he describes a perlocutionary, not an illocutionary act. A speaker can say something and mean it (thus peform an illocutionary act) even though he may not "care a hang" (Searle) whether the speaker believes it.[70] It is thus possible for someone to perform an illocutionary act (secure uptake, reach understanding, be understood) without performing or intending to perform a perlocutionary act (inducing belief, convincing, etc.), even if in most cases we do intend to produce perlocutionary effects as well. Searle's point is that Grice's definition confuses the intention to have an intention recognized with the intention to produce a belief:

> In the case of illocutionary acts we succeed in doing what we are trying to do by getting our audience to recognize what we are trying to do. But the "effect" on the hearer is not a belief or a response, it consists simply in the hearer understanding the speaker. It is this that I have been calling the illocutionary effect.[71]

However, just as Grice's definition of nonnatural meaning could be easily modified to include Strawson's condition of essential avowability, it would seem that Grice could also incorporate Searle's criticism. Jonathan Bennett, in fact, proposes just such a revision in "The Meaning-Nominalist Strategy."[72] Grice would only need to formulate his speaker's primary intention (i–1) as follows: S intends to produce in A the knowledge (or the understanding or the recognition of) that P by X.

Habermas has developed an apparently similar criticism in his claim that meaning-nominalism has failed to do what it set out to do. Rather than providing an account of speaker meaning ("saying something") by shifting from an analysis of illocutionary to perlocutionary acts, meaning-nominalism has instead provided an account of "indirectly giving something to be understood."[73] Habermas further argues that this analysis fails since perlocutionary acts presuppose (or are parasitic upon) illocutionary acts. Thus, far from analyzing speaker meaning, the meaning-nominalist strategy must presuppose acts of direct understanding.

This criticism is not easy to assess, however, in part because Habermas mistakenly identifies perlocutionary acts with concealed strategic action.[74] Many perlocutionary acts (convincing, persuading, comforting) need not be concealed or unavowed, though some certainly must be (for example, hinting, insinuating, or deceiving). (Of course, not all strategic action needs to be concealed either, but it seems particularly forced to equate an overt attempt to comfort someone through words—e.g., a perlocutionary act, with strategic action.) One possible interpretation would be to see Habermas's criticism as a version of Strawson's modification of the Gricean mechanism mentioned above. In support of this view is the fact that Habermas considers a counterexample introduced by Schiffer in his own discussion of Strawson. Schiffer, like Strawson, concludes that cases involving a "sneaky" or hidden intention are not cases of S meaning that P. However, if we follow this interpretation it remains unclear how this account of "indirectly giving something to be understood" presupposes (or is parasitic upon) an illocutionary act as Habermas claims, except in the trivial sense that perlocutionary acts (by definition) rely upon illocutionary acts for their success.[75] Nor are the examples of Strawson and Schiffer easily classified as perlocutionary acts just because they involve a "sneaky" intention. Further, as I noted above, Grice has accepted Strawson's modification and Bennett has suggested that Grice's definition of speaker meaning can easily be accommodated to fit Searle's objection.

Habermas, I want to suggest, is offering a much more fundamental criticism of the meaning-nominalist strategy as a whole, and one that also leads from criticisms of the Gricean mechanism to criticisms of the notion of convention used in this strategy. The question raised at the beginning of this section concerning the task of a theory of meaning reemerges as this point. The shift from an analysis of "saying something" to an analysis of "indirectly giving something to be understood," reflects the assumption that a theory of meaning must be one "which is not in terms of any semantic notions."[76] This formulation of the task is not persuasive, however, unless someone is already committed to the view that a theory of meaning should make no reference to the "internal" perspective of the participant, that is, that speakers' knowledge or belief must be given a wholly objectivistic or physicalistic account. As in Quine's description of the problem of radical translation, Bennett's translator also heads for the jungle, equipped this time with coconuts rather than a translation manual![77]

Habermas develops his own criticism of this "objectivistic" approach to a theory of meaning in connection with Schiffer's notion of mutual knowledge.[78] As I noted earlier, mutual knowledge means not only that everyone knows that P, but also that everyone knows that everyone else knows that P, etc. This definition is required in order to solve various coordination problems in game theory. However, this definition assumes that the parties involved already commonly share certain symbolic expressions. Schiffer's attempt to define common or mutual knowledge without assuming shared symbolic expressions borders on the unbelievable: A and B are sitting at a table, facing one another with a candle on the table between them. A looks through the candle to B, and B looks through the candle to A. Thus A and B both know that there is a candle on the table, and both know that the other knows.[79] If Habermas's argument is sound, meaning-nominalism must already presuppose a notion of symbolic meaning and the attempt to analyze "saying something" in terms of "indirectly giving something to be understood" fails.[80]

Before turning to the second version of communication-intention theories, I want briefly to mention one further criticism of the meaning-nominalist strategy. Both Strawson and Searle have criticized Grice for not paying sufficient attention to the nature and role of conventions or rules in sentence meaning.[81] Grice's account suggests that utterances can mean whatever speakers intend. Conventions are "fossilizations" of intentions, but what is to prohibit a speaker from intending his utterance to mean something other than its conventional meaning? Searle pursues this point in relation to Wittgenstein's question, "Can someone say, 'It's hot' and mean that it's cold?" His claim is that conventionalized sentence meaning cannot be adequately understood in terms of a mutually known regularity in behavior. The rules governing speech acts are not shorthand notations for generalizations in linguistic behavior, but rules that are somehow constitutive of that behavior. I will return to Searle's distinction between these two types of rules below.[82]

A second version of communication-intention semantics is found in the work of J. L. Austin and has been developed by Searle, Strawson, and others (including Habermas and Apel). In this version, like the meaning-nominalist strategy, the basic linguistic unit is not the sentence, but the speech act (sentence meaning being somehow derivative). However, in contrast to the first version discussed, these theorists do not attempt to analyze the basic speech act in terms of game-theoretic or purposive-rational action and choice. The rules constitutive for the different types of speech acts are not conventional regularities of intentions to produce effects, and thus the analysis of "saying something" cannot be carried out through an analysis of "indirectly giving something to be understood." Surprisingly (since we seem to have come so far from Rawls at this point), the first explicit discussion of the two concepts of rules distinguished by Searle (to my knowledge) appears in an article by Rawls.[83] Searle (and Rawls) distinguish between rules that regulate preexisting forms of behavior (such as rules of etiquette) and rules which create or define new forms of behavior (such as the rules of chess). According to Searle, speech acts are a species of constitutive rules and to understand a speech act is to know the rules that are constitutive for the use or employment of acts of that type. Searle formulates his thesis in two parts (which my exposition will follow):

> [Firstly] that speaking a language is performing speech acts such as making statements, giving commands, asking questions, making promises, and so on;...and, secondly, that these acts are in general made possible by and performed in accordance with certain rules for the use of linguistic elements.[84]

Drawing upon the work of Austin, Searle introduces two distinctions that are fundamental for his analysis of speech acts. He distinguishes, first, between the locutionary and illocutionary component of a speech act (roughly Frege's distinction between sense [or meaning] and force); and, second, between illocutionary and perlocutionary acts. Since these distinctions are also important for Habermas's own theory of formal pragmatics, I will comment on each in greater detail.

Meaning and illocutionary acts. In *How to Do Things With Words,* Austin introduced a distinction between locutionary and illocutionary acts: locutionary acts are acts *of* saying something, while illocutionary acts are acts one performs *in* saying something. The former, according to Austin, refer to the sense and reference of the utterance and are apparently the bearers of truth and falsity.[85] Illocutionary acts, on the other hand, indicate the force of the utterance and are determined not by the conditions of their truth or falsity, but by conditions of felicity or infelicity. Although Austin acknowledged that both acts are abstractions from the total speech act, Searle and others have argued the distinction is still not clear.[86] Acts of saying something seem to be illocutionary acts as well (acts of stating, reporting, asserting, etc.) and (most) illocutionary acts also have a locutionary component—in making a promise or a command one promises or commands something. Consequently, Searle has proposed reformulating Austin's distinction not as a difference between two kinds of acts, but as a distinction between the two basic components of any speech act.[87] The locutionary component (or propositional content) refers to the meaning or sense of the utterance and is the bearer of truth and falsity; whereas the illocutionary component specifies the force (or mood) with which the propositional content is uttered. In this view, a speech act is described as having a standard form or "double structure" (Habermas) that can be represented as '$F(p)$'.

Although this reformulation appears to correct certain infelicities in Austin's own account, particularly regarding his notion of truth, it gives rise to at least two problems that I will only mention here. First, it creates the possibility of confusing the meaning of an illocutionary act with the meaning of its propositional content. In fact, much of the confusion in the debate between truth-conditional and communication-intention (or pragmatic) theories of meaning arises from just such a confusion between the meaning of a sentence in this wide or narrow sense.[88] At the same time, it seems that at least some of the issues in this debate can be reframed in terms of this distinction. The central question would then be, "Is the meaning of a sentence (that is, an utterance-type in contrast to occasional speaker's meaning) exhausted by a truth-conditional analysis of the meaning of its propositional content?" Or, conversely (and perhaps further), "Does the analysis of even the propositional content of a sentence lead back to and require an account of what speakers standardly do in making utterances with that content?" Strawson and Habermas, as I see it, answer no to the first question and yes to the second; Searle is more vague but seems to answer no to both questions.[89]

Second, Searle's reformulation leaves it unclear whether explicit performatives can be given a truth-conditional analysis. It is certainly true that
they can in the sense that "I promise I will come" is true if and only if I
promise that I will come. It does not seem to be the case, however, that
knowledge of the truth-conditions of a performative (in this sense) amounts
to the same thing as knowing the (illocutionary) meaning of an utterance.
What is required additionally (or, perhaps, rather) is knowledge of the conditions under which a performative (say, a promise) would be acceptable or
warranted or, in Austin's words, felicitous. Thus, even if a truth-conditional
analysis of performatives is possible, one would not thereby understand the
meaning of a performative, but (at most) the meaning of an assertion that a
particular performative (a promise) had been made.[90]

Illocutionary and perlocutionary acts.   Austin's distinction between
illocutionary and perlocutionary acts, though less controversial than the previous distinction, has also been subject to criticism. According to Austin,
illocutionary acts are essentially conventional in a way that perlocutionary
acts are not; and illocutionary acts aim at "securing uptake" or "Bringing
about an understanding of the meaning and of the force of the locution,"
whereas perlocutionary acts aim at producing an effect in the audience.[91]
Questions have been directed to both of these claimed distinctions. Thus,
while many illocutionary acts are clearly conventional (for example, pronouncing a sentence, bidding in cards, and baptizing), many others do not
seem to be except in the more trivial sense that all linguistic acts are conventional (for example, warning, requesting, or informing).[92] However, as
Strawson has pointed out, Austin's use of the term 'convention' is rather
peculiar. Austin writes, an illocutionary act may "be said to be *conventional*
in the sense that at least it could be made explicit by the performative formula."[93] Illocutionary acts are conventional in the sense that they can be formulated in an explicit performative whereas perlocutionary acts apparently cannot be. Thus, the utterance, "I'll come" may be stated in the explicit
performative "I promise that I will come," or "I warn you that I will come,"
or "I assure you that I will come," depending upon which illocutionary act
the speaker intends to perform. Perlocutionary acts (such as convincing,
insinuating, or frightening) cannot be so formulated and in some cases the
attempt to formulate them as an explicit performative would defeat the perlocutionary aim (for example, hinting or attempting to impress someone).
Further, as I mentioned above, although some perlocutionary aims can be
openly acknowledged, it is not necessary for an understanding of the speech
act performed that they be overtly stated (and in some cases they cannot be).
By contrast, as Strawson's critique of Grice has shown, a feature of an illocutionary act (an act of meaning something) is that it be essentially avow-

able. Searle has developed this insight further in what he calls the "Principle of Expressibility": "Whatever can be meant can be said."[94] Searle's claim is not that a speaker must always explicitly state what he (illocutionarily) means, but that it is in principle possible for a speaker to state what illocutionary act he has performed, either by means of an explicit performative or in some other way.[95] Thus, nonliteral speech acts such as irony or indirect requests ('Can you pass the salt?') do not constitute an objection to this principle.[96]

This clarification of Austin's peculiar usage of the term 'convention' also helps to explain Austin's claim that illocutionary acts aim to secure uptake while perlocutionary acts aim to produce an effect. Understanding is also an effect, but unlike the effects of perlocutionary acts, the effect sought (reaching understanding) is essentially overt and, in a manner I will consider shortly, constitutive for the type of illocutionary act performed. A speaker cannot successfully utter a command, request, or assertion without the hearer recognizing it as an act of that type, and a hearer understands a particular speech act only when she knows the conditions necessary for the successful performance of acts belonging to that type. By contrast, in the case of perlocutionary acts, knowledge of the speaker's perlocutionary intent is not necessary for an understanding of the type of speech act that has been performed and, correspondingly, a speaker need not intend to produce a perlocutionary effect in order to perform a perlocutionary act. A hearer does not need to be frightened in order to understand a threat, or convinced in order to understand an assertion, or appeased in order to understand an apology. Similarly, a speaker need not intend to frighten in order to frighten, need not intend to convince in order to convince, and need not intend to comfort in order to make someone happy. In the serious and literal performance of an illocutionary act, however, a speaker cannot assert something without wanting to tell it, cannot promise something without undertaking to do it, and cannot command something without wanting the hearer to recognize what compliance would involve. In short, the aim of securing uptake or achieving understanding is built into the structure of the illocutionary act, or the act of understanding, whereas perlocutionary aims are incidental and, in this sense, subordinate to them. We can, accordingly, summarize the distinction between illocutionary and perlocutionary acts as follows: An illocutionary act is an act that, when standardly and literally performed, aims at securing uptake or reaching understanding. An essential feature of an illocutionary act is that it be, in principle, wholly overt. A perlocutionary act is an act in which the speaker's saying something produces an intended or unintended effect upon the feelings, thoughts, or actions of her audience beyond or in addition to that of reaching understanding.[97] Perlocutionary acts are therefore by definition dependent upon the success of illocutionary acts. An audience cannot be influenced by what a speaker says unless it has first understood (even if incorrectly) what the speaker says.

With these distinctions in hand we can turn to the second part of Searle's thesis mentioned above, namely, that the successful performance of a particular speech act (or act of meaning something) is possible in virtue of certain rules that govern acts of that type. In keeping with the distinction between constitutive and regulative rules noted above, Searle suggests that the rules governing the types of speech acts can be regarded as constitutive rules, that is, the rules create or constitute the form of behavior which they govern. He formulates the second part of his thesis in more detail as follows:

> The semantic structure of a language may be regarded as a conventional realization of a series of sets of underlying constitutive rules, and that speech acts are characteristically performed by uttering expressions in accordance with sets of constitutive rules.[98]

The central task of *Speech Acts* is to provide a description and summary of these constitutive rules. Searle suggests that there are four main rules or conditions constitutive for the type of speech act performed, the most important of which is the essential rule or rule that specifies the act's illocutionary point or aim. I will briefly summarize these four rules in connection with examples of three basic types of illocutionary acts: "I (S) promise H that p"; "I (S) apologize to H that p"; and "I (S) assert to H that p."[99]

1. Propositional content rule. Although the illocutionary force of an utterance is distinct from its propositional content, in many cases the force imposes constraints or conditions upon the propositional content. In the case of a promise, the content cannot be a past action; in the case of an apology, the content must be something for which S is responsible; in the case of an assertion, only very general conditions are imposed. For example, if S asserts that x is bald, x must exist.

2. Preparatory conditions or rules. These state general conditions which must obtain for a particular type of speech act to be performed. In the case of a promise, H must prefer S's doing p to S's not doing p and S must believe this to be the case; in the case of an apology, S must believe that p is wrong or reprehensible; in the case of an assertion, S must be able to offer some reason or evidence for p.

3. Sincerity rule. Illocutionary acts imply a corresponding psychological state with the same propositional content. Generally, in the

case of a promise, S must intend to undertake p; in the case of an apology, S must regret or feel sorry for p; in the case of an assertion, S must believe that p.

4. Essential rule. An utterance *counts as* a type of illocutionary act in accordance with the aim or point expressed in it. These aims are internal to the structure of the illocutionary act and are independent of other aims or the particular occasional intentions a speaker may have in making the utterance. In the case of a promise, S undertakes to do p; in the case of an apology, S expresses sorrow or regret for p; and in the case of an assertion, S reports or tells how things are (that p).

In any successful (or nondefective) speech act, these rules or conditions must be conformed to or fulfilled. A speaker successfully performs an illocutionary act by virtue of fulfilling the conditions specified by the constitutive rules, and a hearer understands an utterance when he knows the conditions necessary for the successful performance of an illocutionary act of that type. Finally, on the basis of this analysis of the rules constitutive for the different types of speech acts, Searle offers the following reformulation of Grice's notion of nonnatural meaning (see p. 101 above):[100]

S utters sentence T and means it (i.e., means literally what he says)=

S utters T and

(a) S intends (i–1) the utterance U of T to produce in A the knowledge (recognition, awareness, understanding) that the states of affairs specified by (certain of) rules of T obtain (Call this effect the illocutionary effect, IE).

(b) S intends (i-2) U to produce IE by means of recognition of i–1.

(c) S intends (i–3) that i–1 will be recognized in virtue of (by means of) T, that is, by means of the appropriate preparatory, essential, and sincerity rules for the successful performance of T.

Habermas's theory of formal pragmatics is greatly indebted to this analysis of the constitutive rules that determine the meaning of illocutionary acts. Roughly stated, according to Habermas, someone understands the meaning of a speech act when she knows the rules constitutive for speech acts of that type or, to use his phrase, when she knows the conditions that would make it acceptable (*TCA* 1, 297). Despite the apparent similarity between this formulation and truth-conditional semantics, Habermas agrees with the basic criticism of that approach made by Strawson and Searle: The (illocutionary) meaning of an utterance is partly fixed by the rules governing its standard employment, and a speaker's ability to understand an utterance does not consist in objectivistic (or knowledge-transcendent) truth-conditions; that is, truth-conditions whose fulfillment can be determined from the perspective of an observer or third person (*TCA* 1, 115–16). Rather, knowledge of the "conditions of satisfaction" (Searle) or "conditions of acceptability" (Habermas) requires that the speaker/hearer adopt the "performative attitude" of a (possible) participant (*TCA* 1, 298). The basic error of theories of meaning framed in terms of the problem of radical translation is that they either assume that an objectivistic or physicalistic analysis of sentence meaning can be given or presuppose surreptitiously the perspective of the participant (or performative attitude) in their analysis (as in the case of the jungle translator who is already competent in his own language). Even in those truth-conditional approaches that do not cast the problem of meaning as a problem of radical translation, there is a tendency to view the knowledge of truth-conditions in terms of a monological processing of information or application of decision-procedure rules, rather than in terms of the type of commitment or engagement a speaker assumes *vis-à-vis* his audience about the validity of his utterances.[101] It is in this sense that Habermas speaks of the need to move beyond semantics to pragmatics. Pragmatics is thus not an empirical or contextual supplement to semantics, but an analysis of the formal conditions under which speakers can make and understand meaningful utterances.[102]

However, despite his indebtedness to Searle's version of communication-intention semantics, Habermas proposes several clarifications and revisions in developing his own theory of formal pragmatics. Three of these will be considered here: his clarification of Searle's notion of convention, his reformulation of Searle's "essential rule" or illocutionary point of a speech act, and his introduction of a three-world orientation. The last point provides the basis for Habermas's reclassification of the basic types of illocutionary acts.

(1) In emphasizing the role of convention over intention in his critique of Grice, Searle tends to underestimate the nonconventional character of many basic illocutionary acts.[103] Strawson already drew attention to this problem in his discussion of Austin's peculiar usage of the term 'convention'. Searle, too, would undoubtedly want to distinguish between what Habermas calls "institutionally bound" and "institutionally unbound" speech acts.[104] There is an important difference between such illocutionary acts as calling a strike, pronouncing a sentence, or christening a boat and such illocutionary acts as promising, apologizing, and asserting, even if Strawson is correct in claiming that they form two poles of a continuum. If the latter are still regarded as "language-games," they nevertheless possess a "weak" or "quasi-transcendental" status in a way the former do not.[105] Toward the end

of *Speech Acts,* in a comment on Proudhon's remark that "Property is theft," Searle hints at this difference:[106]

> If one tries to take this as an internal remark it makes no sense. It was intended as an external remark attacking and rejecting the institution of private property. It gets its air of paradox and its force by using terms which are internal to the institution in order to attack the institution. Standing on the deck of some institutions one can tinker with constitutive rules and even throw some institutions overboard. But could one throw all institutions overboard? One could not and still engage in those forms of behavior we consider characteristically human. Suppose Proudhon had added (and tried to live by): "Truth is a lie," "marriage is infidelity," "language is uncommunicative," "law is a crime," and so on with every possible institution.

Habermas's description of certain basic types of speech acts as quasi-transcendental is intended to draw attention to their unavoidable character.[107] At the same time, however, as a reconstructive analysis of a speaker's competence, the theory of formal pragmatics is an empirical and thus fallibilistic undertaking. There is no claim to *a priori* knowledge. Further, in contrast to Apel, the transcendental force or necessity of the basic types of speech acts does not of itself imply a moral obligation to conform to those basic types, or that the constitutive rules are themselves moral rules.[108] An attempt to cross the fact/value gap with such a transcendental argument would merely represent a linguistic version of the naturalistic fallacy—one that Searle is himself inclined to make.[109] As I hope to show in the next section, Habermas's strategy, which makes essential use of the notion of communicative action, is quite different.

(2) Habermas and others have drawn attention to the fact that Searle's description of the essential rule or illocutionary point of a speech act amounts to little more than a paraphrase of what speakers generally do in performing speech acts of that type.[110] As such, the rule lacks any explanatory force. By contrast, Habermas suggests that what is constitutive for the basic kinds of illocutionary acts is the specific type of "engagement" or "performative attitude" exhibited in the structure of the act. On the basis of this, the speaker becomes committed to accepting certain consequences of action and to redeeming the validity of his claims should they be contested.

> An utterance can count as a promise, assertion, request or avowal, if and only if the speaker makes an offer that he is ready to make good insofar as it is accepted by the hearer. The speaker must engage himself, that is, indicate that in certain situations he will draw certain consequences for action.[111]

This engagement or performative attitude is not primarily defined in terms of the occasional subjective attitude or intention of the speaker, but in terms of validity claims that correspond to each type of illocutionary act and that are built into the structure of acts of that type. Habermas's analysis of these validity claims is thus intended to function in much the same way as Searle's analysis of the essential rule (or illocutionary point) of the basic speech acts, that is, they are constitutive for the type of speech act in question. Moreover, a speaker's recognition of these validity claims (or conditions of acceptability) is not a purely cognitive matter. The speaker also commits herself to certain consequences of action (for example, undertaking to do some future act, as in promising) and, if the sequence of interaction is to remain undisturbed, to redeeming or making good the validity claims raised in the speech act should the utterance be challenged.

Habermas clarifies the various validity claims constitutive for the basic types of speech acts with reference to the different types of Yes/No responses that an audience can adopt toward them.[112] Thus, for the following four elementary and simple illocutionary acts,

1. I promise you that I will come.
2. I request that you stop smoking.
3. I tell you that the movie has already begun.
4. I confess to you that your actions disappoint me,

the hearer or audience might respond in the following ways,

5. Yes, I shall depend upon it.
6. Yes, I shall comply.
7. Yes, I believe that what you say is true.
8. Yes, I believe that you are speaking sincerely.

In 5 and 6 the hearer's response is directed primarily to a claim about the rightness or appropriateness of the offer made in the speech act; in 7, he is responding primarily to the truth or accuracy of what the speaker asserts; and in 8, he responds primarily to the sincerity or truthfulness of the speaker's intention. Of course, even in these simple examples it is clear that more than one validity claim can be raised in any speech act. Thus, in response to 1 and 2, the hearer may challenge not only the appropriateness of the promise or request, but also the sincerity of the speaker or the accuracy of the facts involved. Similarly, in response to 3, the hearer may challenge not only the accuracy of the assertion but also the speaker's sincerity or the appropriateness of making the assertion on a particular occasion. Finally, in response to 4, the hearer can also challenge the right of the speaker to make such a confession or the facts on which the speaker has formed her opinion. Habermas's claim is that, in addition to the general conditions of intelligibility (such as grammatical well-formedness), there are precisely three validity claims that can be raised in relation to an utterance (truth, rightness, and truthfulness). The priority of the respective claim determines the basic type of speech act performed (*TCA* 1: 307). In constative or assertive illocutionary acts, it is the claim to truth that is constitutive; in regulative illocutionary acts, the claim to its normative correctness or rightness; and, in expressives, the claim to truthfulness or sincerity (see Figure 3-1). To understand the meaning of a particular speech act is to know the conditions under which it would be acceptable (or what would be required to satisfy the validity claims raised). Habermas describes the acceptance of a speech act as "rationally motivated" to the extent that it depends on the recognition and acceptance of the validity claims involved, and illocutionary acts can be said to possess a rationally motivated binding (or bonding) force to the extent that they require speaker/hearer acknowledgment of these validity claims.[113]

(3) Habermas also offers a reformulation of Searle's taxonomy of the basic types of speech acts that makes more explicit the possible world-relations that social actors can adopt.[114] As we saw above in the discussion of communicative action, in seeking to reach an agreement with one another about something in the world, social actors are oriented to either an external world of states of affairs, a social world of interpersonal norms, or a subjective world of experiences.[115] Habermas now proposes that the possible world-relations that speakers can adopt in their attempts to reach agreement with one another be correlated with the three basic types of speech acts and thus used to strengthen his own classification of the latter: In constative speech acts, speakers primarily seek to reach an agreement about the external or objective world; in regulative speech acts, speakers primarily seek to reach agreement about the intersubjective or social world; and in expressive speech acts, speakers primarily seek to reach an understanding about the internal or subjective world (see Figure 3-1). This taxonomy, Habermas argues, also has the virtue of avoiding some of the difficulties encountered by Searle in his attempt to classify speech acts according to their "illocutionary point" (or essential rule) and "direction of fit."[116]

First, "direction of fit" does not seem to be able to explain satisfactorily more than three types of illocutionary acts: neither declaratives nor expressives (as Searle notes) can be discussed in terms of a word-to-world or world-to-word relation. Moreover, directives and commissives (which are not distinguishable in terms of direction of fit) would seem to be better clarified in terms of their relation to an intersubjective world of norms than an objective world of states of affairs. Accordingly, Habermas brings directives, commissives, and declaratives under the more general category of regulatives in order to indicate their common relation to the social world of norms.

SEARLE

Type of Illocutionary Act	Illocutionary Point ("Essential Rule")	Direction of Fit	Psychological Attitude Expressed	Restrictions on Propositional Content
ASSERTIVES	tell someone how things are	word to world ↓	B belief	(P) none
DIRECTIVES	attempt to get the hearer to do something	world to word ↑	W wish	(H does some future A)
COMMISSIVES	commit the speaker to a future course of action	world to word ↑	I intention	(S does some future A)
DECLARATIVES	bring about a change in the world through speaker's utterance	word to world & ↕ world to word	Ø	(P)
EXPRESSIVES	express the speaker's psychic feelings or attitudes	Ø empty (no direction or fit)	(P) variable	S/H and some properties (e.g. S cannot apologize for everything)

HABERMAS

Basic Type of Illocutionary Act	Principle Validity Claim	World Relation	Grammatical Person and Basic Performative Attitude	Illocutionary Aim or Point
CONSTATIVES	Truth	Objective world of facts or 'states of affairs'	3rd Objectivating	Represent a state of affairs
REGULATIVES	Rightness	Social or intersubjective world of norms	2nd Norm-conformative	Establish an interpersonal relation
EXPRESSIVES	Truthfulness	Subjective world of experiences, feelings, or desires	1st Expressive or dramaturgical	Express a subjective experience, feeling or desire
COMMUNICATIVES	—	Reflexive relation to the process of communication	—	Serve the organization of speech
OPERATIVES	—	—	—	Application of generative rules

Figure 3-1: Classification of Basic Types of Speech Acts*

*SOURCES: Searle, *Expression and Meaning*, Chapter 1
Habermas, *TCA* I, Chapter 3

Second, as Habermas and Martinich have noted, Searle's class of expressives is quite diverse and does not seem to be based on any obvious criterion (for example, in addition to avowals, it also includes such acts as thanking, greeting, and congratulating). Habermas suggests that this results from Searle's attempt to find a place for what Austin called behabitives and proposes instead to unify the class of expressives in terms of their relation to the subjective world of feelings, needs, and desires, etc.[117]

Third, Searle's classification leaves no place for what Nicholas Fotion has called "master speech acts" (acts such as replying, objecting, conjecturing, etc.).[118] These are included in the class of what Habermas calls "communicatives" whose point is to serve the organization of speech. They do not have a unique world-relation, but rather have a reflexive relation to the other basic types of speech acts. Similarly, the class of operatives (inferring, calculating, counting, classifying, etc.) don't have a unique world-relation, but rather refer to linguistic acts that employ generative rules in the construction of symbolic expressions.[119]

Since the publication of *The Theory of Communicative Action*, Habermas has modified his analysis of illocutionary acts in one major respect relevant for his attempt to ground a discourse ethics. In *The Theory of Communicative Action*, Habermas sharply distinguished between simple imperatives that reflect mere expressions of will ("Bring me a glass of water") and normatively authorized imperatives that more evidently draw upon socially recognized norms and institutions (such as an airline steward's request that passengers not smoke). Habermas argued that only the latter properly belong to the class of regulative speech acts. Furthermore, in addition to the satisfaction conditions discussed above (i.e., the hearer must know what would be involved in conforming to the request), simple imperatives must also be supplemented by "conditions of sanction," that is, the speaker must know why the speaker thinks she can impose her will on him. In normatively authorized speech acts, these additional conditions of sanction are contained within the illocutionary meaning of the speech act itself: one understands the force of the request because one is also aware of the institutional structure in which such a request can be made. In the case of simple imperatives, however, there are no corresponding social norms or institutions; the conditions of sanction seem to rely solely upon the rewards/threats that the speaker can use to impose her will. For this reason, Habermas was initially inclined to view simple imperatives as strategic actions or as a subclass of perlocutionary acts, rather than as a type of illocutionary act (*TCA* 1: 300f., 329). More recently, however, and partly in response to criticisms of this classification, Habermas has revised his view. He now treats simple imperatives as one extreme in the continuum of regulative speech acts. Except perhaps for the case of direct threats of force, even simple imperatives seem to draw upon sanctions associated with social norms and institutions. To the extent that they do, even if these norms are only habitually recognized or followed, they are connected to the potential for a rationally motivated agreement characteristic of all basic types of illocutionary acts.[120]

IV. THE IDEA AND JUSTIFICATION OF A DISCOURSE ETHICS

With this exposition of the notion of communicative action and the theory of formal pragmatics in hand, we can finally proceed to a clarification of Habermas's moral theory and, more specifically, to his justification of its principle of universalizability (U). As a rule of argumentation that is constitutive for a practical discourse Principle U may be regarded as a communicative or intersubjective reconstruction of Kant's categorical imperative.[121] It stipulates that a social norm is morally justified only if the forseeable consequences that would follow from its general observance could be accepted by everyone affected as in their own interest (see *DE,* 65; ME, 197). I begin with a brief summary of the major features of a discourse ethics by comparing it with Kant's moral theory (A). Following this, I consider Habermas's derivation of the principle of universalizability (B). This derivation occurs in two steps: First, Habermas introduces a set of rules of argumentation gleaned from an analysis of the universal and unavoidable pragmatic presuppositions of argument. These presuppositions themselves depend upon the close connection between meaning and validity established in the theory of formal pragmatics (e.g., we know the meaning of an utterance when we know the conditions under which it would be acceptable). However, the derivation of the principle of universalizability can only be completed when these rules of argumentation are supplemented with the idea of what it means to justify a norm of action (see *DE,* 86, 92; *ME,* 198). This second step in the justification draws upon some of the conclusions arrived at in Habermas's analysis of communicative action. I then offer a comparison between Habermas's discourse ethics and a recent proposal for a contractualist moral theory made by Thomas Scanlon (C). The chapter concludes with an indication of some of the remaining problems and questions to be dealt with in the last two chapters (D).

A. Discourse Ethics and Kant's Moral Theory

In his recent essay "Morality and Ethical Life," Habermas formulates more clearly than earlier the similarities and differences between his version of a discourse ethics and Kant's moral theory. Like Kant, Habermas describes the moral point of view as a position of impartiality, distinct from other personal and/or self-interested perspectives.[122] The central task for a moral theory thus becomes that of clarifying and justifying what it means to adopt a "moral point of view" or impartial standpoint. The further similarities between Habermas's project and Kant's moral theory can be described under four headings.

First, discourse ethics is a *universalistic* moral theory. Its basic principle (U) is not restricted to a particular time period or culture, nor does it merely represent the moral beliefs of, say, liberal white males. Habermas attempts to establish its universality by deriving this principle from the "quasi-transcendental" (and, hence, unavoidable) presuppositions of argumentation: Anyone who seriously enters into argument with others presupposes certain pragmatic rules from which the principle of universalizability can be inferred (when these rules of argument are combined with the notion of justifying a norm of action—see below). Habermas also argues that the rules and structure of argumentation are not a contingent feature of, say, advanced capitalist societies, but belong to the evolutionary development of species-wide competencies. In this sense, the claim to universality of discourse ethics is defended by means of a revised transcendental argument. Still it rejects the stronger claim to *a priori* status; it is fallibilistic and depends upon the empirical validity of its reconstruction of specific human competencies.

Second, discourse ethics is a *formalistic* moral theory. Like Kant's categorical imperative, the principle of universalizability is introduced as a procedure for testing norms. It does not by itself generate any substantive moral norms; rather, it specifies an argumentative procedure that any norm must satisfy if it is to be morally acceptable. Since Hegel's critique of Kant, the distinction between a formal principle and normative content has been difficult to defend and I will consider it in more detail below. Still, in another sense, Hegel's critique missed its target since, as we saw in chapter 1, the categorical imperative was not intended by Kant to generate moral norms, but rather to specify a test procedure for existing maxims of action. Similarly, discourse ethics assumes the existence of a social world of norms; the validity of these norms, however, can only be established by way of real discourses actually taking place. To expect that substantive moral norms can be immediately inferred from a clarification of the moral point of view (in the way, perhaps, that Rawls hopes to derive his two principles) is, according to Habermas, to ask for too much from a moral theory.

Third, discourse ethics is a *cognitivist* moral theory. This characterization is liable to confusion: In one interpretation, cognitivism in ethics is contrasted to subjectivism (or relativism) and then identified with a defense of the objectivity of moral norms and judgments. However, the notion of objectivity that this view seems to imply has been strongly contested and the argument itself seems to rely upon a questionable distinction, at least when it concerns moral questions, between the objective and intersubjective: According to Mackie, for example, objectivity in moral values or judgments means that they are (or that they reflect) "part of the fabric of the world."[123] But Kant, Rawls, and Habermas—to mention only those with whom we have been concerned—all defend cognitivism and yet deny that there are moral facts of the matter to which our judgments should correspond. Kantian constructivism, as we have seen, is not committed to moral realism or the existence of an independently existing moral order (see chapter 2).

In a second interpretation (often not distinguished from the first), cognitivism is contrasted to voluntarism (or decisionism) in ethics. Here the question is not whether there is an independent order of moral facts, but whether there is a significant analogy between moral discourse and scientific discourse that would, for example, allow us to speak of a progress in learning, or of a comparable notion of "good reasons" or argument in both. In this interpretation, cognitivism (which I take to be the position of Kant, Rawls, and Habermas) maintains that there is some analogy between moral discourse and scientific discourse in that we can critically assess reasons and arguments in both domains, and perhaps even speak of a more general "unity of reason." Voluntarism or decisionism, by contrast, is the view that moral norms and judgments are finally based in preferences or expressions of the will that are beyond the reach of rational assessment. Of course, preferences can be assessed in terms of their compatibility or incompatibility with other preferences, but our basic preferences cannot be rationally criticized; they can at most be decided upon. Accordingly, for Ernst Tugendhat as well as most utilitarians, morality is the search for a compromise between competing preferences; preferences themselves, however, are generally accepted as given.[124] Habermas attempts to preserve the Kantian connection between reason and morality by linking the acceptability of norms to the validity claims of regulative speech acts. Norms no less than assertions can be contested, and the validity of both depends upon their capacity to be redeemed through discursive argumentation.[125]

Finally, discourse ethics is a *deontological* moral theory. The contrast between deontological and teleological ethics can be understood in two ways: First, as we have seen, Kant and Rawls both draw a sharp distinction between questions of right and questions of the good life. The basic moral principle must be specified in a way that does not presuppose a specific conception of the good life since that would amount to a disregard for the ethical (*sittliche*) pluralism that characterizes modern societies. As we shall see in the next chapter, Kant, Rawls, and Habermas all attempt to defend this distinction in terms of a notion of practical reason or moral autonomy. In a further sense, the distinction between deontological and teleological theories is closely related to Kant's distinction between categorical and hypothetical imperatives. Kant's view that morality commands categorically means that pure reason is itself practical, that is, moral obligations do not depend upon the presence of nonreason-based interests and desires. A deontological ethic is thus a moral theory that claims moral obligations that do not depend upon the presence of desires or interests other than the "interest of Reason" (Kant). This distinction between categorical and hypothetical imperatives has been widely debated in recent analytic moral philosophy, especially since Philippa Foot's influential essay, "Is Morality a System of Hypothetical Imperatives?"[126] Habermas sides with those who argue that morality consists of categorical imperatives (imperatives that do not require nonreason-based interests or desires), but agrees with critics such as Foot that Kant's defense of such imperatives was not successful. In his own theory, Habermas accounts for the "oughtness" or obligatory character of moral norms in terms of their relation to communicative action: Valid norms are morally binding because of their intimate connection to processes of communication and social interaction that one cannot easily (or even rationally) choose to step out of.[127]

Despite this wide agreement with Kantian moral theory, discourse ethics also differs from Kant in several important respects. (I will mention some of these differences here; their elaboration extends over the remaining chapters.) Perhaps most importantly, like Rawls, Habermas rejects Kant's two-world metaphysics and seeks to reconstruct a Kantian perspective freed from its assumptions (*ME, 203*). For Habermas, this especially means an attempt to reconstruct the notions of reason and autonomy in such a way that they do not presuppose a distinction between a noumenal and a phenomenal world, or between a transcendental and an empirical ego.[128] Reason no longer stands in sharp opposition to needs and interests; rather, reason is defined procedurally in terms of the structure of argumentation and process of communication and the question becomes what interpretations of needs can best withstand discursive vindication. Similarly, autonomy no longer signals the exclusion or repression of interests and desires, but rather the capacity to reflect critically upon them and the willingness to redeem them discursively if their interpretation is contested (see chapter 4, section D).

Second, discourse ethics abandons Kant's monological version of the categorical imperative in favor of an intersubjective or communicative version of the principle of universalizability.[129] Of course, Kant's categorical imperative—especially the "Kingdom of Ends" formulation—already has an intersubjective dimension to it. However, it seems clear that Kant is only able to equate what one person can consistently and rationally will with what everyone could consistently and rationally agree to because of his two-world metaphysics. Only because interests, desires, and inclinations are set over against reason and purged from the Kingdom of Ends can Kant assume a harmony between the individual and the collective rational will. In discourse ethics, by contrast, such simulated thought experiments should ideally be replaced by actual practical discourses. Even though real discourse will always be limited by constraints of space and time and will thus fall short of their ideal, virtual dialogues carried out by a few on the behalf of others are not an adequate substitute.

Finally, discourse ethics rejects Kant's notion of the Fact of Reason in favor of a justification or grounding that appeals to the universal and unavoidable presuppositions of argumentation. This strategy regarding the problem of justification also has the consequence of more clearly moving Kant's moral theory away from intuitionism toward constructivism as this was described by Rawls. Whereas Rawls claims that the original position (as a procedural interpretation of the categorical imperative or moral point of view) is constructed on the basis of a model-conception of the person, Habermas describes his project as an attempt to reconstruct theoretically the intuitive competencies of mature speaking and acting subjects. I will discuss the similarities and differences between these two projects in the next chapter, particularly as they relate to a conception of moral autonomy. At this point, however, we can turn to a closer examination of the two stages in Habermas's attempt to provide a grounding for the principle of universalizability.

B. The Derivation of the Principle of Universalizability

"Presuppositions of argumentation" refer to those pragmatic conditions that speakers implicitly assume whenever they enter into serious argumentation. These presuppositions have a *transcendental* status in the sense that they are unavoidable: anyone who denies them and yet wants to argue seriously involves himself in some form of a performative contradiction.[130] Their unavoidability is thus demonstrated by showing that skeptical critics must presuppose them in the very attempt to deny their existence. Further, these presuppositions are of a *pragmatic* nature. It is not the more narrowly conceived conventional meaning of terms that yields these presuppositions, but rather the connection between the meaning of utterances and the pragmatic conditions of their validity as this was developed in the theory of formal pragmatics. Here, Habermas distances himself not only from Hare, but also from a proposal made by R. S. Peters:[131] The claim is not that normative presuppositions are entailed by the semantics of certain words in our language, but that they are part of the pragmatic conditions of successful or felicitous communication. In this sense, the rules of argumentation that Habermas introduces are closer to Grice's notion of "conversational maxims" and his "Cooperative Principle": "Make your conversational contribution such as is required, at the stage at which it occurs, by the accepted purpose or direction of the talk exchange in which you are engaged."[132] But whereas Grice's rules tend to state all-purpose maxims and expectations given certain agreed-upon aims of communication ("Be informative and don't say what you believe to be false or what you lack evidence for"; "Be relevant"; "Be perspicuous"), Habermas's rules represent those formal pragmatic conditions necessary for reaching understanding or communicative agreement. Habermas offers the following three rules:

1.   Every speaker with the competence to speak and act is allowed to take part in a discourse.

2.   (a)   Everyone is allowed to question any assertion whatever.
      (b)   Everyone is allowed to introduce any assertion whatever into the discourse.
      (c)   Everyone is allowed to express his attitudes, desires, and needs.

3.   No speaker may be prevented, by internal or external coercion, from exercising his rights as laid down in 1 and 2.[133]

Rule 1 states who may participate in a discourse: There are no restrictions other than being an agent capable of speech and action. (I assume that Habermas would claim that individuals who lack this capacity for whatever reason must be appropriately represented by a "trustee.") It thus includes all who are considered "rights-bearing" persons in the contemporary natural law tradition.[134] Rule 2 states that no relevant information can be excluded from a discourse and, more importantly, that only an actual discourse can ultimately determine what information is relevant. Further, no interests, needs, or desires are in principle excluded from the outset. The point is rather that the process of discourse itself will clarify their status (e.g., whether they are generalizable or not, etc.). Agreement is not achieved by excluding particular needs and desires from the discourse, but on the assumption that particular needs and desires can be discursively or communicatively transformed.[135] Finally, rule 3 states that discourses exclude the use of all force—whether in the form of internal structural asymmetries or external threats or sanctions—except the force of the better argument.

Taken together, these rules of argumentation can be seen to represent an "ideal speech situation" (Habermas) or "ideal communication community" (Apel) and, as a representation of the unavoidable presuppositions of argumentation, this ideal is actually assumed whenever anyone argues seriously.[136] However, the ideal speech situation also functions as a "regulative" idea that can be used to criticize actual discourses. Habermas must defend both of these aspects of the ideal speech situation at once:[137] On the one hand, it is not merely a counterfactual ideal, but a real presupposition of all argumentation that, to a greater or lesser extent, is approximated in discursive practices and embodied in social institutions within the lifeworld. We actually make such idealizing suppositions in our discursive practices to the extent that we are open to relevant information, listen to who are concerned, and are ready to be persuaded only by the force of the better argument.[138]

On the other hand, no single discourse can completely fulfill the conditions of an ideal speech situation. Although discourses involve validity claims that transcend the spatial and temporal horizons of their own embodiment, the practice of justifying a claim must always draw upon resources (knowledge, interpretation of needs, etc.) from within the lifeworld. In this sense, as Habermas puts it, "discourses are islands in a sea of praxis."[139] Moreover, any agreement reached today about the validity of a claim does rule out the possibility that tomorrow—in the light of new information, changed social conditions, or reinterpreted needs—it will be necessary to enter again into a discourse about the claim's validity. Thus, the transcendent character that belongs to the notion of an ideal speech situation does not rule out the immanence (and, hence, fallibility) of our discursive practices.

However, to turn now to the second step in the justification of a principle of universalizability, Habermas does not claim that the principle specified in discourse ethics can be derived solely from an analysis of the presuppositions of argumentation. To arrive at a distinctively *moral* principle of universalizability, these presuppositions must also be combined with the idea of what it means to justify a norm of action.[140] The rules of argumentation, of course, possess a normative content, but they do not yet constitute a specifically *moral* principle, where this is understood as defining a category of moral oughtness or obligation (*Sollgeltung*).[141]

As I understand it, Habermas insists upon this point for two reasons: First, the rules of argumentation state the necessary conditions for those who want to engage in a particular social practice, namely argumentation. In this sense they are analogous to the rules of a game: they are constitutive for a practice, but it is not impossible to imagine rejecting the practice as a whole. There also does not seem to be any reason why the normative character of these constitutive rules must be interpreted in moral terms.[142]

Second, as I suggested earlier, Habermas associates moral phenomena with forms of communicative action in general, rather than with its more demanding form as argumentation. Our moral intuitions center around the basic ideas of individual well-being and compassion or sympathy for others that may themselves have arisen from a sense of the fragility and vulnerability of our common life. In any case, Habermas seeks to clarify both of these ideas with reference to the suppositions of mutual reciprocity that is already contained in our communicative interactions and that is so crucial for the formation of both individual and group identities.[143] In this sense the often contrasted ideals of "autonomy" and "solidarity" have a common root in our communicative interactions, and it is from this model of communicative action that the distinctively moral character of norms and obligations arise. There is thus no attempt to derive a moral obligation from the constraints of rational argumentation alone. Rather, the claim is that if a general notion of what it means to justify one's action to others—the notion, that is, of what it means to regulate conflicts of interest in light of the norm of reciprocity implicit in the idea of communicative action—is combined with the more demanding rules gleaned from the analysis of the presuppositions of argumentation, then one can derive a rule of argument constitutive for a practical discourse, namely, Principle U (*DE*, 97). Principle U is thus not a new moral principle introduced on the basis of nonmoral considerations, but an attempt to reconstruct basic moral intuitions already contained in our communicative practices.

Of course, as Habermas notes in a self-correction, the notion of justifying a norm of action introduced in this second step must be understood in a relatively weak sense.[144] More specifically, it must not be understood already to entail the notion of impartiality that should be defined by Principle U. The idea is rather that we can only infer U from the rules of argumentation if we can assume that a person also has some idea of what it means to justify his or her actions, that is, has some general sense of (and interest in) what it means for a social norm to be acceptable to others.

C. Discourse Ethics and Scanlon's Contractualism

In a recent and challenging essay, T. M. Scanlon has argued for a version of contractualism that resembles Habermas's discourse ethics in several respects.[145] I will outline his proposal here in order to indicate how it might strengthen a weakness in Habermas's approach and how it, in turn, can be improved in light of considerations raised by a discourse ethics.

Despite its conflict with many of our everyday moral intuitions, the attraction of utilitarianism as a philosophical theory of morality, according to Scanlon, is found in its account of moral motivation and in the failure of rival theories to offer a description of moral phenomena that does not presuppose utilitarian considerations: The domain or subject matter of morality is closely tied to the notion of individual well-being, and our natural sympathy for others (to the extent that it exists) would seem to provide a better explanation of moral motivation than, say, Kant's notion of pure respect for the Moral Law or doing one's duty solely for duty's sake. Scanlon wants to show that in fact contractualism can provide a satisfactory alternative to utilitarianism on both scores. On the one hand, it can satisfactorily describe the subject matter of morality, that is, "give us a clear account of what the best forms of moral argument amount to and what kind of truth it is that they can be arriving at."[146] On the other hand, contractualism can also offer a plausible account of the nature of moral motivation. This second task, it should be noted, is not the same as offering an account of why it is prudentially rational to act morally—Scanlon, like Habermas, dismisses this formulation of the problem. Rather, the purpose of a philosophical theory of morality is to show what moral reasons or considerations are and to explain why moral reasons or considerations are ones that people can seriously regard as sources of motivation to act.[147] Scanlon's proposal regarding the first task, the description of the subject matter of morality, resembles Rawls's constructivism: moral theory, or, more specifically, its basic norm or principle, does not rest upon a realm of moral facts as "part of the fabric of the world" (Mackie) or a set of nonnatural intuitions. Rather, the subject matter of morality is rooted in, and constructed out of, our conception of ourselves as agents who are interested in finding a basis for agreement about the rules governing our behavior and relations with others. In view of these two aspects of the task of moral theory, Scanlon introduces the following principle as a contractualist account of moral wrongness:[148]

> An act is wrong if its performance under the circumstances would be disallowed by any system of rules for the general regulation of behaviour which no one could reasonably reject as a basis for informed, uncoerced general agreement.

A number of similarities with Habermas's proposal are obvious: First, the norms or "system of rules" that would disallow an action must be based upon an *informed* agreement. In contrast to Rawls's original position, Scanlon's version of contractualism does not in principle exclude any information. Presumably, an individual is free to express whatever needs or interests she wants and is constrained only by a mutually recognized desire to reach an agreement. (However, who determines what information is relevant, and on the basis of what criteria, remains unclear.) Second, Scanlon states that the system of rules in question must not be unreasonable *given* the common interest in finding a basis for agreement. Although I have suggested that Habermas must make a similar assumption—an agent must not only know what it means to act communicatively, but also have an interest in so acting—the virtue of Scanlon's proposal is that it makes explicit the need for this common interest. Further, the presence of the interest in reaching an agreement (or acting communicatively) is crucial for explaining both why moral norms impose a categorical obligation and why someone can reasonably be motivated to act according to those norms. Finally, agreements must be uncoerced. As in discourse ethics, this requirement prohibits structural asymmetries in communication (such as access to information or the opportunity to make assertions, voice needs, etc.), as well as external sanctions or threats.

However, despite these similarities, a significant difference between the two proposals still remains. If I understand it correctly, Scanlon's formulation leaves remarkably unclear the relationship between the "system of rules" for regulating behavior and the rules that describe the general conditions for reaching an informed, uncoerced agreement (what Habermas calls the "rules of argumentation"). At times, he suggests that the rules for regulating behavior are the same as the rules for reaching an agreement, and even the formulation quoted above can be read in this way: it would be much clearer if "as a basis for" were substituted with "in an."[149] I suspect that this confusion is finally attributable to the monological character of Scanlon's formulation: it does not require that real discourses be carried out, but rather asks what an individual cannot reasonably reject—but I will not pursue this objection here. I want to suggest instead that it is mistaken to equate rules for regulating behavior (e.g., social norms) with rules for reaching an agreement. Of course, the rules for reaching an agreement also regulate (a type of) behavior, but many (perhaps most) social norms are not rules for reaching an agreement. Thus, it would seem preferable to distinguish between social norms and the general rules for reaching an agreement and, like Habermas, argue that the former are morally valid only if they conform to the requirements specified in the latter. This does not mean that what counts as an unforced agreement on a particular occasion cannot be a subject of dispute— as Scanlon suggests, this may well account for a large number of moral conflicts. But since the rules for regulating behavior are not limited to rules for reaching an agreement, not all moral conflicts need to be about the terms for reaching an agreement: they can be (and, I think, often are) about the content or subject matter of a common agreement, that is, about what interests are generalizable or capable of general agreement.

If this reconstruction of Scanlon's proposal is plausible, the strength of his theory lies in showing that a contractualist model can offer an account of moral reasoning and moral motivation that does not presuppose utilitarianism. The interest in general human well-being is reinterpreted, so to speak, as a basic interest in achieving agreement among individuals. (This perspective is further strengthened by Habermas's analysis of the close connection between processes of communication and the formation of individual personality.) A norm is morally binding and we can be motivated to act in accordance with it because we believe it could not reasonably be rejected by those who have an interest in reaching an agreement with one another about the general regulation of behavior. The weakness of Scanlon's formulation, however, lies in its failure to distinguish between social norms or rules for regulating behavior, on the one hand, and rules that specify the conditions for reaching an informed, unforced agreement, on the other. I have attempted to show that this is a virtue of Habermas's discourse ethics that draws upon the conclusions and insights of a theory of formal pragmatics.

D. Conclusion

The preceding discussion of the main features and justification of discourse ethics has, at most, only pointed to a number of questions and problems that could be raised in connection with Habermas's project. Some of these will be addressed more directly in the remaining two chapters. By way of a conclusion, however, I would like to outline three of the most prominent issues and the general strategy of Habermas's response.

(1) The question of the scope or domain of morality has been at the center of much recent discussion in moral theory.[150] Should the term 'morality' be restricted to interpersonal conflicts that involve the infringement of norms or violation of rights and that require an impartial resolution, or should the term be extended to include all cases in which difficult existential choices must be made, often at the expense of one valued good over another? At one level, the debate can be seen as primarily a semantic one: It is possible, at least in principle, to reserve the term 'morality' for a specific range of moral phenomena without necessarily prejudicing the treatment of other moral/ethical issues. At another level, however, substantive issues and claims are at stake: It has to do with the question of whether or not at least some (moral) conflicts are capable of a rational and impartial resolution that is equally in the interest of all or whether all moral phenomena are tied to personal choices and specific conceptions of the good life so as to render such a conception of morality suspect. Discourse ethics, I have argued, belongs to the broader Kantian tradition by insisting upon a distinction between normative questions of justice (or morality) and evaluative questions of the good life, and the relative priority of the former over the latter. For discourse ethics, morality is restricted to the impartial regulation of interpersonal conflicts of action (*MCCA*, 116; *ME*, 198). The central question becomes "What norms should govern our common life?" rather than "What sort of person do I want to become?" and the more limited task of a moral theory is to clarify the (impartial) standpoint from which normative disputes could be assessed.[151]

This conception of morality has been criticized from a number of perspectives and for a variety of different reasons. So-called "communitarians" ("neo-Aristotelians" or "neo-Hegelians") have questioned the feasibility as well as the desirability of any sharp distinction between the "right" and the "good," while feminists have called attention to some of the consequences that seem to follow from the distinction—such as a defense of the traditional public/private dichotomy on the basis of certain negative liberties. In response to the "communitarian" objections to the distinction between the right and the good, Habermas would agree that the former cannot be clarified without some reference to the latter, that is, we cannot delineate a set of individual rights without also attending to the broader social context required for maintaining "solidarity." On the other hand, like Rawls, Habermas insists that some distinction between the right and the good is required in a liberal society in which a diversity of conceptions of the good life is affirmed. A theory of (public) morality that is designed to address the legitimacy of the basic social norms that govern collective life should not rely upon a particular (and, hence, sectarian) conception of the good life, nor should it necessarily have something to say to every "ethical" question concerning individual or communal lifestyles. Habermas attempts to defend such a distinction by distinguishing between the general structures of communicative action (which include conditions of "solidarity" as well as "justice") and the plurality of more concrete life-styles or conceptions of the good that are compatible with them. As I shall argue in the next chapter, this distinction still implies a conception of moral autonomy, but one that is conceived differently than Kant's.

Similarly, like some feminist critics, Habermas would also want to challenge the normative grounds of the traditional private/public dichotomy without however abandoning the distinction altogether.[152] In discourse ethics, the private/public distinction is relativized, at least at one level, to what can be agreed to by all concerned in a practical discourse. At another level, however, some model of autonomy (and, hence, individual privacy) is required to ensure that the agreements reached in a practical discourse are in fact agreements reached between free and equal parties. This question, too, will be addressed in the next chapter.

(2) A second, though related, difficulty encountered by Habermas's conception of morality concerns his insistence upon distinguishing between the justification of a norm and its application in specific contexts of action.[153] This distinction has also been challenged by those more sympathetic with a moral theory that emphasizes the role of prudence and judgment (or *phronesis* in Aristotle's ethics).[154] For example, in his extensive reflections on Habermas's discourse ethics, Wellmer argues that the central focus of post-conventional moral reasoning, which presupposes a distinction between morality and legality, is precisely the appropriate interpretation or "application" of the moral point of view.[155] Whereas for legal norms the distinction between a norm's legitimacy and its appropriate application is crucial, for moral norms such a sharp distinction cannot be drawn since moral deliberation is more deeply embedded in particular contexts of action and the inter-

pretation of a norm cannot be made without reference to the particular context. According to Wellmer, most moral debates will thus be about the best or most appropriate formulation of the norm in question in a given situation.

Contrary to Wellmer's interpretation, however, within a Kantian moral theory the distinction between the justification of a norm and its application is not limited to the legal domain. Furthermore, as we saw in our discussion of Kant in chapter 1, although formulating the "relevant description" of the maxim or norm in question requires judgment and is open to conflicting interpretations, a maxim or norm is not so deeply embedded in a particular context of action that the agent cannot abstract it from that context and submit it to the test procedure of the categorical imperative. Similarly, in a discourse ethics as well, practical judgment is required both for identifying the relevant norm that is to be tested in a discourse and for its subsequent application in various contexts of action. Discourses concerning the legitimacy of a norm must also take into consideration a reasonable range of application and the *foreseeable* consequences that would follow from its general observance.[156] Contrary to Wellmer's suggestion, however, this need not imply that norms are tied to the contexts of their application in such a way that reasonable generalizations cannot be made. Although Wellmer rightly draws attention to the importance of judgment in characterizing or describing moral conflicts, he underestimates the extent to which contexts of action are normatively structured and thus the extent to which they can, as required, be described with reference to underlying norms at varying levels of abstraction.[157]

(3) Finally, a third objection raised against Habermas's discourse ethics concerns the ideal of a rational consensus implicit in the criterion of legitimacy it proposes. According to this objection, the notion of consensus is either so exacting that there is no reason to assume any actual norm could satisfy it *or,* should a society approach that ideal to any significant degree, it could do so only at the expense of a plurality and diversity of viewpoints that is to be valued in a liberal political order.[158] In either case, the notion of consensus implies the idea of a fully transparent society that is unrealistic and potentially totalitarian. As I will attempt to show in greater detail in the final chapter, however, this objection misconstrues the way in which the notion of a consensus functions in Habermas's theory. Although it is true that the notion of a rational consensus reflects the ideal that the norms and institutions of a society are legitimate only if they could reasonably be agreed to by all and thus, too, the vision of a society in which in principle nothing needs to be hidden or concealed from its members in order to insure its self-maintenance, neither of these ideals require the interpretation expressed in this objection. First, the notion of a rational consensus does not presuppose that individuals be transformed into perfectly rational agents or that they all participate in one harmonious order in which every aspect of their lives is open to public view and jus-

tification. Rather, what is required is that the norms and institutions of a society reflect, and are publicly known to reflect, a view of its members as free and equal citizens. The notion of consensus does not point to a form of life in which everyone shares the same ideals, but to one in which the ideal of diversity and plurality is publicly affirmed and maintained on the basis of this conception of their democratic autonomy. Second, the ideal of a rational consensus (and related notion of the ideal speech situation) should not be interpreted too concretely. It does not require, for example, that every social norm or public policy receive the unanimous agreement of all who might be affected by it. What is required, however, is that the processes of public decision making and compromise formation be considered fair in the sense that the rules governing those processes also be open to debate and in principle capable of general agreement at a deeper level of justification.[159] The picture of a legitimate order implicit in Habermas's notion of a rational consensus is not that of a society that requires unanimity on every debated issue, but of a society that at a variety of levels and in different forms has institutionalized a network of overlapping and intersecting civic, political, and legal forums in which citizens collectively deliberate about and determine the basic terms of their collective life.[160] In short, the notion of a rational consensus points to a network of institutions that Habermas refers to as the public sphere. This concept of the public sphere is a topic of the final chapter.

4

THE CONCEPT OF THE PERSON, MORAL AUTONOMY, AND GENERALIZABLE INTERESTS

I. INTRODUCTION

In this chapter I take up the difficult question of the relation between moral theory and conceptions of the self. How tight a fit exists between these two areas of philosophical inquiry? To what extent can philosophical theories of the self be set aside on the basis of moral arguments and considerations? Or, conversely, to what extent can a favored moral theory be strengthened and/or criticized on the basis of an independent conception of the person? Or, still again, is it perhaps the case that moral theories are "underdetermined" by any particular philosophical conception of the person, for example, either a "simple" or "complex" view of self-identity (Parfit)? These questions are especially relevant for a Kantian theory that attempts to distinguish between the right and the good—or normative questions of justice and evaluative questions of the good life—on the basis of a (normative) conception of the person (e.g., in relation to a conception of moral autonomy or practical reason). For example, Michael Sandel (along with others) has recently argued that Rawls's theory of justice presupposes a morally unacceptable and philosophically suspect conception of the person; Charles Taylor and Bernard Williams both argue that Kantianism and utilitarianism are to be rejected because of their corresponding conception (or lack of conception) of the self; and Derek Parfit suggests that much of the attraction of deontological theories over utilitarian theories is ultimately due to a philosophically indefensible notion of self-identity. Similarly, recent adherents to a Kantian approach have also sought to find support for their moral theory by appealing to the conception of the person or, more specifically, the notion of practical reason that it implies. Different examples of this strategy can be found in Rawls's Dewey Lectures, "Kantian Constructivism in Moral Theory," Kohlberg's theory of moral development, and Habermas's theory of communicative action. To be sure, these philosophical approaches do not all share the same conception of the self. Some argue for a conception of the person that is relatively independent of normative questions (Parfit), others rely more heavily upon sociological or psychological theories (Kohlberg, Taylor, and Habermas), while still others offer an explicitly "political" or practical conception of the person that is underdetermined with respect to competing philosophical or psychological theories (Rawls).

The question of the relation between moral theories and conceptions of the self has admittedly generated a broad and highly contested array of hypotheses, and I do not intend to take up many of the interesting ideas found within this field of research. Nevertheless, for my own attempt to clarify the normative grounds of social criticism in relation to a notion of practical (communicative) reason, at least two more specific questions should be addressed. First, there is the question of whether a nonnormative conception of the person can provide reasons for rejecting a particular moral theory. I will pursue this question in relation to Parfit's critique of Rawls. Second, there is the question of whether a normative conception of the self (such as Rawls's model-conception) can be used to criticize and/or defend a particular characterization of the "moral point of view" and, eventually, specific principles of justice. Here I want to examine some recent criticisms of Rawls (notably, Michael Sandel's) as well as some attempts to characterize the "moral point of view" differently though still with reference to a comparable conception of the person or practical reason (Kohlberg and Habermas).

This chapter is divided into three sections accordingly: First, I will discuss Rawls's model conception of the person (or moral autonomy), the various ways in which it enters into his theory, and some of the criticisms that have been made of this ideal (II); then I will consider the normative conceptions of the person (or moral autonomy) found in the work of Kohlberg and Habermas (III). My claim is that although they share similar ideals of the person, their characterizations or representations of that ideal in a description of the moral point of view differ. The conception of autonomy as a form of communicative competence that, I shall argue, is implicit in Habermas's theory of communicative action is, in the end, also able to avoid some of the criticisms that have been made of Kohlberg's model of postconventional moral reasoning. In the final section, I will compare the way the conception of the person (or moral autonomy) is used to develop the list of primary social goods in Rawls with Habermas's notion of suppressed generalizable interests (IV). Both of these latter notions are introduced as tools for social criticism that the moral/social theorist is able to employ in an advocacy role.

II. RAWLS'S MODEL-CONCEPTION OF THE PERSON

The conception of the person enters Rawls's theory of justice at a number of different points and is used to achieve a number of different aims. I will list what I consider to be the three most important of these and then turn to a discussion of the first of the two questions mentioned above. First and most importantly, what Rawls calls "the model-conception of the person" is invoked in the construction of the original position and in arguing for the particular features he ascribes to it. This role of the conception of the person is most evident in his Dewey Lectures, but it can already be found in *A Theory of Justice*. As I argued in chapter 2, the original position does not represent a situation of choice based simply on a neutral or nonnormative notion of rationality. Rather, it presupposes the model-conceptions of the well-ordered society and the person. I have already shown how the ideal of the well-ordered society is invoked to justify imposing the various constraints on the original position. In the present context I will therefore only briefly recall this strategy with respect to the model-conception of the person.

Second, the model-conception of the person is invoked in developing a list of the primary social goods. Again, this role is emphasized more strongly in Rawls's later essays, especially "Social Unity and Primary Goods." In fact, I shall argue in section IV that Rawls's justification of the primary goods has undergone substantial revision since *A Theory of Justice:* Whereas in that book he argued for the list of primary goods in terms of those things that any rational person will want whatever else he wants (*TJ,* 92), in his later essays Rawls defends the list of primary social goods more specifically in connection with the two highest-order moral powers of the person.

Finally, the conception of the person enters importantly into part 3 of *A Theory of Justice* where Rawls develops the account of goodness as rationality and attempts to show, via a conception of the person, that a society that realized the two principles of justice would be stable over time.

Each of these tasks is obviously important to the task of *A Theory of Justice,* thus it is also important to specify carefully the conception of the person to which Rawls appeals and to show how it is invoked in each of these places. In the following I will primarily be concerned with the first two uses. I shall begin, however, by reviewing a critique of Rawls's theory that also appeals to a conception of the person, but employs this conception in a manner that is quite different from Rawls's. The criticism I have in mind is one made by Derek Parfit in his essay "Later Selves and Moral Principles," and developed at length in his recent book, *Reasons and Persons.*[1] Parfit's general strategy is to argue that Rawls's theory of justice presupposes a conception of the person or, more specifically, a notion of personal identity, that is philosophically suspect. He then offers an alternative philosophical account of personal identity that, he suggests, is also more compatible with a utilitarian moral theory. Finally, he concludes that on the basis of a nonmoral conception of personal identity, support can be provided for or against a particular moral theory.

From Rawls's reply in "The Independence of Moral Theory," it becomes clear that this criticism misses its target and, more generally, that this sort of strategy is not analogous to Rawls's argument from a normative conception of the person to a particular moral theory.[2] In this essay, Rawls argues that conceptions of personal identity and, more generally, developments in the philosophy of mind, are not sufficient for singling out one moral theory over another, at least not the more widely recognized and contested ones (e.g., utilitarianism, Kantian contractualism, or perfectionism). Moral theories are, so to speak, "underdetermined" by the philosophy of mind.[3] This reply is interesting for the relationship it suggests between moral theory and other domains of philosophical and/or scientific inquiry. I will therefore attempt to spell it out in more detail.

Rawls concedes to Parfit that a Kantian moral theory may require a "stronger" criterion of personal identity than utilitarianism. Since utilitarianism does not value the particular distribution of goods in a society, it does not require a notion of personal identity for this purpose; "whereas for a Kantian this is essential: the links of responsibility and contribution have to be traced through time and distribution suitably related to them."[4] What Rawls claims is that even if one should accept Parfit's "complex view," it would not be sufficient to rule out a Kantian moral theory. It may well be that personal identity is based on such things as psychological continuities, memory, and perhaps even bodily continuity, and thus does not rest upon any deeper "fact of the matter." But it would require a different sort of argument—one that drew upon social theory and psychology, for example—to show that the degree of personal identity required by a Kantian theory could not be realized in this way in any reasonably feasible society. According to Rawls, no degree of personal identity is "natural or fixed"; rather, it depends upon the ideals and values fostered by a society and its institutions.[5] Only an argument that drew upon these sorts of considerations (e.g., the impossiblity or unfeasibility of social institutions creating and maintaining the requisite conditions for a stronger sense of personal identity) would constitute an objection to a Kantian theory. Thus, however relevant they may be in aiding an assessment, insights and arguments from the philosophy of mind *alone* do not seem be be sufficient for selecting between competing moral theories. What Rawls hints at in this reply, but does not develop, is the idea of a cooperative labor between moral theory, other philosophical disciplines (such as the philosophy of mind), and the more empirical sciences (such as moral psychology).[6] What he clearly rejects, however, is the possibility of eliminating alternative moral theories on the basis of an appeal to nonmoral conceptions of the person alone.

To turn now to Rawls's first use of the model-conception of the person—for the construction of the original position—it would seem that this argument concerning the underdetermination of moral theories runs counter to the argumentative strategy employed in *A Theory of Justice*. Some critics of Rawls have, in fact, entered precisely this objection.[7] In *A Theory of Justice*, one of Rawls's central objections to utilitarianism is that it ignores the "distinctness of persons" (*TJ*, 27). This would seem to be an argument on the basis of an independent conception of the person for one moral theory over another, that is, an argument of precisely the sort that Rawls rules out in "The Independence of Moral Theory." On the other hand, it could be that Rawls in fact begins not with a neutral conception of the person, but with a normative "ideal" of the person. The original position becomes, so to speak, an illustration of certain ideals, rather than an independent argument for them.[8] If so, however, the argument from the original position to the specific principles of justice would then appear to lose some of its force. In order to evaluate this objection properly, we must review more closely the way in which the conception of the person enters into the construction of the original position. However, it should already be clear from our earlier discussion that Rawls's strategy is not to argue from a nonmoral or neutral conception of the person for or against a particular moral theory. Rather, it must be that Rawls works from a certain "ideal" of the person that he takes to be less controversial and more widely accepted—though not morally neutral—than the more substantive conclusions about the principles of justice at which he arrives. After reviewing the way in which the conception of the person enters into the construction of the original position, we will be in a better position to evaluate the second general sort of criticism leveled at Rawls's conception of the person, namely, that Rawls invokes an unacceptable *ideal* of the person in arguing for his two principles and that, since the ideal is unacceptable, so too are the principles that he derives from it. This objection, with minor variations, can be found in the criticisms of Williams, Sandel, Taylor, and Benhabib.

Recall from our discussion in chapter 2 that in the model-conception Rawls describes persons as free and equal moral beings. Persons are considered moral in the sense that they possess two highest-order moral powers: the capacity for an effective sense of justice—the capacity to act from principles defining fair terms of social cooperation (whatever they turn out to be)—and the capacity to form, revise, and pursue rationally a conception of the good (whatever it happens to be). Recall, too, that this model-conception of the person enters into the construction of the original position in several ways. What Rawls refers to as the "Reasonable" (including such features of the person as the capacity to have a sense of justice and the freedom and equality

of each) is used in the argument for the various constraints built into the original position. These include the formal constraints on the concept of right
that any conception of justice must satisfy, the veil of ignorance, and the fact
that the parties are choosing principles that are to regulate the basic structure.
Similarly, the "Rational" is also appealed to in the construction of the original position. Here, Rawls has in mind primarily the freedom of citizens in the
well-ordered society and their ability to form, revise, and pursue a conception of the good. These are represented in the original position in that the
parties seek to secure the greatest amount of primary goods possible and
adopt the maximin rule as the suitable principle of rational choice under conditions of uncertainty. Thus, as I argued in chapter 2, Rawls's model-conception of the person forms a central part of the argument for constructing the
initial situation in his philosophically favored form, that is, as the original
position.

It is possible to divide the objections raised against Rawl's ideal or
model-conception of the person into two different groups. On the one hand,
there are those who criticize the ideal itself, arguing that it is not widely
shared (Galston), that it misrepresents or distorts relevant moral phenomena
(Walzer and Williams), or that it implies an abstract, atomistic, and rationalistic conception of the self (Taylor, Sandel, and Benhabib). On the other
hand, there are those who do not criticize the ideal so much as the way in
which Rawls has chosen to represent that ideal in his description of the original position. This I take to be essentially the position of Scanlon, Kohlberg,
and Habermas, as well as others who largely share a Kantian theory of the
self but reject Rawls's specific use of it in the derivation of his two principles
of justice. These two different sorts of criticisms are not always easily distinguished, since a criticism of Rawls's representation of the ideal in the original position may appear to imply a rejection of the ideal itself.[9] However,
since they represent a potentially greater challenge, I will begin with the first
set of objections and then turn to criticisms of Rawls's representation of the
ideal in the original position.

The charge that Rawls's theory presupposes an individualistic and
rationalistic conception of the self has a long history. Teitelman and
Schwartz raised this objection in the initial discussions of *A Theory of Justice,* and Nagel reiterates it in his earlier review.[10] At the same time, however, Rawls has repeatedly claimed that this description fails to consider the
role of his model-conception of the person:

> The theory does not hold that human beings are self-sufficient; nor that
> social life is simply a means to individual ends. Persons' more particu-
> lar desires and preferences are not thought to be given, but, as Teitel-
> man notes, to be shaped by social institutions and culture. The view is

individualistic in the minimal sense of stipulating that society is composed of a plurality of human persons for whom an equal liberty and the right of dissent is to be maintained.[11]

Thus, in order to move beyond this initial impasse, we need to examine more closely the motivations behind this criticism and the details of Rawls's response.

One of the most forceful criticisms of Rawls's conception of the person is found in Michael Sandel's *Liberalism and the Limits of Justice*. Sandel develops his criticism on two levels. First, on a metaphysical level, in a manner similar to Parfit, Sandel argues that Rawls's conception of the person implies a "simple view" of personal identity: His theory presupposes an "antecedent unity of the self," that is, the self attains its identity apart from the particular values, ends, or attachments it has. Second, on a moral level, Sandel suggests that Rawls's conception of the self violates certain deeply affirmed notions of moral desert and responsibility.[12] I will consider each of these criticisms in turn.

According to Sandel, what must be true of Rawls's conception of the self is that the self possess a unity and identity prior to its membership in any particular historical community and prior to its attachment to any specific ends. What is constitutive of the self is not any specific set of ends or attachments, but simply its *capacity* to choose. According to this "thin" view of the self, the self relates to its ends as a mere "system of desires." These desires can perhaps be rationally ordered according to their relative intensity, but they do not essentially define the self's identity.[13] But, Sandel argues, such a distinction between the self and its ends ultimately undermines the very notion of moral agency itself. A self that exists prior to its ends must be a self "wholly without character, without moral depth," and thus "incapable of self-knowledge in any morally serious sense."[14] If all that justice protects is the capacity of an agent to make radically free (e.g., arbitrary) choices, it becomes unclear why it should even be valued as the first virtue of societies. Moreover, according to Sandel, the problem is not merely that the moral agent becomes a subject of radical choice deprived of any "qualitative distinctions of worth between different orders of desires": "where the self is unencumbered and essentially dispossessed, no person is left for *self*-reflection to reflect upon."[15] In MacIntyre's apt phrase, moral agents have become ghosts—and ghosts, of course, don't exist![16]

On the alternative conception advocated by both Sandel and Taylor, human beings are conceived as "self-interpreting animals."[17] This suggests that our relation to our desires is not that of a "simple weigher" of preferences, but that the process of interpreting and evaluating those desires is *constitutive* of who we are. Moreover, our membership in specific historical communities also informs our attempts at self-understanding and shapes our self-identity. Thus, we are "thick" selves in the sense that we exist only *in* our individual and collective self-interpretations.[18]

It is debatable, however, whether Sandel has provided the best reconstruction of the model of the self implicit in Rawls's theory.[19] While Rawls does describe his model-conception of the person as possessing two "highest-order moral powers," including the capacity to form, to revise, and to rationally pursue a conception of the good, he does not deny the great extent to which our identity is socially constituted. As we noted above in his response to Parfit, Rawls agrees that no degree of personal identity is "natural or fixed"; rather, he claims, it depends upon the ideals and values fostered by a society and its institutions. The real question at issue is whether it is possible, in the context of a plausible theory of moral psychology, to distinguish between certain capacities an agent has—such as the capacity to have and revise a conception of the good—and the exercise of those capacities in connection with varying content and within different situations. Sandel does not address this question of a moral psychology. Rather, by simply assuming that we can only have an intelligible model of moral agency if that model incorporates a notion of strong evaluations, that is, preferences that are constitutive of the self, he begs the question at hand. Furthermore, it is doubtful that Rawls must accept the description of his model of the self as "thin" and as a "simple weigher of preferences." A better characterization, I would like to suggest, is found in a model in which the agent possesses a hierarchy of motivations or what Harry Frankfurt has called "first- and second-order" desires and valuations.[20] On this view, moral autonomy is construed as the capacity to assess effective first-order desires in light of higher-order desires as well as the capacity to integrate both levels of desires into a coherent sense of oneself in a reflective manner. My suggestion is that Rawls's description of the two highest-order moral powers more or less parallels this description of a moral agent's second-order capacity to reflect critically upon and revise first-order preferences and desires. As I shall argue below, this model of moral agency could be still further developed in connection with Kohlberg's description of a postconventional level of moral reasoning characterized in terms of the agent's capacity for decentration, differentiation, and reflexivity with respect to moral claims: Autonomous moral agency would then need to be understood not only as the capacity to formulate a coherent sense of oneself in a reflective manner, but also as the capacity to take sufficiently into account the viewpoint of others when assessing a norm or maxim of action.[21] If this reconstruction is at all plausible (as I believe it is), then the conception of the self that underlies Rawls's theory of justice would not be that of a "thin self" but that of an agent endowed with these general capacities for postconventional moral reasoning.

When we turn to the moral side of Sandel's criticism, two further objections can again be identified. The first concerns the notion of individual moral desert and Rawls's claim that the distribution of natural talents should be regarded as a "common asset" (*TJ*, 101, 179); the second questions Rawls's description of the moral point of view as one of impartiality and is made even more explicit in the writings of Taylor and Williams. Both objections, however, finally lead back to a criticism of Rawls's conception of the person.

One of the fundamental assumptions of justice as fairness is that the natural distribution of talents and abilities does not provide an appropriate basis for defining principles of distributive justice:

> The natural distribution [of talents] is neither just nor unjust; nor is it unjust that men are born into society at some particular position. These are simply natural facts.... The basic structure of [aristocratic and caste] societies incorporates the arbitrariness found in nature. But there is no necessity for men to resign themselves to these contingencies. The social system is not an unchangeable order beyond human control but a pattern of human action. In justice as fairness men agree to share one another's fate. In designing institutions they undertake to avail themselves of the accidents of nature and social circumstance only when doing so is for the common benefit. (*TJ*, 102)

As Sandel notes, however, this assumption seems to conflict with widely held beliefs about individual merit and moral desert. It implies, for example, that a person of superior talent or character is entitled to benefit from these only if it results in the benefit of all. An individual has no prior moral claim to such benefits since these attributes arise from the contingencies of nature and social circumstance.

> It seems to be one of the fixed points of our considered judgments that no one deserves his place in the distribution of native endowments, any more than one deserves one's initial starting place in society. The assertion that a man deserves the superior character that enables him to make the effort to cultivate his abilities is equally problematic; for his character depends in large part upon fortunate family and social circumstances for which he can claim no credit. The notion of desert seems not to apply to these cases. (*TJ*, 104)

Sandel suggests that Rawls is able to make this one of our "fixed points" only by drawing a very sharp distinction between the self and its possessions (including character, talent, and abilities). Otherwise, it would conflict not only with our ideas about moral desert, but also with Rawls's own

Kantian view that persons should be treated as ends-in-themselves and never merely as a means:

> Regarding the distribution of natural talents as a common asset does not violate the difference between persons nor regard some as means to others' welfare, because not *persons* but only "their" *attributes* are being used as means to others' well-being. To say that *I* am somehow violated or abused when "my" intelligence or even effort is used for the common benefit is to confuse the self with its contingently given and wholly inessential attributes (inessential, that is, to me being the particular self I am). Only on a theory of the person that held these endowments to be essential *constituents* rather than alienable *attributes* of the self could the sharing of assets be viewed as using *me* as a means to others' ends.[22]

But Sandel's criticism does not end here. To arrive at the idea of common assets it is not enough to deny that natural talents and abilities are essentially related to the self. Rather, Rawls must also claim that they in fact belong to the society (or political community) as a whole. What Rawls takes from individual persons as concrete selves, Sandel argues, he then gives to the community as a whole. "[This] second defense ties the notion of common assets to the possibility of a common subject of possession. It appeals, in short, to an intersubjective conception of the self."[23]

Once again, however, it is not clear that *A Theory of Justice* requires such a metaphysical conception of the person, or that Rawls's notion of common assets must be understood to clash directly with our intuitions about moral desert. Rawls's claim, I take it, would be that these two notions operate at different levels. If we (who must settle the question of justice) agree that the principles of justice should be ones that are fair, there is good reason for disregarding advantages that are due to the contingencies of nature and social circumstance *in the process of deciding what those principles should be*. This is precisely what the imposition of the veil of ignorance is intended to accomplish. This does not mean, however, that notions of merit or desert have no place in a well-ordered society. In fact, the priority of the basic liberties and the guarantee of fair equality of opportunity are presumably designed to account for these notions in various ways. At the same time, the decision is made from the perspective of the parties in the original position— that is, from the perspective of the representation of citizens as free and equal moral persons—in order to limit the individual benefits that arise from such an arrangement to what is also for the benefit of all.

One further remark in Rawls's defense might also be offered at this point: Apart from the guarantee of basic liberties and equality of opportunity, it is not at all clear how a notion of moral desert (or what Taylor calls "the contribution principle") is relevant to questions of distribution.[24] Libertarians have long recognized that it is virtually impossible to distinguish between economic gain that results from individual initiative, effort, and hard work (those things that we would normally call meritorious) and gain that results from simply having what the market wants or "being in the right place at the right time."[25] If this is so, it is not possible to reward strictly on the basis of merit within a market economy (as Taylor and Sandel seem to imply). Rawls's strategy, by contrast, is to limit the extent to which market distributions should be allowed to influence life chances by regulating the role of the market in a society according to principles agreed to by citizens regarded as free and equal persons.

The second specifically moral objection to Rawls's model-conception of the person is more difficult to assess. Although it can be found among Sandel's arguments, it is more explicit in essays by Bernard Williams and Charles Taylor. It concerns Rawls's notion of a rational life plan, his apparent Kantian assumption that such a plan will not involve any deep moral conflicts, and the connection between this assumption and the notion that the moral point of view can be described as one of impartiality. Thus, in contrast to Rawls's notion of deliberative rationality, Taylor suggests that Kant's formalism and rationalism distort our understanding of moral phenomena (and moral reasoning) by giving rise to the illusion that there is a single, consistent domain of the moral and that there is one set of considerations (or one model of calculation) that defines what is morally right.[26] He suggests further that there exists a "diversity of goods" (personal integrity, charity, justice, liberation, rationality, etc.), all of which are central to our conception of ourselves as moral agents but that may not be coherently united into one rational life plan in which justice plays the predominant role. Rather, it may be the case that these goods place incompatible demands upon us, even though we feel we cannot repudiate or deny any one of them. Part of our understanding of moral agency consists precisely in the fact that a language of "qualitative contrast" is essential to it and cannot be avoided.[27]

Similarly, Bernard Williams argues that the sorts of "deep attachments" and "ground projects" necessary for our lives to have meaning and purpose will at times conflict with the Kantian ideal of impartiality. At the same time, however, it would be irrational for us to deny them. This leads Williams to conclude that the ideal of impartiality cannot be a complete description of the moral point of view and thus that Kant's (and Rawls's) conception of the person distorts or "misrepresents" the domain of moral phenomena.

It follows that moral philosophy's habit, particularly in its Kantian forms, of treating persons in abstraction from character is not so much a legitimate device for dealing with one aspect of thought, but is rather a misrepresentation, since it leaves out what both limits and helps to define that aspect of thought.[28]

It is difficult to know what would count as an adequate response to these objections, since it is unclear exactly where their force lies.[29] On the one hand, Rawls does not claim that the perspective of the original position provides a suitable framework for resolving all moral conflicts and questions—he specifically limits it to the task of finding principles of justice (TJ, 17). On the other hand, Rawls does invoke a conception of the person with which he attempts to distinguish questions of justice from questions of the good life. If the recognition of our "deep attachments," "ground projects," and languages of "qualitative contrast" renders this conception of the person implausible, then Rawls's attempt to distinguish justice as the "first virtue of social institutions" from other aspects of morality (such as personal integrity, friendship, and the like) would seem to be jeopardized as well. However, as I have already suggested above (and as I will attempt to support in the consideration of Kohlberg and Habermas below), recognition of the diversity of ends and attachments does not make it impossible to distinguish between certain capacities of the moral agent (say, the capacity to form, revise, and pursue a conception of the good, and the capacity for a sense of justice) and the particular ends or goods to which an agent may be attached. Rawls's conception of the person does not deny that individuals have such attachments; he only argues that in attempting to find principles of justice that are fair it is reasonable to expect that we abstract from these aspects of the person.[30] Of course, whether this conception of the person (with its ideal of impartiality) is best represented in Rawls's description of the original position is a separate question—one to which I will now turn. The problem then is less the adoption of impartiality as an ideal than the more specific way in which impartiality is characterized in his theory.

The second broad set of objections mentioned previously (p. 128) is directed not so much against Rawls's model-conception of the person, as against its representation in the original position. In this respect, the criticisms of Scanlon, Kohlberg, and Habermas differ from the criticisms of Sandel, Williams, and Taylor. These critics do not object to the ideal of impartiality as a characterization of the moral point of view, but instead criticize Rawls's representation of it via the notion of self-interested choice behind the veil of ignorance. For example, Scanlon—who in an earlier essay endorses Rawls's ideal of the person—has recently questioned Rawls's characterization of the original position as an interpretation of the moral point of view and develops his own version of contractualism.[31] In a careful analysis of the transition from the ideal of impartial acceptance of principles (P) for regulating the basic social structure to the idea of a self-interested rational choice of principles from behind a veil of ignorance, Scanlon suggests that there is a confusion between two apparently similar notions that are in fact quite different. The ideal of impartiality suggests that "I must believe that I would have a reason to accept P no matter which social position I were to occupy," and this in turn suggests at least a minimal notion of the idea of choosing or agreeing to P in ignorance of one's social position, tastes, and preferences, etc.[32] For if it is a principle that *all* could reasonably agree to then the reasons cannot be those that are *essentially* tied to any of those features. (In this sense, too, the notion of choosing from ignorance is the same as Kohlberg's notion of "moral musical chairs": the principle(s) in question must be one(s) that anyone could accept irrespective of her own particular social position, etc.) However, as Scanlon points out, "the idea of what it would be unreasonable for people to reject given that they are seeking a basis for general agreement" is not the same as Rawls's idea of "what it would be rational for a self-interested person to choose or agree to under the assumption of equal probability of being anyone."[33] In the second case, it is precisely the individual's concern to advance their own interests (rather than to find a basis for general agreement) that determines "in the first instance" what principles they will adopt. In short, in the first case the individuals are already motivated to find a generally agreed solution to a problem, while in the second case they are motivated by rational self-interest alone.

Habermas, too, apparently does not question Rawls's conception of the person or its ideal of impartiality so much as the way in which Rawls represents it in the original position.[34] But Habermas's acceptance of a conception of the person similar to Rawls's model-conception does not mean that he also accepts the uses that Rawls makes of it. On the one hand, as we have seen, he attempts to provide a stronger justification for the moral point of view via a "transcendental-pragmatic argument"; on the other hand, he has more modest expectations about what can be gained from a philosophical clarification of the moral point of view. Thus, he does not believe that it is possible to derive substantive principles of justice from its description in the way that Rawls attempts. At most, he suggests, Rawls's two principles can be viewed as the proposal of one citizen in the debate, not as a definitive solution provided from the standpoint of the philosopher. A clarification of the moral point of view alone cannot yield substantive principles of justice; these require actual discourses being carried out among those concerned (or, in their absence, virtual discourses conducted by moral theorists or social critics in an advocacy role). In the next section I will attempt to clarify Habermas's conception of the person (or moral autonomy) over against the characterizations of both Rawls and Kohlberg.

III. MORAL AUTONOMY AS
COMMUNICATIVE COMPETENCE

Like Rawls, Habermas defends a cognitivist theory of morality. That is, moral conflicts are amenable to rational argument and discursive resolution, and moral reasoning can be viewed, more generally, as a developmental learning process in which the agent acquires "the ability to make use of interactive competence for *consciously* processing morally relevant conflicts of action."[35] In contrast to Rawls, however, Habermas draws more explicitly upon the insights and conclusions of moral psychology, especially the work of Lawrence Kohlberg. This is most evident in his defense of a "postconventional" level of moral reasoning. Habermas, to be sure, also modifies Kohlberg's proposals in several respects. Nevertheless, as I shall argue, he shares a conception of the person and ideal of moral autonomy that is similar to both Kohlberg's and Rawls's. Various characteristics of the moral agent (or structural features of practical reasoning) can be identified independently of the particular ends or conceptions of the good life that a moral agent might hold at any given time, and moral judgments (in contrast to the broader category of ethical judgments) are ones that are oriented primarily to conflicts concerning the conditions necessary for the realization and exercise of this capacity for practical reasoning, such as individual autonomy and social solidarity. Moreover, the moral point of view, as a standpoint of impartiality, is defined with reference to these features of moral agency or practical reasoning. Where Habermas parts from Rawls and Kohlberg is thus not so much in his acceptance of this ideal of the person as in the subsequent use to which it is put in describing or operationalizing the moral point of view (e.g., he offers his model of discourse and the ideal speech situation as an alternative to both Rawls's original position with its veil of ignorance and Kohlberg's ideal role-taking as "moral musical chairs").[36] In short, the disagreement is not that Rawls and Kohlberg assume an atomistic conception of the person whereas Habermas works with a socially interactive one; rather, the disagreement between these Kantian moral theorists is about how the moral point of view is best represented and defended. I will therefore briefly review several important features of Kohlberg's theory of moral development and some of the criticisms that have been raised against it. We will then be in a better position to evaluate Habermas's reception of Kohlberg, as well as his own attempt to reconstruct a notion of moral autonomy in connection with a theory of communicative action.[37]

(1) Kohlberg has described his theory of moral development as an attempt to reconstruct scientifically the stages of moral reasoning through which all individuals progress, given certain basic social and environmental conditions. He claims that these stages reflect a species-wide and invariant hierarchy of cognitive structures that remain constant despite social and cul-

tural variations in the content of the moral problems. He thus also claims that they are "hard" or Piagetian stages and do not merely reflect a particular orientation to moral questions that is shaped by social and cultural contingencies or by the self-reflective preferences of the moral agents themselves.[38]

This description of the stages of moral reasoning, especially those at the postconventional level, as hard or Piagetian has been contested for a number of different reasons: First, the empirical confirmation of stages 5 and 6 does not seem to be as strong as for the earlier stages. There is also some evidence of regression from these stages to earlier ones. This would violate one of Piaget's criteria for a hard stage. Second, unlike the earlier stages, the postconventional stages cannot be defined solely with reference to the psychic representations or "manifest thought operations" of the moral agent. This too suggests that they may not be "natural" in a Piagetian sense since the stages thereby acquire a more hypothetical status. Finally, the postconventional stages seem to involve a degree of self-reflective intervention on the part of the moral subject, something that also runs counter to Piagetian criteria. As many critics have noted, stages 5 and 6 appear greatly indebted to (socially and historically conditioned) philosophical theories of morality. In light of these objections, it has been suggested that the postconventional stages are "soft" or existential rather than hard or natural.[39] It has also been suggested that this may be due at least in part to the fact that at this level the asymmetry that existed between the moral subject and moral theorist at earlier stages now breaks down. At least in terms of competence, the moral subject is on an equal footing with the theorist in reconstructing her moral intuitions.[40] However, although Kohlberg has in response modified some of his claims (for example, by introducing a stage 4 1/2 and by assigning stage 6 a more hypothetical and tentative status), he has himself continued to describe his stages of moral reasoning as hard or Piagetian stages.[41]

(2) In addition to the claim that his stages are Piagetian, Kohlberg has also claimed that his theory bridges the traditional fact/value dichotomy in a way that makes it possible to infer from the fact that moral development does proceed in this way to the conclusion that moral subjects should reason in this way. Originally, he defended this claim by arguing that an adequate psychological explanation of why a person moves from stage to stage was at the same time an adequate philosophical account of the moral superiority of the higher stages: "The scientific theory as to why people factually *do* move upward from stage to stage, and why they factually *do* prefer a higher stage to a lower is broadly the same as a moral theory as to why people *should* prefer a higher stage to a lower."[42] However, in response to the objection that this argument is still susceptible to the naturalistic fallacy—including a criticism by Habermas—Kohlberg now more clearly endorses a complementary relationship between moral psychology and moral theory:

> While moral criteria of adequacy of moral judgment help define a stan-
> dard of psychological adequacy or advance, the study of psychological
> advance feeds back and clarifies these criteria. Our psychological theo-
> ry as to why individuals move from one stage to the next is grounded
> on a moral-philosophical theory which specifies that the later stage is
> morally better or more adequate than the earlier stage. Our psychologi-
> cal theory claims that individuals prefer the highest stage of reasoning
> they comprehend, a claim supported by research. This claim of our
> psychological theory derives from a philosophical claim that a later
> stage is 'objectively' preferable or more adequate by certain *moral* cri-
> teria. This philosophic claim, however, would for us be thrown into
> question if the facts of moral advance were inconsistent with its psy-
> chological implications.[43]

Thus, moral psychology must draw upon the insights and arguments of
philosophical theories of morality for the construction of its own theory (for
example, in describing the formal properties of postconventional reasoning),
but philosophical theories of morality can also be criticized if their claims
find little or no support in the psychological data. "Science, then, can test
whether a philosopher's conception of morality phenomenologically fits the
psychological facts. Science cannot go on to justify that conception of morality as what morality ought to be."[44]

   (3) Finally, a third feature of Kohlberg's theory relevant to our discussion is his decision to restrict the domain of investigation to reasoning about
issues of justice and rights and his claim that the stages of moral development reflect this preference for a deontological moral theory.

> In other words, I assumed that the core of morality and moral develop-
> ment was deontological, that is, it was a matter of rights and duties or
> prescriptions. My assumption about the deontological form of mature
> moral judgment was associated with the assumption that the core of
> deontological morality was justice or principles of justice. My assump-
> tion concerning the centrality of justice derived directly from Piaget's
> (1932) own study of the development of moral judgment and
> reasoning.[45]

This decision also leads Kohlberg to conclude that the highest stage of moral
reasoning is one of principled reasoning about the resolution of social conflicts: "At the highest level of moral reasoning, reversibility implies a conception of justice as 'moral musical chairs,' a conception which requires
each person to systematically take the position of everyone else in the situation until a solution emerges that is balanced fairly."[46]

Kohlberg's preference for regarding moral questions as questions of justice and rights has also been sharply criticized, most notably perhaps by Carol Gilligan. In a manner reminiscent of other critiques of a Kantian moral theory, she claims that this exclusive orientation to justice distorts the moral domain by excluding other relevant phenomena. She also argues that the description of the highest stage of moral reasoning in terms of questions of justice and rights creates a gender bias in Kohlberg's theory.[47] According to Gilligan, women tested under Kohlberg's Scoring Manual consistently score lower than men and not as many women attain postconventional levels of moral reasoning.[48] Following recent neo-Freudian work on early childhood development, she suggests that this is due to the fact that women are socialized to think about moral questions in terms of such values as caring, nurturing, and responsibility, rather than fairness, rights, and duties. Finally, in response to Kohlberg, she suggests that there are two "tracks" of moral development, one leading to a highest stage of justice reasoning and another leading to a more contextualist stage of postconventional moral reasoning.[49]

Kohlberg has responded to these criticisms in a number of different ways.[50] He suggests, first, that when educational and occupational differences are accounted for, empirical research does not support Gilligan's conclusion that women fail to score as high in his tests. He also suggests that Gilligan's research is oriented to a different object-domain, and thus that her findings do not conflict with his own. Whereas he is primarily concerned with questions of justice and rights, Gilligan focuses on personal moral choices or questions of the good life that do not allow for principled reasoning in the same way. Finally, he suggests that, when properly understood, Gilligan's discovery of an ethic of care and responsibility in fact complements and goes beyond his own analysis of stages of justice reasoning. Her work focuses on the various "soft" or existential orientations that individuals can adopt toward certain (personal) moral issues, especially at the postconventional level of moral reasoning. However, these orientations nevertheless remain limited or constrained by the principled reasoning captured in the hard, Piagetian stages that he has identified.

Since Kohlberg's first response is an empirical question about which there is still a great deal of disagreement, I will limit my own comments to the second two responses.[51] However, the disagreement concerning the possible gender bias of Kohlberg's research is no doubt also due to the fact that there is not a consensus about what his stages demarcate—for example, hard stages or complementary orientations.[52]

Kohlberg's claim that Gilligan's analysis does not conflict with his own findings follows from his assumption that she has studied a different object-domain. Whereas Kohlberg has focused on moral reasoning about issues of justice and rights, Gilligan's own research has been directed to issues of personal decision making or questions of the good life.

> The difference between the Frankena [and Kohlberg] and the Gilligan sense of the word *moral* is captured by the distinctions that many Americans make between the sphere of personal moral dilemmas and choices and the sphere of moral choice that is not considered personal, that is, the sphere captured by our justice dilemmas. The spheres of kinship, love, friendship, and sex, all eliciting considerations of care, are usually understood to be the spheres of personal decision making, as are, for instance, the problems of marriage and divorce.[53]

As this passage suggests, the distinction between justice dilemmas and personal moral dilemmas (or normative questions of justice and evaluative questions of the good life) has a long tradition. Kohlberg attempts to provide additional support for it on the basis of two different sorts of considerations. On the one hand, he defends the distinction on what might be called "essentialist" grounds: The postconventional justice reasoning on which his studies focus satisfies the Piagetian criteria for classification as hard stages, whereas the kind of moral reasoning studied by Gilligan does not.[54] At other times, however, he defends the distinction on more procedural grounds in terms of whether or not the questions raised are amenable to resolution based on principled reasoning to which all could agree.[55] In either case, however, the claim is that Gilligan has not identified a separate developmental track, but has at most widened the range of phenomena to which a stage model is applicable. Furthermore, the personal moral dilemmas on which her studies focus allow for a variety of possible resolutions and thus require room for toleration within the limits or constraints of justice.

> At the post-conventional level of justice reasoning the distinction between these two kinds of dilemmas is understood. Reasoning at this postconventional level leads to a tolerance about the resolution of personal dilemmas of special obligation while at the same time upholding a general framework of nonrelative justice that provides the context within which individually varying personal moral decision making takes place.[56]

What remains unclear from this response to Gilligan's research, however, is whether her insights require a reinterpretation or redescription of the normative endpoint of moral development (e.g., the moral point of view). Are there still two moral points of view, one connected with the hard stage of justice reasoning and stressing the attributes of impartiality and universalizabilty, and another, connected to the soft stage of reasoning about personal or evaluative questions, emphasizing the values of compassion and care? Or do Gilligan's findings require a redescription of the moral point of view in a way that tempers or modifies the ideals of impartiality and universalizability? In other words, even if there are not two different moralities, is it still the case that justice reasoning remains unscathed by Gilligan's studies, or must the moral point of view be reinterpreted to correct for certain distortions in Kohlberg's description? My own proposal is that while Kohlberg (for the most part) believes that his description of the moral point of view remains unaffected by Gilligan's research, Habermas's position has from the outset been more disposed to incorporate certain insights contained within it (while, at the same time, continuing to insist upon some distinction between normative questions of justice and evaluative questions of the good life). The challenge for Habermas, as we shall see, is to clarify how this distinction can be maintained *without* invoking Kohlberg's essentialist claim that it is because the stages of justice reasoning are hard, Piagetian stages.

Habermas's reception of Kohlberg's theory has been both constructive and critical. At the same time, his own appropriation of Kohlberg's theory has been modified in light of more recent criticisms and empirical findings.[57] The three features of Kohlberg's theory identified above provide a good point of departure for summarizing Habermas's own reception of it.

First, in connection with the relationship between moral psychology and moral philosophy, Habermas emphasizes the complementary relationship that exists between them. In fact, he regards Kohlberg's theory of moral development as a prime illustration of the cooperative division of labor that should exist between philosophy and empirical research and an example of his own model of a reconstructive science.[58] At the same time, Habermas has also attempted to provide further support for Kohlberg's theory by drawing attention to parallels between it and Selman's theory of social perspective-taking and his own theory of social interaction.[59] Structural analogies exist among all three of these research domains, particularly with respect to the delineation of preconventional, conventional, and postconventional levels of reasoning and interaction.[60]What emerges from these studies is thus indirect support for a conception of moral autonomy (or a normative conception of the person) that can be clarified in connection with his own theory of communicative action.

Second, in a more critical spirit, Habermas rejects Kohlberg's description of the postconventional stages as hard stages.[61] Unlike the earlier stages of moral reasoning, Habermas argues that postconventional moral reasoning does not satisfy Piaget's criteria for a hard stage. Rather, adopting a suggestion made by Tom McCarthy, Habermas suggests that the explication and delineation of postconventional stages necessarily depends upon philosophical arguments and assessments about how to best reconstruct our moral intuitions.

The suggestion I should like to advance is that Kohlberg's account places the higher-stage moral subject, at least in point of competence, at the same reflective or discursive level as the moral psychologist. The subject's thought is now marked by decentration, differentiation and reflexivity which are the conditions of entrance into the moral theorist's sphere of argumentation. Thus the asymmetry between the pre-reflective and the reflective, between theories-in-action and explications, which underlies the model of reconstruction, begins to break down. The subject is now in a position to argue with the theorist about questions of morality. This discursive symmetry might help to explain why Kohlberg's attempt to get from "is" to "ought" (in part) by establishing the "naturalness" of the higher stages has struck moral philosophers as questionable. He has to adopt and defend a specific position on the very meta-ethical issues they spend their lives debating; the appeal to empirical-psychological considerations brings no dispensation from participation in this debate. This is not to deny the significance of such considerations for moral theory; it is only to say that they will have to make themselves felt *within* moral-theoretical argumentation.[62]

Third and last, with respect to the distinction between justice dilemmas and personal morality (or the right and the good), Habermas parts with Kohlberg in the latter's response to Gilligan. Like Kohlberg, Habermas does not believe that Gilligan's research warrants hypothesizing a separate track of moral reasoning. But whereas Kohlberg's attempt to incorporate some of Gilligan's insights into his characterization of the highest stage of moral reasoning seems rather *ad hoc,* Habermas's model, since it begins with a notion of reciprocity or mutual recognition as a basic moral intuition, is better able to incorporate these insights. In particular, questions of solidarity (or care) as well as questions of individual rights or justice more narrowly conceived constitute an appropriate matter for a practical discourse.[63] At the same time, however, Habermas retains a procedural distinction between normative questions of justice (including solidarity), on the one hand, and evaluative questions of the good life, on the other (*MCCA,* 178, 180; *DE,* 108). Only the former are amenable to a rational resolution in the context of a practical discourse; the latter, by contrast, since they are more deeply embedded within the context of particular cultural traditions and alternative value systems, allow for a greater range of possible resolutions. For Habermas, the distinction between questions of justice and questions of the good life is ultimately a distinction that must be drawn within a discourse itself—depending on whether or not the conflict involves a generalizable interest. At the same time, or so I would want to argue, the general social conditions necessary for realizing the possibility of practical discourse, including the various competencies associated with a communicative model of autonomy, should also be considered a matter of justice (see above, p. 68).

This different analysis of the distinction between justice and the good life also leads Habermas to a different characterization of the two postconventional stages of moral reasoning. Rather than distinguishing between a utilitarian and deontological stage, Habermas distinguishes between a stage of principled moral reasoning and a stage of procedural reasoning about the justification of norms (a discourse) (MCCA, 177). Whereas Kohlberg characterizes the highest stage of moral reasoning in terms of a notion of "moral musical chairs," Habermas describes it as a highly reflective form of communicative action, namely, the discursive vindication of contested norms and principles (MCCA, 130).

Furthermore, whereas Kohlberg contrasts justice and benevolence, equating the first with hard stages of moral reasoning and the second with soft, existential orientations, as we have just seen, Habermas argues for a closer correlation between justice and solidarity *within* the characterization of the moral point of view.[64] Concern for the equal rights of all cannot be entirely divorced from concern for the welfare of each individual, since individual identity (and autonomy) is shaped through interaction with others. Nor does solidarity (or benevolence) simply mean empathetic good will toward others; rather, a dimension of "communicative reason" is exhibited in it as well, thus requiring respect for the individual integrity of the other. The notion of mutual reciprocity built into the structure of communicative action requires attending to the conditions of solidarity as well as justice.

With this critical reception of Kohlberg's theory in hand, I would now like to outline the model of moral autonomy (or the normative conception of the person) implicit in Habermas's characterization of postconventional moral reasoning and, more generally, his discourse ethics. This model can be summarized around three features: (1) the intimate connection between autonomy and socialization; (2) the capacity to adopt a hypothetical and reflective attitude; and (3) the notion of a communicative access to, and interpretation of, needs.

(1) In contrast to conceptions of autonomy that regard socialization as a hindrance to the exercise of one's autonomy, Habermas stresses the close tie between the formation of individual identities and processes of socialization.[65] The autonomous self is not someone who has emancipated him- or herself from the effects of socialization, but rather someone who has acquired various competencies through a process of socialization and who thus stands in a certain relation to that process.[66] There is thus no core primordial (or noumenal) self prior to socialization from which choices must arise if they are to be regarded as the agent's own; rather (following Mead),

Habermas regards the self as someone who is constituted in his or her inter-actions with others. The autonomous self is a complex (and fragile) construc-tion shaped by specific forms of reciprocity (or mutual recognition) that are themselves symbolically (linguistically) mediated. This suggests that the fea-tures of autonomous agency should themselves be clarified in connection with general competencies acquired in the process of socialization and that, in some sense, reflect that process. Again following Mead and, more recent-ly, Selman, Habermas has attempted such a clarification in connection with the general developmental structures of social perspective-taking.[67] Moral autonomy is thus identified with the exercise of various interactive compe-tencies acquired in the process of socialization.

A further consequence of such a conception of autonomy is that it is from the outset conceived as something that is fundamentally intersubjective. It is not simply a question of whether an individual can consistently will that his maxim become a universal law, but a question of whether an individual has sufficiently considered how acting on that maxim or norm would affect others. In the last analysis, this capacity to adopt the standpoint of the other and to assess the consequences of one's actions from all relevant points of view is a capacity that can be acquired only through participating in actual practical discourses.

(2) A second feature of the conception of moral autonomy implicit in Habermas's writings is the capacity to adopt a hypothetical attitude at a vari-ety of different levels: First, an autonomous person has acquired the capacity for a decentered understanding of the world, that is, he is able to differentiate between the natural, social, and subjective worlds and identify the different types of validity claims associated with each (*MCCA,* 138). Second, with respect to the social world of norms, an autonomous person is able to abstract a contested norm from its embeddedness in social life and adopt a reflective attitude toward it (*DE,* 125; *MCCA,* 125). If a norm is contested, an autonomous person is one who is able to enter into a practical discourse to determine its validity. This implies that the person is also able to distinguish between the social acceptance of a norm and its ideal validity (*MCCA,* 126, 177). Finally, the capacity for adopting a hypothetical attitude is expressed in the ability to engage in ideal role-taking or, to use Kohlberg's more whimsi-cal phrase, "moral musical chairs." However, in connection with a theory of communicative action, the notion of ideal role-taking is understood more in terms of a capacity for argumentation and responsiveness to reasons, than merely the capacity for empathetic insight.[68] Ideal role-taking is from the outset understood as a highly reflective form of communicative action, that is, argumentation.

(3) Finally, in contrast to a model in which autonomy is set in opposi-tion to individual needs and desires, a communicative conception of autono-

my implies a reflective attitude toward the interpretation of one's own needs and interests and a capacity to render them "communicatively fluid." Autonomy does not imply the subjection of desires to the demands of reason, but the communicative interpretation and transformation of needs within a discourse. Moreover, individual needs and preferences are no longer viewed as given, rather, attention shifts to the social interpretation of needs and, when a conflict about the interpretation of needs arises, competent moral subjects are ready and able to enter into a discourse regarding them.[69] Similarly, individual preferences and desires do not constitute a private realm tamed but protected by principles of right; rather, needs can be made communicatively fluid in a discourse, thus suggesting that (at least at some level) the distinction between public and private is not permanently fixed.

> Inner nature is rendered communicatively fluid and transparent to the extent that needs can, through aesthetic forms of expression, be kept articulable [*sprachfähig*] or be released from their paleosymbolic prelinguisticality. But that means that internal nature is not subjected, in the cultural preformation met with at any given time, to the demands of ego autonomy; rather, through a dependent ego it obtains free access to the interpretive possibilities of the cultural tradition. In the medium of value-forming and norm-forming communications into which aesthetic experiences enter, traditional cultural contents are no longer simply the stencils according to which needs are shaped; on the contrary, in this medium needs can seek and find adequate interpretations. Naturally this flow of communication requires sensitivity, breaking down barriers, dependency—in short, a cognitive style marked as field-dependent, which the ego, on the way to autonomy, first overcame and replaced with a field-independent style of perception and thought. Autonomy that robs the ego of a communicative access to its own inner nature also signals unfreedom. Ego identity means a freedom that limits itself in the intention of reconciling—if not of identifying—worthiness with happiness.[70]

If these three features of a communicative conception of moral autonomy are joined with the characterization of autonomy offered above in our discussion of Rawls—a higher-order capacity to reflect critically upon and revise first-order preferences and desires—what emerges is a model of autonomy conceived as a complex set of competencies with which an individual is able to resolve moral conflicts and establish a rational life plan. This model does not presuppose an opposition between a noumenal and phenomenal self, nor does it disregard the importance of socialization for the formation of individual identities. Rather, it offers a procedural model of autonomy that emphasizes the ideas of reciprocity and mutual recognition that are already implicit in everyday forms of communicative action. As I now hope to show, such a conception of moral autonomy is also relevant for normative social criticism.

IV. PRIMARY GOODS AND GENERALIZABLE INTERESTS

The second broad area (mentioned in section II) in which Rawls's model-conception of the person is invoked is in the elaboration of the list of primary social goods or, as Rawls puts it in *A Theory of Justice,* those goods that every rational person wants whatever else he wants (*TJ,* 62, 260). The notion of primary goods is crucial to Rawls's theory, especially in providing an "objective" criterion for the interpersonal comparison of welfare. At the same time, it (like the conception of the person) is often criticized as both too abstract and individualistic and biased in favor of particular conceptions of the good.[71] In this section I will review Rawls's account of primary social goods and its various uses in his theory of justice. I will then offer a comparison between *some* of the uses Rawls makes of it and Habermas's own model of suppressed generalizable interests. My claim is that some such notion is crucial for the possibility of normative social criticism. The major difference between Rawls and Habermas, however, is that while Habermas introduces the model of suppressed generalizable interests as a fallibilistic tool to be used by the social critic in her advocacy role, Rawls's account of primary social goods ascribes a privileged position to the external perspective of the philosopher or social theorist.

The notion of primary goods serves at least two functions in *A Theory of Justice.* Most importantly, it is introduced as a criterion of interpersonal comparison so that the relative well-being of representative members of a society can be determined. An indexing of the primary goods, for example, enables the least-advantaged representative group to be identified (*TJ,* 91). According to Rawls, such an index is necessary in order to decide whether the basic structure of a society satisfies the Difference Principle (or second principle of justice). More generally stated, this means that the notion of primary social goods provides a tool that can be used by the social critic in assessing social institutions.

The second major function of the notion of primary goods is more specific to a problem generated within Rawls's own theory: In the original position, the parties are denied knowledge of their own particular conceptions of the good. However, if the deliberation and choice of the parties in the original position are to be rational, Rawls argues that they must take place in light of some set of goods. The notion of primary goods fulfills this need: the parties assume that they want more rather than less of these goods (*TJ*, 142). Even though (once the veil of ignorance is lifted) some parties may not want as much of these goods as others, Rawls believes this strategy is acceptable because the list specifies goods that everyone will want whatever else they want. Since I have already offered some reservations about the extent to which Rawls's original position can be viewed as an adequate representation of the moral point of view, I will limit my discussion of the notion of primary goods to the first function, that is, as a standard for the interpersonal comparison of welfare. It is clear, however, that the problems encountered in the second function assigned to the primary goods are largely due to the fact that there is a discrepancy between the constructed identities of the parties in the original position and the real identities of those who have to agree upon the principle of justice. This discrepancy does not arise within the context of a discourse ethics.

In response to numerous criticisms, Rawls has revised his justification of the list of primary goods, though apparently (and somewhat curiously) without at all altering the list itself. In *A Theory of Justice,* he argued for the list of primary goods in terms of quasi-empirical social and psychological assumptions about what any person needs in order to carry out a rational life plan. In "Social Unity and Primary Goods," however, Rawls shifts his strategy and argues for the list of primary goods with reference to his model-conception of the person. Thus, "the primary goods are necessary for realising the powers of moral personality and are all-purpose means for a sufficiently wide range of final ends."[72] To be sure, the account still presupposes "various general facts about human wants and abilities, their characteristic phases and requirements of nurture, relations of social interdependence and much else," but the weight of the argument now depends essentially upon the notion of moral autonomy or the model-conception of the person.[73] I will discuss in a moment whether this shift in justification should also lead to a change in the list of primary goods itself; but first I want to consider some of the reasons for introducing it as a standard of interpersonal comparison.

In "Preference and Urgency," Scanlon distinguishes between "subjective" and "objective" criteria of interpersonal comparison. A subjective criterion is one in which the well-being of a person is determined "solely from the point of view of that person's tastes and interests."[74] Harsanyi's principle of maximum average utility and Sen's principle of maximum equal satisfaction are examples of such a criterion. An objective criterion, by contrast, is one that provides a basis of comparison that is independent of a person's particular tastes and preferences. Rawls's account of primary social goods is an example. An objective criterion need not renounce any consideration of subjective preferences, but it does imply that not all interests be given the same consideration and that the intensity or strength of a preference is not a sufficient reason for giving it greater consideration. One important reason for this, offered by Rawls, is the assumption that individuals are not simply "assailed" by preferences and desires over which they have no control. Rather, they are responsible for at least some of their preferences. Of course, not all preferences are "voluntary" in this sense—for example, special medical needs, and the like—but others, such as exotic tastes, are clearly ones that despite their intensity do not provide an approriate basis of interpersonal comparison for settling questions of distributive justice.

Scanlon's own suggestion is that in making such interpersonal comparisons we should assess not only the preferences that individuals have, but also the *reasons* people can or might offer for them.[75] What he hopes will emerge from a consideration of such reasons is "a kind of schematic picture of a range of variation of normal lives," in which some preferences will appear more urgent and others relatively peripheral. Of course, not only individual preferences but also the reasons offered for them will vary from society to society. For this reason, Scanlon describes his approach as "conventional" rather than "naturalistic": there is no claim that the preferences regarded as urgent correspond to an objective moral order. Rather, the ordering appeals to the notion of a rationally motivated (hence, ideal) consensus. It represents "the best available standard of justification that is mutually acceptable to people whose preferences diverge."[76] It is along this line too, I want to suggest, that Habermas's notion of generalizable interests is most fruitfully understood.

As I have just indicated, Rawls's notion of primary goods should be viewed as an "objective" criterion of interpersonal comparison. The representative least-advantaged group is not defined according to an indexing of subjective preferences (as in utilitarianism), but according to an indexing of primary goods specified in terms of the model-conception of the person. At the same time, however, it is not clear whether Rawls would accept Scanlon's attempt to provide a consensual grounding for an account of primary goods (or urgent preferences).[77] Rather than resting the account of primary goods upon the idea of what all could reasonably agree to under suitable conditions of debate, Rawls argues for the list through a direct appeal to the model-conception of the person, which is itself regarded as a "fundamental intuitive idea" implicit in our public culture. Although this appeal to a conception of the person is certainly relevant, in severing the list of primary goods from a notion of what all could agree to, Rawls once more unnecessarily privileges the external perspective of the philosopher. Nevertheless, it is also clear from his specific list of primary goods that they rely heavily upon the tradition and institutions of liberal democratic societies, thus leaving him open to the charge of relativism. In his most recent discussion, Rawls offers the following list (together with some of the most important considerations for them):

1. The basic liberties (freedom of thought and liberty of conscience, etc.) are the background institutions necessary for the development and exercise of the capacity to decide upon and revise, and rationally to pursue, a conception of the good. Similarly, these liberties allow for the development and exercise of the sense of right and justice under political and social conditions that are free.

2. Freedom of movement and free choice of occupation against a background of diverse opportunities are required for the pursuit of final ends as well as to give effect to a decision to revise and change them, if one so desires.

3. Powers and prerogative of offices of responsibility are needed to give scope to various self-governing and social capacities of the self.

4. Income and wealth, understood broadly as they must be, are all-purpose means (having an exchange value) for achieving directly or indirectly a wide range of ends, whatever they happen to be.

5. The social bases of self-respect are those aspects of basic institutions that are normally essential if citizens are to have a lively sense of their own worth as moral persons and to be able to realise their highest-order interests and advance their ends with self-confidence.[78]

In his "special conception" of justice (which I discuss in the next chapter), Rawls draws a fairly sharp distinction between the primary goods listed in the first category and those specified subsequently. Roughly stated, the liberties listed in 1 are protected by the first principle of justice; while those contained in 2 through 5 are regulated by the second principle of justice (the Difference Principle). As several critics have noted, this division reflects the traditional liberal distinction between the public and private spheres or, more specifically, between politics and the market.

Habermas introduces his own notion of "the model of the suppression of generalizable interests" in *Legitimation Crisis* (pp. 111–17). The idea is to employ a notion of generalizable interests for the purpose of social criticism. Generalizable interests, or interests that express the common good, are those interests that all participants in a practical discourse could accept with good reasons, that is, those interests that admit of a "rationally motivated consensus." The model thus already assumes the idea and justification of a discourse ethics as outlined in the last chapter, that is, it assumes that practical questions are open to rational justification and that, ideally, such justification takes the form of a practical discourse.

As I suggested above, there is a broad similarity between Scanlon's attempt to develop an objective criterion of interpersonal comparison and Habermas's notion of generalizable interests. In each case, the idea is to identify those interests or preferences that from an impartial standpoint could be rationally agreed to by those concerned as worthy of recognition or in the "common good." However, posed in these terms, Habermas's formulation gives rise to an apparent dilemma: On the one hand, it is only by carrying out an actual discourse in which the participants accept and reject reasons for regarding certain interests as generalizable that anything even remotely resembling Rawls's list of primary goods might be constructed. Short of such actual discourses, the model is abstract and indeterminate.[79] On the other hand, any actual discourse will necessarily be limited and subject to the various constraints of space, time, and resources—not to mention unidentified power relations. Thus, any list of generalizable interests arising from it will be tentative and subject to future discursive vindication. With respect to any actual discourse, it will also be open to question among the participants whether disagreement about specific generalizable interests is a reasonable one or one that results from the veiled influence of existing power relations.

Habermas's proposal is that in the absence of actual discourses (or with reference to fundamental disputes within the public forum) it is the task of a critical social theory to carry out virtual or counterfactual discourses to help differentiate between generalizable and nongeneralizable interests, thereby identifying areas where real generalizable interests have been suppressed. This "advocacy" role of the critical social theorist is analogous to Scanlon's notion of hypothetically constructing a "schematic picture of a range of variation of normal lives" and then using that scheme to criticize social institutions. It also supplements the internal perspective of the participant with the external perspective of the social theorist, thereby enabling a different account of the possible sources of disagreement. According to Habermas, the question the critical theorist must address in her advocacy role is:

How would the members of a social system, at a given stage in the development of productive forces, have collectively and bindingly interpreted their needs (and which norms would they have accepted as justified) if they could and would have decided on the organization of social intercourse through discursive will-formation, with adequate knowledge of the limiting conditions and functional imperatives of their society? (*LC*, 113)

This model has both advantages and disadvantages: On the one hand, it is less tied to the traditions and institutions of a particular society than Rawls's list of primary goods. This enables it to be both more critical and more utopian. On the other hand, the hypothetical thought experiment it enjoins is quite abstract and the sorts of considerations that would need to be taken into account are tremendous. Here Rawls's theory seems to have an advantage. My own suggestion is that the two theories can be combined in a way that provides a tool for the critical social theorist. Rawls's list must be regarded as tentative and hypothetical, subject to the criterion of what all would agree to if they were to enter into a discourse about the interpretation of their needs and interests. At the same time, however, Habermas's model of the suppression of generalizable interests needs to be more closely connected to specific institutions and traditions if it is to be very useful as a tool of social criticism. The idea is that a list of primary goods or generalizable interests (now interpreted as a hypothetical and fallible list of what the participants themselves would rationally agree to as a standard for interpersonal comparison) can serve as a tool for social criticism. In either case, implicit appeal is made to a normative conception of the person or, more specifically, those general social conditions that are necessary for the realization of the freedom and equality of citizens. Nevertheless, since it is likely (and desirable) that some reasonable disagreement even about generalizable interests or the common good will persist in a liberal democratic regime, the most useful task for the model of suppressed generalizable interests may be to emphasize the need for strengthening those institutions in the public sphere where debate and deliberation about the common good and collective need interpretation take place.[80] This is the topic of the final chapter.

5

FROM DISTRIBUTIVE JUSTICE TO NORMATIVE SOCIAL CRITICISM

So far, I have not discussed in any detail the content of Rawls's two principles of justice. In chapter 2 we were primarily concerned with the first of the two main parts of *A Theory of Justice,* the interpretation and justification of the initial choice situation or original position (OP), (*TJ,* 15, 54). This chapter, by contrast, begins with an analysis and critique of the two principles. However, our earlier discussion of the OP, and in particular of the problems related to its interpretation as a situation of rational choice under uncertainty, already suggests an important consequence for the two principles: the relationship between the OP and the two principles is neither "strictly deductive" nor an example of rigorous "moral geometry," at least not when the construction and design of the OP is considered as a whole (*TJ,* 121). Rather, as Rawls expresses it in "Kantian Constuctivism," the OP is a "device of representation" that mediates between the model-conceptions of the person and the well-ordered society, on the one hand, and the specific formulation of the two principles, on the other (*KC,* 520, 533). As such, the OP is best viewed as an element of moral constructivism, as part of a legitimation procedure for substantive proposals concerning social justice.[1] This reconstruction has the advantage of drawing a sharper distinction between the procedure of legitimation that any norms or principles must satisfy (e.g., Rawls's OP or Habermas's discourse ethic), and the substantive proposals themselves (e.g., Rawls's two principles).[2] It also suggests that the two principles need not be viewed as principles that would be chosen *sub specie aeternitatis* (*TJ,* 587), a conclusion with which Rawls would now apparently agree.[3]

After offering an internal criticism of the two principles (I), I again take up Rawls's notion of the basic social structure as the primary subject of justice. Despite the importance of the "principle of publicity" for Rawls's Kantianism, I argue that he neglects to thematize the institution(s) of a public sphere *within* civil society in his description of the basic social structure (II).

This neglect, in turn, surfaces in the ambivalent status of democratic participation in his theory of justice (III). In the final section, these criticisms lead to the conclusion that a theory of social justice should be developed in closer connection with a specific model of democracy. After suggesting why ideals implicit in Rawls's theory of justice are not compatible with the two most prevalent models of democracy—pluralism and neocorporatism—I introduce a model of "deliberative" democracy as a third alternative.[4] This third model of democracy, I argue, can be clarified with reference to Habermas's notion of the public sphere (IV). I conclude with a summary of some (slightly) more specific suggestions on how this third model might best be pursued.

I. RAWLS'S TWO PRINCIPLES OF JUSTICE

Rawls's two principles have already been the subject of extensive debate and criticism. My own discussion will therefore be more or less limited to (1) the implications of Rawls's more recent attempt to justify them with reference to the model-conceptions of the person and the well-ordered society and (2) some unresolved difficulties related to their clarification and interpretation. In this way I hope to provide an immanent critique that will move Rawls's liberalism in a more egalitarian and social-democratic direction.

The most recent formulation of the "special conception" of the two principles reads as follows:

> Each person has an equal right to a fully adequate scheme of equal basic liberties which is compatible with a similar scheme of liberties for all (the Principle of Equal Liberty).

> Social and economic inequalities are to satisfy two conditions. First, they must be attached to offices and positions open to all under conditions of fair equality of opportunity; and second, they must be to the greatest benefit of the least-advantaged members of society (the Difference Principle).[5]

This "special conception" of the principles of justice differs from the "general conception"—"All social primary goods are to be distributed equally unless an unequal distribution of any or all of these goods is to the advantage of the least favored" (*TJ*, 303)—in two respects: First, it distinguishes between the basic rights and liberties (contained in the first principle) and the other primary social goods (regulated by the second principle). And second, it claims priority for the first principle over the second principle, and for the first part of the second principle over the second part. Thus, the Difference

Principle strictly speaking (e.g., the second part of the second principle) is only applied to background social institutions after the basic liberties and equality of opportunity have been secured; in a society with only moderate scarcity of social wealth, it would be unjust to equalize the distribution of other social goods by more than that specified by the Difference Principle. The claim for the priority of the first principle of justice is also found in Rawls's claim that the basic liberties can only be restricted for the sake of a more fully adequate scheme of basic liberties and not, say, on the basis of utilitarian considerations about the common good. This further claim has a long standing in the liberal tradition, and I will consider Rawls's defense of it in reference to the interpretation of the two principles.

Contrary to the interpretation of some critics, Rawls does not begin with the conception of negative liberty familiar to the liberal tradition since Hobbes—liberty as the absence of coercion rather than liberty as self-determination or self-government (the "positive" conception).[6] Rather, he sidesteps this controversy (at least for the moment) by making use of the triadic definition of freedom introduced by MacCullum and by Oppenheim: A person is free (or not free) from this or that constraint to do (or not do) so and so (*TJ*, 202). This formulation avoids the problems that arise when a sharp distinction is drawn between the two conceptions, yet it is still quite formal and leaves unspecified the sorts of things that might properly be regarded as constraints or obstacles to freedom. The attempt to "fill out" this formal definition of liberty with the list of basic liberties included in the first principle is a central task of *A Theory of Justice*.

The first question to raise concerning the "special" conception of justice is how Rawls specifies the particular set of liberties to be included in the first principle. In the earliest formulation found in "Justice as Fairness" (1958), Rawls stated that an individual has an equal right to "the most extensive liberty compatible with a like liberty for all."[7] This formulation differs from that found in *A Theory of Justice,* which refers not to a concept of liberty in general, but to a "system of basic liberties" (*TJ,* 302). To my knowledge, Rawls nowhere discusses the reason for this change, but in a perceptive analysis of the liberty principle, H. L. A. Hart suggests that it might be due to a problem noted long ago by Sidgwick (and one that we have already encountered in our discussion of Kant):[8] If there is a basic right to liberty in general, it is difficult to see how a more specific set of rights and liberties could be derived from it since such rights would presumably impose in total an even greater number of restrictions.[9] For example, the right to private ownership imposes restrictions upon the freedom of everyone else. As we saw, Kant attempted to resolve this difficulty by introducing an abstract (and debatable) notion of a "limitation upon a limitation," and even then only as a "permissive law" that required (in principle) the agreement of all concerned (cf. chapter 1, section III). Rawls apparently avoids this problem by beginning not with a right to liberty in general, but with a right to the most extensive (or fully adequate) scheme of basic liberties. Among these he includes "political liberty (the right to vote and be eligible for public office) together with freedom of speech and assembly; liberty of conscience and freedom of thought; freedom of the person along with the right to hold (personal) property; and freedom from arbitrary arrest and seizure as defined by the concept of the rule of law" (*TJ*, 61). However, as Hart observes, this merely postpones some of the difficulties, for Rawls is now obliged to provide an argument for each of the specific liberties he introduces, as well as an argument for those he excludes. In short, what liberties should be considered basic, and why?

This question is related to a second difficulty contained in Rawls's claim that liberty can be restricted only for the sake of a more fully adequate scheme of basic liberties. As even sympathetic critics have noted, a scheme of basic liberties may not only conflict with other social values but may also contain internal conflicts within itself.[10] The claim that liberty can be limited only for the sake of liberty would seem to be unable to provide any guidance for resolving such conflicts. When one person's freedom to own property, for example, conflicts with another person's freedom to speak, is it possible to find a resolution without appealing to other social values?

Finally, critics have drawn attention to the possible ideological implications of Rawls's distinction between liberty and the *worth* of liberty (*TJ*, 204). Although the Principle of Equal Liberty provides that all have an equal right to the most fully adequate scheme of basic liberties, the worth or value of those liberties can vary greatly according to a person's social position, wealth, and access to various resources. Consequently, critics have charged that this distinction makes the basic liberties merely formal—the rich and the poor may have an equal right to eat in an expensive restaurant, but this right will be of value only to the rich.[11] Since this distinction between liberty and its worth is closely related to the Difference Principle (which regulates acceptable inequalities of the worth of most liberties), I will consider the first two problems here, and reserve the third until the discussion of the Difference Principle.

Rawls treats these and related problems at length in his 1981 Tanner Lecture, "The Basic Liberties and Their Priority" (hereafter, *BL*). His central strategy is to argue for the basic liberties on the basis of their relation to the model-conception of the person first discussed in "Kantian Constructivism." As we saw in the previous chapter, Rawls characterized the person in terms of two highest-order moral powers: the capacity for a sense of justice (that is, the capacity to understand and be moved by a desire to act from principles of justice as the fair terms of social cooperation) and the capacity to form, revise, and rationally pursue a conception of the good (*KC*, 525). In "Kantian Constructivism," Rawls referred to these two capacities as the Reasonable and the Rational, respectively, and showed how each played a role in the construction and design of the OP. In "Basic Liberties," he argues that this model-conception of the person is also crucial in framing the list of principles from which the parties in the OP must choose. Ideally, the "fully adequate scheme" of basic liberties specified by the first principle is justified to the extent that it defines the essential conditions for the development and exercise of the two highest-order moral powers (*BL*, 7).

However, this ideal is immediately qualified in three important respects. First, a list of specific basic liberties obviously cannot be inferred directly from the model-conception of the person; rather, "we" who construct the list "survey the constitutions of the democratic states and put together a list of liberties normally protected, and we examine the role of those constitutions which have worked so well" (*BL*, 6; on the use of "we," see *KC*, 534). Second, Rawls argues (as he did in *A Theory of Justice*) that only the general form and content of the basic liberties are specified by the first principle; the details of how they fit together into a fully adequate scheme, as well as how they mutually limit one another, are reserved until the subsequent constitutional, legislative, and judicial stages of Rawls's four-stage sequence (*TJ*, 195; *BL*, 12; see also Figure 2–1, p. 54 above). For example, while the right to personal property is included among the basic liberties because "the role of this liberty is to allow a sufficient material basis for a sense of personal independence and self-respect, both of which are essential for the development and exercise of the moral powers" (*BL*, 12), whether this right is best realized in the form of capitalist property rights or as a right to equal participation in the control of natural resources and means of production that are socially owned is a question that cannot be settled until the stage of the constitutional convention when more specific social and historical factors are taken into consideration (*BL*, 12; *TJ*, 274). Third, even at the constitutional level Rawls acknowledges that a "criterion of significance" is required in order to fit the potentially conflicting liberties into a fully adequate scheme. He suggests, however, that this criterion of significance can be drawn from the model-conception of the person, rather than from considerations of social utility (as Hart proposes) (*BL*, 50).

The sort of justification of the basic liberties that Rawls has in mind can be briefly illustrated with reference to the two moral powers. Liberty of conscience and freedom of assembly are recognized as basic because of their central importance for the development and exercise of the capacity to form, revise, and pursue a conception of the good. Without these liberties the social conditions necessary for the development of this moral power would not be secure. Further, although the parties in the OP are denied knowledge of their own particular conception of the good, they know that they have a conception and hence it would be irrational for them to deny priority to the conditions necessary for its realization.

Likewise, freedom of speech is defended on the basis of its relation to the conditions required for the realization and maintenance of a sense of justice. A society that restricts (in contrast to regulates) this liberty risks undermining the conditions of publicity necessary for its citizens to maintain a sense of justice and the belief that the rules governing the basic structure rest on fair principles of cooperation (*KC*, 539). However, more specific issues relating to the freedom of speech, such as seditious libel, prior restraint, or the "clear and present danger rule," cannot be settled by appeal to the model-conception of the person alone. These are questions to be resolved at the stage of the constitutional convention where the delegates have more knowledge of the history of constitutional doctrine and past experiences.

How successful is this new strategy as a response to the problems raised by Hart (e.g., the criterion for specifying the liberties to be contained in the first principle, and the problematic claim that liberty can be limited only for the sake of liberty)? Several remarks are in order: First, it is clear once again that Rawls's defense of the basic liberties is quite far from the notion of self-interested rational choice under uncertainty and firmly within the tradition of a Kantian model of autonomy as outlined in the last chapter (see *BL*, 21 n.20). The model-conception of the person is invoked not only in the construction of the OP, but is also used to specify the general form and content of the liberties contained in the first principle, and it is invoked again at the subsequent stages of the constitutional convention, legislative assembly, and judicial review. It also serves as a criterion of significance in light of which the various liberties can be weighed and fit into a coherent scheme.

On the other hand, however, the defense of the liberties does not rest on a particular conception or ideal of the good life, but on those conditions necessary for having a conception of the good (e.g., the moral powers). If our reconstruction of the model-conception of the person as a notion of communicative autonomy in the previous chapter is sound, then Rawls may be read as providing an argument for basic rights in terms of those conditions necessary for the protection and institutionalization of processes of discursive will-formation. Rawls's constructivism is thus an alternative to both natural rights doctrine and pure proceduralism with respect to the defense and interpretation of basic constitutional rights.[12]

Finally, Rawls's admission that only the general form and content of the basic liberties can be provided at the stage of the OP and that their more specific details (private property capitalism or market socialism, for example) can only be settled at later stages in the four-stage sequence tends to support the distinction I have attempted to draw between a principle of legitimation and substantive proposals. However, rather than acknowledging such a distinction and arguing, for example, that substantive proposals about rights need to be defended with reference to a notion of communicative autonomy, Rawls allows substantive issues and historical tradition—"those constitutions that have worked so well"—to slip in surreptitiously as he slowly lifts the veil of ignorance at each successive stage. As a result, the basic rights and their priority appear as the conclusion of philosophical arguments rather than as proposals to which "we," the affected, must (in principle) all agree.

I would now like to return to the third problem mentioned above: the distinction between liberty and its worth. To repeat the criticism, such a distinction seems to make the basic liberties merely formal since the worth of the liberties can apparently vary significantly. But since, according to Rawls, inequalities in worth are regulated by the Difference Principle, whether it does vary *significantly* depends crucially on the interpretation of this principle. Yet, this is where Rawls encounters difficulties: the Difference Principle is (perhaps unavoidably) unable to measure differences in the worth of liberty beyond a rough correlation between that worth and income. Before taking up the interpretation of the Difference Principle, however, I should mention one further complication that Rawls introduces—one that could make much of the discussion about the Difference Principle moot.

Although it has not been widely noted by his critics, Rawls argues in *A Theory of Justice* (and again in "Basic Liberties") that measures should be taken to insure the fair value (or worth) of the political liberties, *including* political speech and assembly:

> What is necessary is that political parties be autonomous with respect to private demands, that is, demands not expressed in the public forum and argued for openly by reference to a conception of the public good.... Historically one of the main defects of constitutional government has been the failure to insure the fair value of political liberty. (*TJ*, 226; cf. also 356, and *BL*, 41f.)

If inequalities in the distribution of social goods cannot be so great that they upset the fair value of political liberties, then Rawls would seem to have much more in mind than the guarantee of formal rights; in fact, it becomes hard to see why the Difference Principle, as an additional principle for regulating inequalities in social wealth, needs to be introduced at all. Of course, Rawls quickly notes that the guarantee of fair value applies only to political liberty (e.g., there is no attempt to insure the fair value of religious liberty or the right to own personal property), but unless Rawls makes the implausible assumption that substantial social and economic inequalities do not translate into unequal political advantage, it is difficult not to conclude that this notion of the fair value of political liberties would entail profound social changes in modern welfare-state democracies. Perhaps the Difference Principle is really quite radical: It requires that *after* social and economic inequalities are restricted so that they do not upset the fair value of political liberty—including the fair value of forming and expressing public opinion—such inequalities are *still* only permissible if they benefit the least advantaged. The difficulty with this view, however, is that at just the point where the Difference Principle would come into play, it would lose most of its value. Once the fair value of political liberty (in the wide sense) is assured, public debate (I suspect) would no longer be about the distribution of wealth and social goods, but about what Habermas has termed "the grammar of lifeforms," that is, questions about the quality of life and individual and collective self-definition that cannot be addressed solely through the compensatory measures of the welfare state (see *TCA* 2:392). The more likely interpretation, which I develop in the next two sections, is that Rawls tends to limit political liberty or the "principle of participation" to the right to vote and run for political office. The task of protecting autonomous public spheres recedes into the distant background of his theory and a more significant division of labor between the principles sets in: the first guarantees the traditional political and civil liberties, the second regulates the distribution of income and wealth.

The Difference Principle states that inequalities in the distribution of primary social goods (other than the basic liberties secured by the first principle) are justified only to the extent that they result in a greater amount of these goods for the least advantaged. The Difference Principle is satisfied when there is no alternative institutional arrangement of the basic structure that would lead to a more equitable distribution of primary goods without worsening the situation of the representative least advantaged in that arrangement. The representative least advantaged is defined not by an index of preferences (as used in welfare economics), but by a measure of primary social goods. (Recall from the last chapter that the primary goods are defined as the social background conditions and all-purpose means necessary for the development and exercise of the two highest-order moral powers; in addition to the basic liberties, they include freedom of movement and choice of occupation, powers and prerogatives of office and positions of responsibility, income and wealth, and finally, but most importantly, the social bases of self-respect.[13]) The task is thus to develop an index of the primary goods in order to make interpersonal comparisons, define the position of the least advantaged, and compare alternative arrangements of the basic structure. Rawls quickly concedes, however, that it would be difficult (if not impossible) to develop an index in which such a diversity of goods could be coordinated (*TJ*, 93f, 97). There is no guarantee that the least advantaged with respect to freedom of movement will also be the least advantaged with respect to the social bases of self-respect or even income, nor is it clear that these goods can be fit into a *single* index. Consequently, Rawls introduces a "simplest form": the representative least advantaged is defined solely in terms of income and wealth.[14] Further, rather than measuring the distribution of wealth at any given point in the life span of a (representative) individual, the index measures the lifetime expectation of the representative least advantaged. However, whatever the "simplest form" gains in usefulness, it seems to lose in terms of its relation to the model-conception of the person (on the basis of which the primary goods were defined). Unless one assumes that the worth of each of the basic liberties rises and falls relative to an increase or decrease in material wealth (which Rawls does—*TJ*, 97), the "simplest form" permits an increase in wealth at the expense of the worth of the basic liberties (since only the former is measured). It allows for material growth and prosperity while permitting a decline in the worth of basic liberties for the least advantaged.[15]

Finally, it should be clear by now that the distinction between the two principles of justice and the claim for the priority of the first—the heart of what Rawls calls the "special conception"—corresponds to a fundamental division in the basic structure, namely, the distinction between the public and the private, between political and civil rights (guaranteed by the first principle) and social and economic inequalities (regulated by the second principle). What I hope to show in the next section is that this division of the basic structure results in the systematic neglect of a public sphere *within* civil society.

II. THE BASIC STRUCTURE AND NORMATIVE SOCIAL CRITICISM

In chapter 2 I argued that a distinctive feature of Rawls's theory of justice is that it regards the basic social structure as the primary subject of justice. In contrast to libertarian conceptions of justice, Rawls focuses attention on the background social institutions that shape the expectations and opportunities of representative members within that society. The primary subject of justice is not the contractual agreements between persons (as with Nozick), but the fundamental arrangement of major social institutions in the context of which other associations form and individual transactions take place.[16] As we saw, this has several advantages: first, it is not possible to assess whether individual agreements are fair without examining the nature of the social institutions in which they occur; second, it recognizes the "social nature" of persons, that is, the extent to which individual expectations and desires are shaped by social institutions; and finally, it reflects the fact that the (hypothetical) agreement to the original social contract is quite different than other types of contractual agreements—this was a central feature of Hegel's critique of Kant (see *BS*, 53). Despite these advantages, I now want to argue that Rawls's discussion of the basic social structure fails to thematize the public sphere within civil society. His analysis of the basic structure retains the traditional liberal distinction between the public and private sphere, and this results in undesirable consequences for his theory of social justice.

Recall that Rawls defines the basic structure as "the way in which major social institutions fit together into one system, and how they assign fundamental rights and duties and shape the division of advantages that arises through social cooperation" (*BS*, 47). In *A Theory of Justice,* he also refers to it as "a public system of rules defining a scheme of activities that leads men to act together so as to produce a greater sum of benefits and assigns to each certain recognized claims to a share in the proceeds" (84). A society is just only if its basic structure is arranged so that it satisfies the two principles *and* if it is publicly recognized that the basic structure satisfies these principles (see *KC*, 521). This public knowledge plays an important role in the development and maintenance of a sense of justice and the belief that the terms of social cooperation are fair; it is thus also central to the stability of a well-ordered society. However, despite the importance of this publicity requirement, Rawls nowhere explicity discusses the need for, and importance of, institutions of the public sphere within the basic structure. In fact, his brief discussions of the basic structure are conspicuous for their omission of such institutions.

From his scattered remarks throughout *A Theory of Justice,* it can be inferred that Rawls includes the following institutions within the basic structure: the political constitution (7, 304–9), the nuclear family (7, 300, 511), the competitive market (7, 304–9), an autonomous legal system—"the rule of law" (235), and an interventionist welfare state (275). He also suggests that the basic structure can be divided into two fundamental parts, corresponding to his two principles of justice (61–3, 199). Thus, the Equal Liberty Principle is embodied in the political constitution and guarantees an equal right to political participation, while the Difference Principle is primarily responsible for regulating inequalities that arise within the private sphere. What is noticeably absent from Rawls's treatment of the basic structure, however, is a critical discussion of what institutions are to be included within it (or excluded from it), as well as any discussion of how the institutions he includes within the basic structure might influence one another (either at present, or in a well-ordered society). The first deficiency indicates once more that, despite his intentions, historical assumptions and traditional categories constantly enter into his description of the original position and influence the choice of the parties. This is most evident in the fact that there is no explicit recognition of the need for autonomous, self-organized associations within civil society to curb the regulatory power of the state. Admittedly, Rawls might reply that such institutions are covered by the right to free speech and assembly, as well as the guarantee of the fair value of political liberty. And I concede that many of my objections would lose their force if these aspects of Rawls's theory were emphasized. But they do not receive systematic consideration by Rawls, as is suggested by the fact that many of his critics do not even note these features. Rawls's assumption that the basic structure divides into two basic parts also supports my interpretation. The second deficiency, I suggest, underlies Rawls's assumptions about how social justice could be realized and maintained, namely through the active intervention of the welfare state into the private sphere or civil society. After a brief description of Habermas's alternative approach to the basic structure, I will illustrate this second deficiency with respect to current debates about the crisis of the welfare state and the growth of legal regulation or juridification (*Verrechtlichung*).

Rawls's concept of the basic structure corresponds roughly to Habermas's notion of the "institutional framework of a society" (in "Technology and Science as Ideology"), as well as to the network of institutions implicit in the idea of abstract "principles of organization" (in *Legitimation Crisis*). But the moment this comparison is made, a major difference becomes evident: Whereas Rawls assumes the existence of major institutions within the basic structure, Habermas attempts to thematize their historical evolution and mutual interaction in order to identify potential "crisis tendencies" within them. Thus, rather than assuming that the market (and wage labor) will perform a significant role in any society, Habermas analyzes the shifting importance of the market for social integration, first with the rise of liberal captialism and again with the transition to advanced capitalist societies.[17] Similarly, he is able to trace the changing interaction between different institutions within the basic structure, such as the relations between the state, the economy, and civil society. Finally, the central theme of *The Theory of Communicative Action*—that social rationalization means not only an increased differentiation between social subsystems and the expansion of instrumental reason, but also the possibility for new forms of (communicative) rationalization within a lifeworld (civil society) that has been freed from the functional imperatives of social subsystems, lies completely beyond the reach of Rawls's analysis of the basic structure. Of course, Rawls could again reply that such a social-theoretic analysis of the basic structure is not the task of a theory of justice, but my claim is that the failure to take such social-theoretic analyses into consideration has implications for the substantive content of the principles of justice. I have already suggested this is evident in his neglect of the public sphere within the basic structure; a similar argument could be made about his exclusion of welfare rights from the constitution or his lack of emphasis on the freedom of association. I will develop some of these criticisms in the next section when I consider Rawls's views on democratic participation. I would now like to show how Rawls's assumptions about how social justice can be maintained run into difficulties.

In view of the institutions Rawls explicitly includes within the basic structure, it may be assumed that the principal mechanism for achieving social justice is the interventionist welfare state, in connection with the legal system. This assumption is further supported by his discussion of "Background Institutions for Distributive Justice" (*TJ*, par. 43). In this section, Rawls distinguishes between four different branches of the government in terms of the function each is to perform in regulating the basic structure: the allocative and stabilization branches are responsible for keeping the market system competitive, arranging tax structures to correct for the failure of the market to accurately measure social benefits and costs, and taking steps to insure full employment of the labor force; a transfer branch is responsible for guaranteeing a social welfare and income minimum (through cash supplements, a "negative income tax" or "in kind" provisions); and a distributive branch has the task of correcting for unequal distributions of wealth (in accordance with the Difference Principle) and raising revenue to meet the costs of social justice (through tax policies and adjustments in property rights, etc.) (*TJ*, 275f.).

As libertarian critics have been quick to point out, these activities require an extensive intervention of the state into what has traditionally been considered the private sphere.[18] In more recent years, however, criticisms of the welfare state have also been voiced by those more sympathetic with its expressed aims.[19] Attempts to achieve greater social justice have simultaneously resulted in the fragmentation, bureaucratization, and monetarization of a civil society traditionally integrated through other means. Although these critics do not necessarily call for a complete rollback of the welfare state and a reinstitution of the traditional public/private distinction, they recognize that its gains have been ambiguous: In addition to undermining the traditional sources of its own legitimation, it imposes demands upon itself that it is increasingly unable to meet.[20] Further, given the limited methods available to it, a bureaucratic administration is often compelled to substitute the demand for social goods and services with monetary compensations, further exacerbating tendencies toward disintegration in the lifeworld (federal housing, unemployment compensation, early retirement payments, and aid to families).[21] Finally, in the effort to meet demands placed upon it, the welfare state threatens the identity of those institutions on which it depends—this has been particularly thematized in discussions about the repoliticization of the legal system and instrumentalization of law.[22]

In *The Theory of Communicative Action,* Habermas offers an analysis of the dilemmas of the welfare state along the lines already begun in *Legiti-*

mation Crisis. He still traces these crises back to "the contradiction of socialized production for nongeneralizable interests" (*LC,* 39; see *TCA* 2:345), but he now describes the phenomena more generally in terms of conflicts arising from a one-sided process of social rationalization. The political and economic subsystems, which in modern societies have achieved a large degree of independence from the communicatively structured lifeworld and whose central institutions are primarily regulated by their own functional imperatives, now turn back on the lifeworld and, via the media of money and political power, threaten to "colonize" it in pursuit of their own self-maintenance. The requirement of the administrative state to secure conditions for economic growth *and* retain legitimacy necessitate further and more extensive interventions into the lifeworld, thereby inhibiting the potential for self-organization and control from arising from within the lifeworld itself.

> From the start, the *ambivalence of guaranteeing freedom and taking it away* has attached to the policies of the welfare state.... The net of welfare-state guarantees is meant to cushion the external effects of a production process based on wage lagor. Yet the more closely this net is woven, the more clearly ambivalences of *another sort* appear. The negative effects of this [process of juridification] do not appear as side effects; they result *from the form of juridification itself.* (*TCA* 2:361–2)

As this quotation already suggests, the ambivalent character of state interventionism can be illustrated in connection with the recent discussions concerning the growth of legal regulation or juridification (*Verrechtlichung*).

With the growth of the welfare state, the legal system has been increasingly relied upon to achieve social goals as well as to protect individual constitutional rights. The result has been not merely a quantitative increase in the amount of legislation enacted, but a qualitative change in the nature of law—frequently described as its "instrumentalization" or "materialization." To the extent that law becomes an instrument for realizing social ends, it is repoliticized and its own autonomy is threatened. A legal system that had first differentiated itself from the lifeworld—the positivity of law—in turn becomes a *medium* through which informal institutions of the lifeworld are juridified, bureaucratized, and monetarized; that is, they are colonized by the economic and political subsystems:

> The *dilemmatic structure of this type of juridification* consists in the fact that, while the welfare state guarantees are intended to serve the goal of social integration, they nevertheless promote the disintegration of life-relations when these are separated, through legalized social

intervention, from consensual mechanisms that coordinate action, and are transfered over to media such as power and money. (*TCA* 2:364)

However, as Habermas argues, law is not only a medium that displaces communicatively structured domains of interaction; as an *institution* it is also anchored in the norms and traditions of the lifeworld, in moral conscious- ness, common law, and constitutional rights. Against positivists who regard law as a self-contained procedure or set of rules, Habermas argues that the legitimacy of the legal system depends upon these institutional roots in the lifeworld. The question thus becomes: How can the function of law as a *medium* be contained and prevented from undermining the very institutions in the lifeworld on which it depends for its legitimacy?[23]

Various attempts to deal with this dilemma can be found in the discus- sions calling for a new type of "responsive," "reflexive," or "procedural" law.[24] Habermas's own somewhat paradoxical proposal is that law can be used as a means to limit the juridifying effects of the law if it operates in a more reflective and self-restrained manner. In connection with an understand- ing of its own rationality requirements contained in the ideal of the rule of law, the law should aim at ensuring that the modes of exchange among the various institutions and corporate bodies of the state, the economy, and the public at large conform to standards of impartiality and procedural fairness.[25] At the same time, however, "the juridification of communicatively structured areas of action ought not to go beyond the enforcement of the principles of the rule of law; beyond the legal institutionalization of the *external* constitution of, say, the family or of the school. The place of law as a medium must be replaced by procedures for settling conflicts that are appropriate to the struc- tures of action oriented by mutual understanding—discursive processes of will-formation and consensus-oriented procedures of negotiation and decision making" (*TCA* 2:371). In relation to communicatively structured institutions such as the family and schooling, for example, the aim of legislation should be to secure these domains from the effects of the subsystems of the economy and the administrative state rather than to convert them into formally orga- nized institutions. To the extent that the latter has already occured, what is required is a "dejuridification" of these domains and the creation of processes of conflict resolution more appropriate to these contexts of interaction.[26]

This brief digression into Habermas's thesis of the colonization of the lifeworld is intended only to illustrate some of the problems connected with Rawls's assumption that social justice can be achieved through welfare-state intervention into civil society. The response that the analysis of such phe- nomena lies beyond the task of a theory of justice would miss the point, since the failure to consider them leads to deficiencies in the substantive pro- posals themselves. I have tried to indicate this both with respect to Rawls's neglect of the public sphere within civil society in his discussion of the basic structure, and his assumption about how social justice can be achieved. I will now turn to a more specific discussion of the relation between justice and democracy in Rawls's theory, and argue for the importance of a normative concept of the public sphere(s).

III. JUSTICE, DEMOCRATIC PARTICIPATION, AND THE PUBLIC SPHERE

Perhaps no topic in *A Theory of Justice* is more ambiguous or conflict-ridden than the role of democratic participation (both political and nonpolitical) in Rawls's vision of a just society. Even his most able critics cannot agree: Hart concludes that Rawls's argument for the priority of liberty rests on a latent ideal conception of the good life, "that of a public-spirited citizen who prizes political activity and service to others as among the chief goods of life and could not contemplate as tolerable an exchange of the opportunities for such activity for mere material goods or contentment."[27] Amy Gutmann, by contrast, concludes that liberal egalitarianism has two faces, a commitment to distributive justice (emphasized by Rawls) and a commitment to maximizing participatory activities (neglected by Rawls but found, for example, in the work of Mill and Cole).[28] Finally, Carole Pateman suggests that *A Theory of Justice* can be viewed as a misguided attempt to divorce political obligations from the notion of participation and consent, thereby justifying a liberal democracy with a passive citizenry.[29] Our own interpretation helps to make these conflicting readings understandable: democratic participation is important to Rawls not because he holds to a *particular* conception of the good life, but because his model-conception of the person finally implies a notion of communicative autonomy and discursive will-formation as a condition for the realization of a wide variety of alternative conceptions of the good life (see chapter 4). On the other hand, Rawls does not make a principle of democratic participation central to his notion of social justice. This is most evident by the absence of a public sphere as a specific institution (or set of institutions) within the basic structure. The result is that Rawls's discussion of democratic participation is vague and fragmented; at times it seems to be an indispensable element of his theory (for example, when he discusses the need to insure the fair value of political speech), at other times it seems that a society democratic only in form might still satisfy the two principles of justice. After examining some of the considerations that might have caused Rawls to diminish the importance of democratic participation, I will consider the two most current proposals for democracy in a large-scale, complex society: pluralism and neocorporatism. I then suggest that, on one interpretation at least, some of Rawls's remarks on the value of democratic participation could best be pursued in connection with Habermas's concept of the public sphere. This leads to a third model of democracy, which has recently been described as "deliberative democracy."

There are a number of considerations that might be responsible for the (explicitly) diminished role of political participation in Rawls's theory of justice. First, contrary to Hart's interpretation, Rawls claims that a life devoted to political activity is only one form of the good and, moreover, not one that is likely to be chosen by many citizens (*TJ*, 227; *BL*, 88). More often, citizens will consider political liberties to be a means for securing other ends. A self-restriction of political liberties to the right to vote might be compensated for by other goods such as wealth and leisure (what Habermas calls civil and familial privatism). This view, which holds that political participation is only one particular conception of the good life, is, however, complicated by Rawls's model-conception of the person. The two highest-order moral powers are introduced by Rawls not as a particular conception of the good life, but as more general conditions of moral agency. To the extent, then, that the development and exercise of these powers requires participatory activity, such activity cannot simply be viewed as optional. Although I think these features of moral agency can be better clarified with reference to Habermas's model of communicative autonomy, in chapter 4 I argued that this interpretation of Rawls's conception of the person is to be preferred over others. Moreover, without some such distinction between (communicative) autonomy as a general condition for the good and particular conceptions of the good, Rawls's attempt to defend the priority of the right over the good is hampered.[30]

Second, a diminished view of political participation is also evident in Rawls's attempt to draw a distinction between the natural duty of political obedience and political obligation: whereas the latter is incurred in proportion to one's participation in and benefit from political life, the former applies to all citizens and is a natural duty based on the "principle of fairness" and the hypothetical agreement within the OP (*TJ*, par. 51, 52). This natural duty is then used to explain why individuals have an obligation to a just state, even though they may not have actively participated in its political life. Whether Rawls's argument is convincing or not, it clearly seems to imply a two-tiered citizenry—reminiscent of Kant's distinction between passive and active citizens—that greatly minimizes the need and value of participation for some.[31]

Third, Rawls is (correctly) of the opinion that more participation does not necessarily imply more justice. This conviction is related to the so-called "paradox of democracy" (Wolin)—democratic procedures need not yield democratic results—and is aired by Rawls in his discussion of the appropriate limits that can be imposed on the principle of majority rule (*TJ*, par. 54).

Rawls argues that the principle of majority rule is appropriately limited in several ways—separation of powers, bicameral legislation, bill of rights, judicial review, etc.—in accordance with notions of justice. However, this paradox is at least partially mitigated by the fact that majority rule is not by itself a full expression of the democratic procedure. Every restriction on majority rule is not *per se* a restriction on democracy and the use of majority rule as a binding decision-procedure is only legitimate when other conditions are also fulfilled.[32] Thus, the appropriateness of imposing restrictions on the principle of majority rule is not itself an argument for the diminished importance of political participation.

Finally, some of Rawls's reservations about the importance of political participation seem to be based on the more pragmatic consideration that in large-scale mass societies extensive participation is neither feasible nor required (cf. *BL,* 13). One is reminded of Oscar Wilde's remark that the problem with socialism is that it would take up too many evenings during the week. These more pragmatic reservations carry a certain weight and suggest, at least, that means other than direct representation or frequent town meetings must be sought for realizing the ideal of political participation.

These considerations are not all of equal weight, and I should mention again that in other passages (some of which I have already cited) Rawls does emphasize the importance of political participation and states that measures should be taken to insure its fair value. What they do suggest, however, is that there is a need to reconsider the possibilities for democratic practice in large-scale and complex societies and to adjust some of our normative criteria accordingly.[33] The two major contenders in contemporary discussions about democratic theory are pluralist-elite theories (Downs, Dahl, and Schumpeter) and, more recently, neo-corporatism (Schmitter, Cawson). Before turning to Habermas's conception of the public sphere, I would like to indicate briefly why I believe neither of these models of democratic practice would be fully compatible with Rawls's normative ideals.

Definitions of pluralism (or polyarchy) are "essentially contestable," so the following will also be open to objection (perhaps especially concerning its ambiguity between normative and descriptive statement). Nevertheless, I believe it is a definition that even many "pluralists" could accept without major revisions. For pluralists, democracy is primarily a method, a means for securing other ends, rather than an end-in-itself (self-rule or participation). It is a procedure by which voters periodically elect leaders from a relatively small group of political elites who have organized themselves into two or more competitive parties. Citizens are free (have the right) to organize into groups to give effective voice to their interests; if leaders are not responsive, they are also free to form new political parties. Political leaders, on the other hand, are responsible for the formation and implementation of public policy;

their desire for reelection insures that they will be reasonably responsive to the interests of the citizens who elected them. There is, however, no 'common good' or 'general will' which it is the task of the elected leaders to ascertain or represent; what is important is only that the leaders be sufficiently effective in implementing policy so as to maintain the degree of voter loyalty necessary to remain in office.

Criticisms of pluralist theory are by now well known and do not need to be developed here. I will briefly recall five of these for purposes of our own discussion. First, pluralists either naively assume that preferences are formed in relative independence from political parties and the political system (Downs, Dahl), or pessimistically imply that it doesn't matter (Schumpeter). In either case, no effort is made to correct for the extent to which voters' preferences become a function of the party and political system, rather than the result of processes of discursive will-formation.[34] Second, it assumes that mass political parties are suitable vehicles for the representation of voters' interests. This follows from the assumption that voters have a reasonably equal opportunity to express their preferences at some point in the decision-making process. (Dahl is, admittedly, less confident about this.) Third, it assumes that political parties are reasonably competitive among themselves, that they do not engage in collusion, and that there are no significant class or institutional biases built into them. Fourth, it rejects as mere fiction the notion of a common good or generalizable interests; the state is accordingly conceived as a neutral arena in which competing interest groups vie for power. Finally, it assumes that interest group pluralism is a reasonably effective way of achieving responsive public policy. This assumption has been dealt a major blow in recent years by empirical studies on the "ungovernability" of modern democratic regimes.[35]

Partially as a response to this critical analysis of pluralist-elite democratic theory, neocorporatism has received increasing attention in recent years.[36] As a theory of the relationship between the state and society as a whole, corporatism (or neocorporatism) is not particularly new. For example, Hegel's theory of the corporation anticipates it in many ways.[37] What is new, however, is the recognition of the trend toward corporatism (in contrast to pluralism) in advanced capitalist democracies, together with the question of whether it opens up new possibilities for growth and a new age of democratic practice.[38]

Philippe Schmitter, a leading theorist of corporatism, defines it as "a mode of policy formation, in which formally designated interest associations are incorporated within the process of authoritative decision making and implementation."[39] In contrast to pluralism, it represents both a new mode of interest *representation* or "intermediation" (Schmitter) and a new means of policy *implementation*. At the level of interest representation, diverse and competing interest groups are replaced by a limited number of quasi-official functional organizations (e. g., labor and capital). At the level of implementation, authority is partially delegated to these organizations so that the state no longer bears sole responsibility. Functional interests are thus brought into the process of policy formation and implementation; and the state is "relieved" of excessive demands placed upon it by competing interest groups. Cawson summarizes its difference from pluralism well:

> Corporatism is a specific socio-political process in which organizations representing monopolistic functional interests engage in political exchange with state agencies over public policy outputs which involves those organization in a role that combines interest representation and policy implementation through delegated self-enforcement.[40]

In a sense, corporatism may be viewed as an attempt to make a virtue out of the vices of pluralist theory: Associations thus assume a more explicit role in shaping the preferences of their members; to the extent that they are nonvoluntary, members are not free to "exit" (Hirschman) and must conform their interests to those of the organization. As a result, corporatism is more capable of *formulating* public policy. Similarly, whereas in pluralism interest groups do not directly enter into negotiation with the state but attempt to exert influence upon politicians, in corporatism, interest groups take part in policy formation and assume responsibility for its implementation. This frees government from certain tasks and allows politicians to spread the blame if policy fails. In this way, corporatism is considered to be more efficient in *implementing* policy. Finally, corporatism seems to have a more honest assessment of the nature of the state than pluralism: the state is neither a neutral arena for competing interest groups, nor does it merely represent the interest of a ruling class; rather, it is seen as a semi-autonomous institution in that it is able to facilitate negotiations between functional organizations (labor and capital), but yet is not autonomous enough to impose its own independent interests upon factional interest groups.

However, despite the success corporatism may have in responding to various crisis tendencies within the modern welfare state by paving the way for more efficient decision making (and hence, economic growth), a number of questions regarding its relation to democratic theory remain. First, corporations are even more hierarchically structured than pluralist interest groups. Further, they exercise more control over interest formation and provide less opportunity for "exit."[41] Second, as Offe and others have argued, for a number of reasons corporatism does not necessarily do away with class bias: on the one hand, workers' interests are less unified than capitalists; on the other hand, however, labor unions tend to exert greater control over their members than do capitalist "corporations." Moreover, the state also has its own reasons for protecting the interests of capital.[42] Third, and finally, efficiency is no replacement for legitimacy.[43] The fact that corporatist practices make complex societies more "governable" does not mean that those societies are therefore more legitimate. This trend toward a displacement of questions of legitimacy by questions of efficiency is perhaps most evident in discussions concerning the "end of the individual" and "post-individualist theories of democracy," but, more generally, it reflects a shift in democratic theory away from the (normative) "art of association" (de Tocqueville) to the (anormative) "science of organization."[44]

Apart from whatever else might be said in behalf of neocorporatist theory, it clearly provides an impetus for a reexamination of the traditional liberal distinction between the state and "civil society" (Hegel), as well as a reconsideration of the possibilities for democratic practice in complex modern societies.[45] I propose to address both of these topics in connection with Habermas's concept of the public sphere. My aim is to indicate the ways in which his model of the public sphere can contribute to the articulation of a third model of democracy, one, namely, that would be more adequate to Rawls's normative ideals (including the model-conception of the person) than either pluralism or neocorporatism. As I understand it, this model bears a close affinity with some recent attempts to develop a model of "deliberative democracy" or modern form of civic republicanism.[46]

IV. HABERMAS'S CONCEPT OF THE PUBLIC SPHERE

The concept of the public sphere has been either an explicit theme or *leitmotif* in almost all of Habermas's writings, but, I want to suggest, it is only in *The Theory of Communicative Action* (and subsequent political essays) that his normative arguments and social-theoretic categories converge in such a way that the rough contours of a posttraditional public sphere can be discerned.[47] In *The Structural Transformation of the Public Sphere* (1962), Habermas traces the emergence of a bourgeois public sphere which, at least for a time, offered the prospect of an arena that would mediate between state and society by curbing (and legitimating) the forces of the former and providing a forum for the public debate, deliberation, and discursive transformation of "private interests" within the latter.[48] Rooted in the social and economic conditions of liberal capitalism, the "bourgeois public sphere" refers to those sociocultural institutions that arose in the eighteenth century in opposition to the absolutist powers of the state—private clubs and coffeehouses, learned societies and literary associations, publishing houses, journals, and newspapers. Taken as a whole, these institutions constituted a "public realm of reasoning private persons" that was partially secured through the subsequent enactment of various constitutional rights and liberties. In theory and, to a much more limited extent, in practice, this public sphere was distinct both from the private sphere of the market and the family (on which it, of course, relied) and from the political authority of the state.[49] It designated a sphere that comes about whenever private persons reason collectively about their common interests and its function was both to restrain and legitimate the political power exercised by the administrative state. It is this idea of the bourgeois public sphere that Kant, in "What is Enlightenment?" thematized in his somewhat idiosyncratic contrast between the public and private use of reason.[50]

Habermas's thesis, however, is that this idea of the public sphere had a very limited life span, ideologically as well as historically. At the level of theory, Hegel already expressed deep ambivalence toward public opinion and introduced a system of corporate representation into his legislative assembly. His interpretation of civil society as a "system of [conflicting] needs" was also taken over by Marx in the latter's own identification of civil society with commercial society, the realm of necessity, and the pursuit of individual self-interest. In liberal theory, too, the idea of the public sphere is often exhausted with the formal guarantee of a limited set of "natural" civil and political rights.

As an historical phenomenon, the bourgeois public sphere suffered an equally unfortunate fate. Rather than providing a basis for the expansion of political and civil liberties to include all members of the demos and the elimination of those social inequalities that restrict the scope of the public sphere, its normative claims retreated further and further from empirical reality. In connection with what he refers to as the "refeudalization" of civil society that occured during the latter part of the nineteenth century, Habermas traces the commercialization of civil society, the bureaucratization of political and non-political authority, and the growth of a manipulative or propagandistic mass media. A "repoliticized social sphere" erodes the real distinction between state and society that is a necessary social condition for the bourgeois public sphere; a society oriented to consumption and a politics based on the competition and bargaining between interest groups emerges in the place of a public sphere formed by an enlightened citizenry. Although Habermas never abandons the normative claims expressed in the bourgeois ideal, the conclusion of *The Structural Transformation of the Public Sphere* is extremely cautious about the possibility for a renewed public sphere under the altered conditions of late capitalist society.[51] Habermas is also quite ambivalent about what more specific institutional forms a renewed public sphere might take and, in particular, the role that the social welfare state might play.[52]

In *Legitimation Crisis* (1973), Habermas addresses the problem of the public sphere at both the normative and social-theoretic level. He introduces social-theoretic categories with which he is able to analyze possible crisis tendencies under the radically altered conditions of advanced capitalist societies. He considers, for example, how crises of capital accumulation might be compensated for by the policies of an interventionist state, but only at the cost of opening the way for other potential crises at the level of administrative rationality, motivation, and/or legitimacy (see *LC,* part 2). At the same time, Habermas also introduces the beginnings of what will later develop into the theory of discourse ethics (*LC,* 102ff.). In *Legitimation Crisis,* however, the normative ideal is still, so to speak, suspended above the social theoretic analyses of institutions.[53] That is, Habermas is as yet unable to show how institutions that would contribute to a form of deliberative democracy—in contrast, say, to a more technocratic political order—might arise from the sort of crisis tendencies he analyzes.

In *The Theory of Communicative Action* (1981), Habermas finally brings his normative and social-theoretic categories together in such a way that the rough contours of a posttraditional public sphere can be discerned and its importance for normative social criticism clarified. This is achieved primarily through the introduction of (1) an analysis of social rationalization from the dual perspective of society as system and lifeworld, and (2) a clarification of the way in which the normative principle of discourse ethics, via the model of communicative action, is reflected (to varying degrees) in institutions of the lifeworld. Since I am primarily interested in the contribution these aspects of Habermas's social theory make to normative social criticism, my treatment will be limited and tailored to this concern.[54]

(1) The system/lifeworld distinction is introduced by Habermas both as a distinction between two analytic perspectives that the social theorist can adopt and as a real distinction between two different institutional orders in modern societies: institutions that are largely integrated through consensually accepted norms (society as lifeworld) and institutions that are largely defined by their capacity to respond to the functional requirements imposed by the environment (society as system).[55] Despite the criticisms it has received, Habermas has insisted that this distinction is crucial for his analysis of the crisis tendencies that can be found in modern societies: in short, social pathologies arise whenever the attempt to meet the requirements of system maintenance spill over into domains of the lifeworld properly integrated on the basis of normatively secured or consensual interactions. Habermas refers to this process as the "colonization" of the lifeworld (*TCA* 2:355).

The distinction between system and lifeworld is also important in that it enables Habermas to identify two different sides to the process of social rationalization: On the one hand, rationalization is conceived as the differentiation of subsystems from the sociocultural lifeworld (and from each other) and an increase in system complexity—this is the aspect of social rationalization predominant in the work of classical sociologists such as Weber, Durkheim, and Parsons. On the other hand, Habermas also speaks of the potential for increased (communicative) rationalization within a lifeworld that has to a large degree been relieved of tasks taken over by the subsystems. What is central to this second aspect of social rationalization is not the expansion of formal or instrumental reason to further dimensions of social life, but an opening up of processes of symbolic reproduction to consensual agreement among autonomous individuals in light of criticizable validity claims.

Habermas describes this second aspect of social rationalization, or "the rationalization of the lifeworld," in connection with three related processes: (a) the structural differentiation of its basic components (culture, society, and personality); (b) the separation of form and content; and (c) the increasing reflexivity of symbolic reproduction (*TCA* 2:145–46).

(a) The structural differentiation between culture *and* society consists in "the gradual uncoupling of the institutional system from worldviews"; between society *and* personality, in "the extension of the scope of contingency for establishing interpersonal relationships"; and between culture *and* personality, in "the fact that the renewal of traditions depends more and more on individuals' readiness to criticize and their ability to innovate" (*TCA* 2:146). In the wake of such societal differentiation, the various structural components of the lifeworld become less concretely homogeneous and "interpenetrate" (Parsons) one another in more general and abstract ways.[56]

(b) Second, a separation of form and content accompanies this differentiation of the structural components of the lifeworld:

> *On the cultural level,* the core, identity-securing traditions separate off from the concrete contents with which they are still tightly interwoven in mythical worldviews. They shrink to formal elements such as world-concepts, communication presuppositions, argumentation procedures, abstract values, and the like. *At the level of society,* general principles and procedures crystalize out of the particular contexts to which they are tied in primitive societies. In modern societies, principles of legal order and morality are established which are less and less tailored to concrete forms of life. *On the level of the personality system,* the cognitive structures acquired in the socialization process are increasingly detached from the content of cultural knowledge with which they were at first integrated in "concrete thinking." (*TCA* 2:146)

In short, the symbolic reproduction of society, which is achieved through the interpretive activity of its members, draws increasingly upon abstract cultural norms and values, formal principles and institutionalized procedures of social order, and decentered forms of intellectual, social, and moral cognition. It also becomes possible to criticize and revise these interpretive accomplishments in light of norms, principles, and individual competencies that have become embodied in the differentiated institutional complexes.

(c) Finally, the processes of symbolic reproduction—cultural transmission, social integration, and socialization—which are associated with each of the structural components of the lifeworld become increasingly reflective and are also, in various ways, given over to treatment by professionals. This occurs not only, as Weber observed, in connection with the transmission of culture (in the differentiated spheres of science and technology, law and morality, and art and art criticism), but also in connection with the creation of social and political solidarities (through democratic forums of will-formation) and the socialization of the young (with the development of formal systems of education and pedagogical sciences) (*TCA* 2:147).[57]

Habermas's claim is that to date (and to a large extent as a result of the capitalist economy), the process of social rationalization has so far been extremely one-sided, taking place largely in response to the imperatives of instrumental (or functional) reason (*TCA* 1:342–3). However, analyses that emphasize only this side of modernization (e.g., Weber's "iron cage," Adorno and Horkheimer's "totally administered society," or Foucault's "panopticism") overlook the real potential for the development of new forms of social learning and communicative rationality opened up *within* the lifeworld.

> The rationalization of the lifeworld makes possible, on the one hand, the differentiation of autonomous subsystems and opens up, at the same time, the utopian horizon of a civil society in which the formally organized spheres of action of the bourgeois (economy and state apparatus) constitute the foundations for the posttraditional lifeworld of *l'homme* (private sphere) and *citoyen* (public sphere). (*TCA* 2:328)

It is in connection with this second aspect of social rationalization, or "the rationalization of the lifeworld," that Habermas speaks of the still largely untapped ("utopian") potential of a reconstituted civil society. It is here too that the the rough contours of a posttraditional public sphere are to be found.

(2) In Habermas's vision of a posttraditional civil society, the ambiguities latent in the liberal public/private distinction are removed with the introduction of a tripartite model that distinguishes between the two subsystems of the economy and the administrative state, on the one hand, and the (informal) institutions of the lifeworld (or "civil society"), on the other (see Figure 5-1).[58] Civil society is no longer so closely identified with the economic subsystem that any regulation of the latter is automatically deemed a violation of private or subjective rights; nor is the public sphere equated with the administrative state or formal political system. Rather, *within* a more or less ratio-

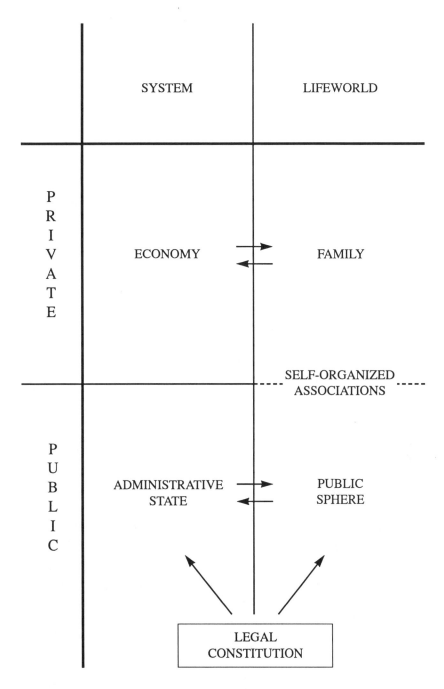

Figure 5-1
Habermas's Concept of the Public Sphere

nalized lifeworld the institutional bases for a public sphere that is opposed to both the political and economic subsystems can be identified. As I understand it, the indications for a more "deliberative" democracy are primarily to be found within this "reconstructed" concept of civil society.

At the center of this concept of civil socity is the notion of a broadly conceived and pluralist public sphere in which citizens define the terms and conditions of their common life and in which debate and argument about collective norms, social policies, and political decisions takes place. What is unique about this understanding of the public sphere is the view that the formation of public opinion should take place within informal institutions or "secondary associations" that are sufficiently shielded from the colonizing effects of the capitalist economy and administrative state. A major weakness of both pluralist theories and neocorporatism was their failure to address adequately the question of how public opinion and voter preferences can be shaped by these sub-systems. In a deliberative model, by contrast, this question is thematic: The formation of public opinion should take place, in Habermas's phrase, "below the threshold" of the mass political party apparatus and formal political system.[59] Measures need to be implemented to insure that public opinion is not simply a commodity manufactured by advertising agencies for the capitalist economy, nor something that can be readily manipulated by campaign managers whose primary allegiance is to the party elite.

Public opinion (or, more generally, "solidarity") is thus conceived as a third resource that, in contrast to money and (administrative) power, is the product of autonomous, informal ("secondary") associations within the lifeworld.[60] Such associations provide forums for discussion and debate and for the formation (and transformation) of the preferences and interests of the individual members of a society. Understood in terms of this model, the challenge for a more radical democratic practice is to find ways in which the growth of this third resource or "solidarity" can be encouraged and then employed to curb or control the resources of money and power that are the primary media of the market and administrative state.

Two questions immediately arise in connection with this understanding of the public sphere and democratic practice. First, what measures can or should be taken to insure that such self-organized and autonomous associations are themselves democratically organized or at least congruent with other democratic values? And second, how can these associations within civil society exercise any control over the formal institutions of the market and administrative state without either being absorbed by them or producing the "mischiefs of faction" (Madison) within them? By way of a conclusion, I would like to draw attention to three more specific suggestions contained in Habermas's writings that at least begin to answer these difficult questions.

(a) In several recent essays, Habermas has spoken of the need for social movements and autonomous associations within civil society to exercise a delicate combination of "power and intelligent self-restraint" with respect both to the state and the market.[61] In contrast to the model of corporatism presented above, the idea is not so much to accord certain key functional groups (e.g., labor and business) privileged access to the decision-making processes of government, but to find ways to encourage the growth of a wide range of civil and political forums, provide them with access to relevant forms and sources of information, and develop mechanisms such that the deliberative conclusions reached in them have an effect in setting the agenda and in shaping the policies and proposals considered within the more traditional forum of parliamentary representation. These associations of the public sphere should not attempt, however, to take over all the tasks that are performed by the formal political system since that would threaten their identity as informal associations. Rather, they should attempt to exercise only an *indirect* influence upon the political system through the supply of loyalties and legitimations or reasons (*Gründe*).[62]

(b) Habermas does not argue that the formal political system, together with its mass political parties, should simply be *replaced* by a more highly decentralized form of democratic rule based solely on such secondary institutions. What he insists upon, rather, is that the former relinquish one of their functions—the generation of mass loyalty.[63] In complex modern societies, proposals for more highly decentralized and pluralistic decision making processes encounter two specific sorts of difficulties: On the one hand, they threaten to undermine concern for the common good on a broad territorial scale or the preservation of basic rights and liberties. These are the "mischiefs of faction" described by Madison in the *Federalist Papers*. On the other hand, they would also most likely weaken the possibility for accountable decision making with respect to any large-scale problems that arise within modern societies.[64] Thus, rather than calling for the dismantling of the formal political system, Habermas has instead spoken of the need for secondary associations of the public sphere to surround and "besiege" it, without however conquering it.[65] Although this metaphor is not particularly instructive for identifying the specific modes of exchange that should exist between institutions of the public sphere and the state, the basic intuition is relatively clear: The informal associations within civil society responsible for the production of solidarity should exercise an indirect influence upon the formal political system through the production of loyalties and legitimations; at the same time, however, the political system, including its territorially based form of representation, should provide appropriate mechanisms for accountable decision making and guarantee adequate concern for the common good of the republic as a whole.

(c) Similarly, along with the legislative body, the judiciary or "forum of principle" (Dworkin) also plays an important role in this conception of the public sphere. One of its main tasks should be to facilitate the growth of autonomous associations by insuring that such associations relate to each other and to the various governmental bodies in ways that conform to the constitutional provisions of fairness and equality. At the same time, in attempting to secure constitutionally recognized rights or the fair administration of the law and governmental policies, the courts must guard against an excessive materialization of the law and thereby an erosion of their own source of legitimation within the framework of a larger democratic process. With respect to the process of legal regulation discussed briefly above, what is crucial is that such legal rights be interpreted and applied so as to secure communicatively structured domains of action against incursions from the market or administrative state (*TCA* 2:371). It is reasonable to assume, however, that the law can fulfill this function only to the extent that it is not construed solely as a semi-autonomous branch of the political system, but itself remains pervious to the kinds of practical discourses that it is designed to protect.[66]

The model of a public sphere envisioned by Habermas is thus by no means limited to proposals for reforming the traditional institutions of parliamentary debate. Rather, as I understand it, the public sphere must be broadly conceived as a vast array of institutions in which a wide variety of practical discourses overlap. It ranges from the more or less informal movements and associations in civil society where solidarities are formed, through the various institutions of the public mass media, to the more formal institutions of parliamentary debate and legal argumentation. Although the idea of a practical discourse in which the entire citizenry participate as free and equal persons is not directly realized within any one of these forums, the entire network of institutions should be designed in such a way that this idea is appropriately mirrored in them. It is in this sense, too, that Habermas has spoken of a "proceduralization" of the Rousseauean conception of popular sovereignty in which the notion of a localized sovereign body is replaced with that of an anonymous network of communication processes comprised of autonomous associations, independent mass media, and other institutions of the public sphere.[67] On this model the "moment" of deliberation, so to speak, does not reside primarily with the judiciary (Sunstein) nor with the body of elected representatives (Madison), but is dispersed throughout a vast communicative network.[68]

In light of this summary of Habermas's conception of the public sphere, it also becomes clear why reflection upon the normative grounds of social criticism invariably leads to reflection upon "the conditions and presuppositions of the activity of justification itself:"[69] Since the normative ground of criticism I have attempted to defend in this work is that of the reasonable agreement of free and equal persons, it is necessary to address the question of the general institutional arrangements under which such consent could come about. As Rawls would acknowledge, the hypothetical agreement of parties in the original position is only binding if we recognize a conception of ourselves as free and equal citizens in that choice situation.[70] The task of social criticism and justification is thus a public task in a strong sense. It requires a robust and multifaceted model of the public sphere in which individuals can deliberate about the collective terms and conditions of their common lives. This model of the public sphere is, of course, itself a normative conception defined with reference to a conception of public practical reason or the idea of a reasonable agreement among free and equal citizens. I see no alternative, however, to the paradoxes to which this conception of normative grounds gives rise: Anything else would either be less than democratic, or would not be a justification.

NOTES

NOTES TO INTRODUCTION

1. See, for example, Don Herzog, *Without Foundations: Justification in Political Theory* (Ithaca: Cornell University Press, 1985); Michael Walzer, *Interpretation and Social Criticism* (Cambridge: Harvard University Press, 1987); and Richard Rorty, "The Priority of Democracy to Philosophy," in *The Virginia Statute of Religious Freedom,* ed. M. Peterson and R. Vaughan (New York: Cambridge University Press, 1988), 257–82.

2. Rorty, *Philosophy and the Mirror of Nature* (Princeton: Princeton University Press, 1979), 390; see also Rorty, *Contingency, Irony and Solidarity* (New York: Cambridge University Press, 1989); Jean-Francois Lyotard, *The Postmodern Condition* (Minneapolis: University of Minnesota Press, 1984); and Rorty, "Habermas and Lyotard on Postmodernity" in *Habermas and Modernity,* ed. Richard Bernstein (Cambridge: MIT Press, 1985).

3. This notion of Kantian constructivism is taken, of course, from John Rawls, *KC;* for further discussion, see Samuel Freeman, "Reason and Agreement in Social Contract Views," *Philosophy and Public Affairs* 19 (1990): 151ff., and Onora O'Neill, *Constructions of Reason* (New York: Cambridge University Press, 1989), especially p. 206ff.

4. This is perhaps the most frequently cited attribute of "foundationalism;" see, for example, Herzog, 20: "One way to characterize [foundationalism's] salient feature is this: any political justification worthy of the name must be grounded on principles that are (1) undeniable and immune to revision and (2) located outside society and politics."

5. For a discussion of some of the weaknesses in this sort of foundationalism, of which Hobbes is a classical example, see Arthur Ripstein, "Foundationalism in Political Theory," *Philosophy and Public Affairs* 16 (1987): 115–37.

6. See *KC,* 554ff.; for a good discussion of the normative conception of reason in Kant and Habermas, see Albrecht Wellmer, "Intersubjectivity and Reason," in *Perspectives on Human Conduct,* ed. L. Hertzberg and J. Pietarinen (New York: E. J. Brill, 1988), 128–163.

7. This is also how I would interpret Habermas's remark that modernity must create its own normativity out of itself. See *The Philosophical Discourse of Modernity*, trans. F. Lawrence (Cambridge: MIT Press, 1987), 7.

8. Walzer, 64.

9 . For this interpretation of the role of the original position in Rawls's theory, see chapter 2.

10. Walzer, 30 n. 21.

11. With only minor reservations, I am even prepared to accept Bernard Williams's characterization of the Kantian project (which he of course criticizes): "What we are looking for, then, is an argument that will travel far enough into Kant's territory to bring back the essential conclusion that a rational agent's most basic interests must coincide with those given in a conception of himself as a citizen legislator of a notional republic; but does not bring back the more extravagant metaphysical luggage of the noumenal self," *Ethics and the Limits of Philosophy* (Cambridge: Harvard University Press, 1985), 65.

12. For a careful attempt to defend Kant against such a reading see Barbara Herman, "On the Value of Acting From the Motive of Duty," *The Philosophical Review* 90 (1981): 359–82; see also the interpretation of Kant's categorical imperative developed by Onora (Nell) O'Neill (discussed in chapter 1).

13. Compare Kant, "Perpetual Peace," *KPW*, 126, and "Theory and Practice," *KPW*, 79.

14. See especially *KC*, 537f.; TJ, 175–82; "The Idea of an Overlapping Consensus," *Oxford Journal of Legal Studies* 7 (1987): 1–25.

15. For a careful and convincing discussion of the idea of agreement in Rawls, see Samuel Freeman, "Reason and Agreement in Social Contract Views," *Philosophy and Public Affairs* 19 (1990): 122–57.

16. See, most recently, "The Priority of Right and Ideas of the Good," *Philosophy and Public Affairs* 17 (1988): 251–76.

17. For such a relativist interpretation of Rawls's method of reflective equilibrium, see Richard Rorty, "The Priority of Democracy to Philosophy." Whether or not he is finally successful, it is clear that Rawls wishes to avoid such an interpretation, see especially, "The Domain of the Political and Overlapping Consensus," *New York University Law Review* 64 (1989), 251.

18. Jeremy Waldron, in a provocative essay, has also suggested that a distinguishing feature of liberalism lies in a certain view about the justification of social arrangements: "Liberals demand that the social order should in principle be capable of explaining itself at the tribunal of each person's understanding," "Theoretical Foundations of Liberalism," *The Philosophical Quarterly* 37 (1987): 149.

NOTES TO CHAPTER ONE

1. For Kant's remarks on the need for practical philosophy to be "at one with itself," see his essay "Perpetual Peace" (*KPW*, 121–2); see also R. Dreier, "Die Einheit der praktischen Philosophie Kants," in *Recht-Moral-Ideologie* (Frankfurt: Suhrkamp, 1981), 286–315. Kant, of course, also spoke of a larger unity of practical and theoretical reason in which practical reason has primacy (*GMS*, 391; *KpV*, 125–6; *Critique of Pure Reason*, B167n.).

2. "Perpetual Peace," *KPW*, 125.

3. Ibid., 99n.

4. P. Riley, *Will and Political Legitimacy* (Cambridge: Harvard University Press, 1982), 129.

5. His teleological assumptions concerning natural history, at a minimum, seem to buttress his confidence in "reform from above" in contrast to revolution, as well as his relative complacency concerning the status of "passive" citizens.

6. See also Dick Howard, "Kant's Political Theory: The Virtue of His Vices," *Review of Metaphysics* 34 (1980): 325–50.

7. These two phrases are not obviously equivalent. Briefly stated, I equate them because the notion of pure practical reason implies that the will is determined by reason rather than desire; that is, its maxims conform to the categorical imperative. Agents whose maxims conform to the categorical imperative are autonomous or free. To regard individuals as equally capable of such action is to regard them as free and equal moral beings.

8. See C. B. MacPherson, *The Political Theory of Possessive Individualism* (New York: Oxford, 1964); for an application of this concept to Kant's theory of property rights (hence one with which I disagree), see R. Saage, "Besitzindividualistische Perspektiven der politischen Theorie Kants," *Neue Politische Literatur* 17 (1972): 168–93.

9. For a discussion of the difference between classical and modern natural law, see. L. Strauss, *Natural Right and History* (Chicago: University of Chicago Press, 1953); for a careful discussion of Kant's attempt to derive basic normative constraints from the structure of practical reason, see T. Hill, "Kant's Argument for the Rationality of Moral Conduct," *Pacific Philosophical Quarterly* 66 (1985): 3–23, and "Kant's Theory of Practical Reason," *The Monist* 72 (1989): 363–83.

10. H. Williams, *Kant's Political Philosophy* (New York: St. Martin's Press, 1983), 93, and P. Riley, *Will and Political Legitimacy,* 132, 148f. where he contrasts the idea of agreement (in the social contract) to Kant's natural right theory.

11. See Saner, *Kant's Political Thought* (Chicago: University of Chicago Press, 1973); and H. Arendt, who approvingly quotes Schopenhauer: "It is as if it

were not the work of this great man, but the product of an ordinary common man [*gewöhnlicher Erdensohn*]," in *Lectures on Kant's Political Philosophy* (Chicago: University of Chicago Press, 1982), 8. For Schopenhauer's remarks on Kant's senility, see the citation in Kersting, "Freiheit und intelligibler Besitz," *Allgemeine Zeitschrift für Philosophie* 6 (1982), 49.

12. One of the more notable ones, which I will only mention here, is Kant's rather forced attempt to create a novel category of "real personal rights" by combining two distinct kinds of rights in Roman law: the "real" rights to own or possess things, and "personal" rights which arise from contracts between individuals. As a "real personal right" marriage is not simply a mutual contractual relationship, but the right of the husband to have his wife under his control and physically brought back to him if she should run away.

13. See also *Religion*, 23; Kant's "moral personality" thus parallels Rawls's model-conception of the person characterized by two highest-order moral powers (the capacity to form a conception of the good and the capacity to have a sense of justice); see *KC*, 525.

14. See also *Religion*, 21n.

15. The term 'claim-right' stems from Wesley Hohfeld, *Fundamental Legal Conceptions* (New Haven: Yale University Press, 1923), 38; for a discussion of the concept see Henry Shue, *Basic Rights* (Princeton: Princeton University Press, 1980), 14f.; and Alan Gewirth, *Human Rights* (Chicago: University of Chicago Press, 1982), 2: "A claim-right of one person entails a correlative duty of some other person or persons to act or to refrain from acting in ways required for the first person's having that to which he has a right."

16. Dieter Henrich argues that Kant has in mind his own attempt at a deduction in the *GMS*; see "Der Begriff der sittlichen Einsicht," in *Die Gegenwart der Griechen im neueren Denken*, ed. D. Henrich, et al. (Tübingen, 1960), 77–115.

17. Ameriks argues that the doctrine of the Fact of Reason was an effort on Kant's part to make a virtue of necessity in light of his failure to provide a theoretical proof of freedom, and that at the end of his career Kant expressed regret that his moral philosophy remained "dogmatic." Cf. "Kant's Deduction of Freedom and Morality," 67, 72. For a more reconciliationist account of the relation between the *GMS* and the *KpV*, see D. Henrich, "Die Deduktion des Sittengesetzes," in *Denken im Schatten des Nihilismus*, ed. A. Schwan (Darmstadt: Wissenschaftliche Buchgesellschaft, 1975), 55–112, and "Der Begriff der sittlichen Einsicht." In the *Metaphysics of Morals* and "Theory and Practice," *KPW*, 69n., Kant rejects the idea of a "theoretical proof" without, however, voicing any regret.

18. For the references to the "Fact of Reason" in *KpV*, see 6, 31, 42, 43, 47, 91 and 105; in later works, there are two clear references in *KU* (468, 474) and in the *MdS* (252, 400).

19. Riley, *Kant's Political Philosophy*, 8; see also Ameriks, 72.

20. Cf. *KpV*, 70–71, for Kant's attempt to steer between "empiricism" and "mysticism" (or a dogmatic rationalism) in his moral philosophy. See also Rawls, "Themes in Kant's Moral Philosophy," in *Kant's Transcendental Deductions*, ed. Eckart Forster (Stanford: Stanford University Press, 1985), 97.

21. See Kant's remarks in "Perpetual Peace," in *KPW*, 99n.

22. Cf. Henrich, "Ethik der Autonomie," in *Selbstverhältnisse* (Stuttgart: Reclam, 1982), 22, and "Das Prinzip der kantischen Ethik," *Philosophische Rundschau* 2 (1945/5): 26f.

23. A proper answer to this question would demand a detailed study of the third section of the *GMS*, something which cannot be provided here; for an argument that Kant never offered, nor intended to offer, such a strong theoretical proof in the *GMS*, see D. Henrich, "Die Deduktion des Sittengesetzes"; for the contrasting view that Kant provides a stronger theoretical deduction even in the second *Critique*, see Beck, 109f., and T. Hill, "Kant's Argument for the Rationality of Moral Conduct," *Pacific Philosophical Quarterly* 66 (1985): 3–23.

24. *Critique of Pure Reason*, A807/B835; for a careful discussion of the problems of Kant's notion of a Fact of Reason in relation to the historical evolution of moral consciousness, see P. Stern, "The Problem of History and Temporality in Kantian Ethics," *Review of Metaphysics* 39 (1986): 505–545.

25. For a discussion of the use of juridical metaphors in Kant, see Henrich, "Die Deduktion der Sittengesetzes," 79.

26. See *Religion*, 21n.; see also T. Hill, "Kant's Theory of Practical Reason," *The Monist* 72 (1989).

27. See D. Henrich, "Die Deduktion des Sittengesetzes," 81, and Kant, *Prolegommena to Any Future Metaphysic*, par. 4 for the distinction between the strong and weak sense of a deduction; see also H. Allison, "Morality and Freedom: Kant's Reciprocity Thesis," *The Philosophical Review* 95 (1986): 393–425.

28. See, for example Aune, *Kant's Theory of Morals* (Princeton: Princeton University Press, 1979), 131, 137–8; Gregor, *Laws of Freedom* (Oxford: Blackwell, 1963), 41; and Nell, *Acting on Principle*, 44; Nell's further comment on 67 acknowledges that what is going on in the *Rechtslehre* is much more complicated, but it is still misleading.

29. For determining duties of virtue, Kant offers the following principle: "Act according to a maxim whose ends are such that there can be a universal law that everyone have these ends" (*MdS*, 395).

30. See Kant's review of Hufeland as cited in Kersting, *Wohlgeordnete Freiheit*, and the discussion in Kersting, 29–35.

31. For example, cf. *Reflexion* 6988, cited in Kersting, *Wohlgeordnete Freiheit*, 32, and other *Reflexionen* contained in R. Bittner, ed., *Materialen zu Kants 'Kritik der Praktischen Vernunft'* (Frankfurt: Suhrkamp, 1975), 95–6.

32. The UPJ is sometimes also referred to as "the law of external freedom" or "the principle of justice."

33. Kant himself draws a distinction between a "narrower" and "wider sense" of right or justice (*MdS*, 234); the authorization to use coercion is connected only with the narrower sense of justice. Thus, it seems Kant recognizes certain duties of justice (the right of equity, for example) where the authorization to use force does not obtain.

34. Aune, 134, also expresses frustration in interpretating the UPJ and, on 136, refers to it as a "somewhat garbled statement." A difficulty is already evident, for example, in the conditions listed above since whether an external action violates the freedom of others can only be decided by applying the CI-procedure to the *maxim* of that action.

35. Kersting, *Wohlgeordnete Freiheit*, 9.

36. Cf. Kersting, 37–42 for other representatives and a critique of the independence thesis; for a similar critique of Yovel, see Riley, 81.

37. Yovel, 189 (italics in original).

38. For a recent critique of Yovel's interpretation along the same lines, see H. van der Linden, *Kantian Ethics and Socialism* (Cambridge: Hackett, 1988), 145ff.

39. *KPW*, 125.

40. The question of a "critical turn" in Kant's theory of history is more problematic than Yovel suggests. Many texts which make the "uncritical" assertion are very late (see *KU*, par. 83; *Religion*, 86, 88; "Perpetual Peace," *KPW*, 121n.; "Conflict of the Faculties"; and *Anthropology from a Pragmatic Point of View* (trans. Gregor), 181; see also Arendt, 18, and Fackenheim, "Kant's Theory of History" *Kant-Studien* 48 (1956/57): 381–98.

41. Gregor, *Laws of Freedom*, 31.

42. (Totowa, N.J.: Rowman and Littlefield, 1983).

43. Riley, 16, 56–7, 67–8; for a criticism of this reading of objective ends, and a constructivist interpretation, see John Atwell, "Objective Ends in Kant's Ethics," *Archiv für Geschichte der Philosophie* 56 (1974): 156–171.

44. Riley, 4; see also 14, 98, 135.

45. (New York: Columbia University Press, 1975), pagination in the text refers to this book.

46. Ibid., 12; for a similar formulation of the problem in Kant but a rejection of Kant's solution, see Kenneth Milkman, "Hare, Universalizability and the Problem of Relevant Description," *Canadian Journal of Philosophy* 12 (1982): 19–32, and Hare, "Relevant Description" in *Morals and Values*, ed. Goldman and Kim.

47. Cf. R. Bittner, "Maximen," *Akten des 4.Internationalen Kant Kongresses,* ed. V. Funke (Berlin, 1974), 489.

48. On the need for judgment, see *GMS,* 407; *MdS,* 446; *Reflexion* 1164 in Bittner, *Materialen,* 119; and *Anthropology from a Pragmatic Viewpoint* (trans. Gregor), 71.

49. This is not a trivial assumption, but one that Kant seems nevertheless to make, cf. Nell, 63, and for a discussion of some of the problems (e.g., agent ignorance, bias, and self-deception), see 112–117.

50. Paton, *The Categorical Imperative,* 162, and Beck, *A Commentary on Kant's Critique of Practical Reason* (Chicago: University of Chicago Press, 1960), 160–62; Paton's claim that Kant passes easily from a notion of the formal law of nature to teleological laws of human nature does not seem to be supported by this passage nor by other remarks Kant makes about the typic (see especially *Kant: Philosophical Correspondence, 1759–99,* trans. and ed. A. Zweig [Chicago, 1967], 194).

51. Cf. Paton's remarks, 160.

52. In response to a letter from J. S. Beck requesting a clarification of the notion of a *typus,* Kant writes: "As for the question, Can't there be actions that are incompatible with the existence of a natural order and that yet are prescribed by the moral law? I answer, Certainly! If you mean, a *definite order of nature,* for example, that of the present world. A courtier, for instance, must recognize it as a duty always to be truthful, though he would not remain a courtier for long if he were. But there is in that *typus* only the form of a *natural order in general,* that is, the compatibility of actions as events in accord with *moral laws,* and as [events] in accord with *natural laws,* too, but merely in terms of *their generality,* for this in no way concerns the special laws of any particular nature" (*Kant: Philosophical Correspondence,* 194).

53. Nell discusses some of these problems, such as the possibility of self-deception (see p. 122f.); others have been raised in interpretations otherwise congenial to her own. Rawls, for example, argues that Kant's application of the CI-procedure in the example of benevolent acts only "goes through" if we assume a notion of minimal basic human needs and impose other epistemic constraints upon the deliberating agents, see "Themes in Kant's Moral Philosophy," 85–6.

54. Nell, 61; see also her article, "Consistency in Action," in *Morality and Universality,* ed. N. Potter and M. Timmons (Boston: Reidel, 1985), 174–81.

55. Kant, even in *MdS,* does not strictly equate the perfect/imperfect distinction with the distinction between duties of justice and duties of virtue, since he considers some duties of virtue (e.g. suicide and lying) to be perfect; see W. Kersting, "Der kategorische Imperativ" for criticism. On the history of these terms, see his *Wohlgeordnete Freiheit,* 83 n. 178; and for a discussion of the distinction between perfect and imperfect duties, cf. Gregor, *Laws of Freedom,* chap. 7, especially p. 96.

56. For this objection, see J. W. Gough, *The Social Contract* (Oxford, 1936), 173.

57. G. Lehmann, "Kants Besitzlehre," in *Beiträge zur Geschichte und Interpretation der Philosophie Kants* (Berlin: de Gruyter, 1969), 210; K. Lisser, *Der Begriff des Rechts bei Kant, Kantstudien* (Ergänzungsheft 58), 39; and R. Saage, "Besitzindividualistische Perspektiven der politischen Theorie Kants," *Neue Politische Literatur* 17 (1972): 168–93. For the most helpful discussions of Kant's theory of property rights in English, see Herbert Marcuse, "A Study on Authority," in *Studies in Critical Philosophy* (Boston: Beacon Press, 1972), 79–95; Howard Williams, *Kant's Political Philosophy* (New York: St. Martins' Press, 1983), chap. 4; and Mary Gregor, "Kant's Theory of Property," *The Review of Metaphysics* 41 (1988): 757–87.

58. In referring to the natural law tradition, I primarily mean the work of Hugo Grotius (1583–1645) and Samuel Pufendorf (1632–94). For a discussion of their views, see R. Tuck, *Natural Right Theories* (New York: Cambridge University Press, 1979) and James Tully, *A Discourse on Property: John Locke and his Adversaries* (New York: Cambridge University Press, 1980), chap. 4.

59. See *MdS*, 230–31.

60. J. Locke, *Second Treatise*, chap. 5, par. 28.

61. W. Kersting, "Kant und der staatsphilosophische Kontraktualismus," *Allgemeine Zeitschrift für Philosophie* 8 (1983): 12.

62. "The body is mine since it is a part of my self (*Ich*) and is moved by my will. The whole animate and inanimate world that does not have its own will is mine insofar as I can master it and influence it through my will.... Whatever is supposed to be a good will must not invalidate itself if it is to be universal and actual; for that reason someone else should not call his what I have made, for otherwise he would presuppose that his will moves my body," cited in *Eigentumstheorien von Grotius bis Kant*, ed. R. Brandt (Stuttgart: Cannstatt, 1974), 177 (my translation).

63. Kant develops this antinomy in much greater detail—and in a slightly altered fashion—in the "Vorarbeiten to the *Metaphysik der Sitten*" (*GS* 23); for a discussion of the antinomy in its various formulations, see Lehmann, ibid., 200f., and W. Kersting, *Wohlgeordnete Freiheit*, 119–27.

64. M. Gregor, *Laws of Freedom*, 58.

65. See the brief comment by Reiss in *KPW*, 195 n. 3, and Klaus Hammacher, "Über Erlaubnisgesetze und die Idee socialer Gerechtigkeit im Anschluss an Kant, Fichte, Jacobi und einige Zeitgenossen," in *Erneuerung der Transzendentalphilosophie im Anschluss an Kant und Fichte*, ed. K. Hammacher (Stuttgart, 1979), 121–41.

66. *KPW*, 97f.

67. *KPW*, 98n.

68. R. Brandt, "Das Erlaubnisgesetz, oder: Vernunft und Geschichte in Kants Rechtslehre," in *Rechtsphilosophie der Aufklärung*, ed. R. Brandt (Berlin: de Gruyter, 1982), 233–85.

69. See *MdS*, 323, and "Perpetual Peace," *KPW*, 118.

70. *KPW*, 118n.

71. See, for example, R. Saage, "Besitzindividualistische Perspektiven der politischen Theories Kants," *Neue Politische Literatur* 17 (1972): 168–93.

72. See also the passage from Kant's working notes in *GS*, 23, 219, cited by Kersting, *Wohlgeordnete Freiheit*, 146.

73. *MdS*, 250, 262; for a discussion of the proper location of this passage in the *MdS*, see B. Ludwig, "Der Platz des rechtlichen Postulats der praktischen Vernunft innerhalb der Paragraphen 1–6 der kantischen Rechtslehren," in *Rechtsphilosophie der Aufklärung*, 218–32.

74. This passage is from Feyerabend's notes of Kant's lectures on natural law in 1784–85, now contained in Kant's *Gesammelte Schriften* 27:1342, cited in Kersting, *Wohlgeordnete Freiheit*, 166.

75. For a brief discussion of the notion of *facultas moralis*, see K. Olivecrona, "Locke's Theory of Appropriation," *Journal of the History of Ideas* 35 (1974): 229.

76. Locke, *Second Treatise*, par. 123, 124, 94.

77. K. Borries, *Kant als Politiker* (Leipzig, 1928), 108, cited approvingly by G. Lehmann, 210; see also Lisser, 38.

78. Rousseau, *The Social Contract*, 1:9:57; Locke, par. 31, 37.

79. Locke, par. 27; for a contemporary reformulation of this "Lockean Proviso," see R. Nozick, *Anarchy, State and Utopia* (New York: Basic Books, 1974), 178f.

80. See *MdS*, 315, and "Theory and Practice," *KPW*, 75–6.

81. This interpretation of Kantian contract theory has been developed more recently by Rawls in "Kantian Constructivism in Moral Philosophy," *Journal of Philosophy* 77 (1980): 515–72.

82. See, for example, Kant's remarks in "Perpetual Peace," *KPW*, 113. Thus, I believe that Wayne Booth's attempt to distinguish between Kant's philosophical history and theory of justice in terms of two different explanatory standpoints is ultimately unsuccessful, as the status of a "permissive law" in Kant's political morality already suggests, see *Interpreting the World: Kant's Philosophy of History and Politics* (Toronto: Toronto University Press, 1986), 132, 143.

83. See Rawls's similar remarks on the difference between the agreement underlying the original social contract and voluntary agreements within society in *BS*, 59–61.

84. *KPW*, 73; *MdS*, 315.

85. *KPW*, 74–8; *MdS*, 314.

86. *KPW*, 74.

87. *KPW*, 75–6.

88. *KPW*, 78; *MdS*, 314.

89. For a discussion of this paradox, see M. Riedel, "Transcendental Politics? Political Legitimacy and the Concept of Civil Society in Kant," *Social Research* 48 (1981): 606f.

90. See *MdS*, 315, and "Theory and Practice," *KPW*, 76.

91. *KPW*, 79.

92. *KPW*, 80, 85; see also "Contest of the Faculties," *KPW*, 187–8.

93. See *KPW*, 100, 184.

94. *MdS*, 315; Kant refers to the state of nature as "the ideal of Hobbes," (*Gesammelte Schriften*, v. 19, *Reflexion* 6593).

95. *MdS*, 312; see also *Religion*, 89n.

96. On the critical function of the idea of the social contract, see Kersting, "Kant und der staatsphilosophische Kontraktualismus," *Allgemeine Zeitschrift für Philosophie* 8 (1983), 3.

97. For a discussion of Rousseau's profound influence on Kant, see Beck, *A Commentary on Kant's 'Critique of Practical Reason'* (Chicago: University of Chicago Press, 1960), 165n.

98. *MdS*, 223; "Perpetual Peace," *KPW*, 99n.

99. *On the Social Contract*, 1:8:56 (Master's translation).

100. Ibid., 1:6:53.

101. See L. W. Beck, *Commentary on Kant's 'Critique of Practical Reason'*, 200f., and "Kant's Two Conceptions of the Will in their Political Context," in *Studies in the Philosophy of Kant* (Indianapolis: Bobbs-Merrill, 1965), 226.

102. *On The Social Contract*, 1:8:56 (Master's translation).

103. Ibid., 2:15:102.

104. See Kant's remarks in "Contest of the Faculties," *KPW*, 183n, for his distinction between the right and the good and the plurality of the latter.

105. *On the Social Contract*, 2:15:101.

106. See *KPW*, 101.

107. *The Social Contract* (Oxford: Oxford University Press, 1936), 173; for a discussion of this problem see also Kersting, "Kant und der staats-philosophische Kontraktualismus," *Allgemeine Zeitschrift für Philosophie* 8 (1983): 1–27.

108. *KPW,* 126.

109. *KPW,* 79.

110. Ibid., 85; for a discussion of the principle of publicity as the mediating concept between politics and morality in Kant, see J. Habermas, *The Structural Transformation of the Public Sphere* (Cambridge: MIT Press, 1989), sec. 13.

111. For an excellent discussion of Kant's notion of the public use of reason, including its idiosyncracies, see Onora O'Neill, "The Public Use of Reason," *Political Theory* 14 (1986): 528–30.

112. L. W. Beck, "Kant and the Right to Revolution," *Journal of the History of Ideas* 32 (1971): 421–2, and T. Seebohm, "Kant's Theory of Revolution," *Social Research* 48 (1981): 557–87.

113. *KPW,* 84, 126–7.

114. "Perpetual Peace," *KPW,* 118n.; see also Habermas, 134.

115. For a subtle discussion of this "appeal to heaven," see Michael Walzer's "The Obligation of Oppressed Minorities," in his *Obligations* (Cambridge: Harvard University Press, 1970), 68–69; for a contrasting interpretation of the effects of commercial trade, see Michael Doyle, "Kant, Liberal Legacies and Foreign Affairs," *Philosophy and Public Affairs* 12 (1983).

NOTES TO CHAPTER TWO

1. For example, see Stephen Darwall, "Is There A Kantian Foundation for Rawlsian Justice?" in *Rawls' Theory of Justice;* S. Darwall, "A Defense of the Kantian Interpretation," *Ethics* 86 (1976): 164–70; Otfried Höffe, "Ist Rawls' Theorie der Gerechtigkeit eine kantische Theorie?" *Ratio* 26 (1984): 88–104; Thomas Pogge, "The Kantian Interpretation of Justice as Fairness," *Zeitschrift für philosophische Forschung* 35 (1981): 47–65; William Galston, "Moral Personality and Rawls' 'Dewey Lectures'," *Political Theory* 10 (1982): 492–519; and Arnold Davidson, "Is Rawls a Kantian?" *Pacific Philosophical Quarterly* 66 (1985): 48–77.

2. See especially, "Kantian Constructivism in Moral Theory," *Journal of Philosophy* 77 (1980): 515–72; "Justice as Fairness: Political Not Metaphysical," *Philosophy and Public Affairs* 16 (1985): 223–51; and "The Idea of an Overlapping Consensus," *The Oxford Journal of Legal Studies* 7 (1987): 1–25.

3. H. E. Mason, "On the Kantian Interpretation of Rawls' Theory," *Midwest Studies in Philosophy* 1 (1976): 47–54; Oliver Johnson, "Heteronomy and Autonomy: Rawls and Kant," *Midwest Studies in Philosophy* 2 (1977): 277–79, and "The Kantian Interpretation," *Ethics* 85 (1974): 58–66; see also the replies by Darwall, ibid.; and B. Baumirin, "Autonomy in Rawls and Kant," *Midwest Studies in Philosophy* 1 (1976):

55–7, and "Autonomy, Interest and the Kantian Interpretation," *Midwest Studies in Philosophy* 2 (1977): 280–82.

4. A. Levine, "Rawls' Kantianism," *Social Theory and Practice* 3 (1974): 47–63; contrast, however, Rawls's own remarks in "Social Unity and Primary Goods" in *Utilitarianism and Beyond,* 164–67, that the list of primary goods depends "essentially" on the model-conception of the person.

5. Levine, ibid., 51; O. Johnson, "The Kantian Interpretation," 63; and R. P. Wolff, *Understanding Rawls,* 114–15; for a more general discussion of this point, see P. Foot, "Morality as A System of Hypothetical Imperatives," *Philosophical Review* 81 (1972), and my own discussion of this question in chapter 3, sec. IV.

6. M. Sandel, *Liberalism and the Limits of Justice* (New York: Cambridge University Press, 1982), 13; B. Williams, *Ethics and the Limits of Philosophy* (Cambridge: Harvard University Press, 1985), c. 4; and C. Taylor, "The Diversity of Goods," in his *Philosophical Papers,* v. 2 (New York: Cambridge University Press, 1985).

7. For a discussion of these recent "communitarian" critiques of Rawls, see my "The Liberal/Communitarian Controversy and Communicative Ethics," *Philosophy and Social Criticism* 14 (1988): 293–313.

8. This is the strategy adopted, for example, by T. M. Scanlon in "Contractualism and Utilitarianism," where he rejects Rawls's introduction of the "veil of ignorance" as a feature of the original position; John Harsanyi, in "Morality and the Theory of Rational Behavior," also argues that a utilitarian principle would be chosen in a situation of initial choice similar to Rawls's original position. Both of these essays are in Sen and Williams, *Utilitarianism and Beyond* (New York: Cambridge University Press, 1982).

9. This criticism is developed in a number of different articles, most forcefully by Mary Gibson, "Rationality," *Philosophy and Public Affairs* 6 (1977): 193–225, and Seyla Benhabib, "The Methodological Illusions of Modern Political Theory: The Case of Rawls and Habermas," *Neue Hefte für Philosophie* 21 (1982): 47–74.

10. For a good discussion of this strategy, see J. B. Schneewind, "Moral Knowledge and Moral Principles" in *Knowledge and Necessity,* ed. G. Vesey (London: Macmillan, 1974), 249–62. Knowledge of moral principles, according to Schneewind, does not mean certainty based on first principles, but "our reasoned confidence that they, or something very close to them, will, of those available for consideration, come out best in relation to all the evidence, future as well as past" (p. 262). Schneewind's stipulation that moral principles "must be capable of calling forth agreement in a potentially unlimited community of moral agents" (p. 262) anticipates Habermas's discourse ethics, which is perhaps not surprising since both philosophers have been influenced by the work of C. S. Peirce.

11. For Rawls's discussions of the notion of a well-ordered society, see *TJ,* 453–62; *KC,* 521–22; and "Reply to Alexander and Musgrave," *Quarterly Journal of*

Economic 88 (1974): 633–55, especially pp. 633–37; in order to emphasize the continuity between *TJ* and *KC,* I will provide references to both essays in the text.

12. In a recent essay, Rawls explicitly repudiates this interpretation: "Thus it was an error in *Theory* (and a very misleading one) to describe a theory of justice as part of the theory of rational choice, as on 16 and 583. What I should have said is that the conception of justice as fairness uses an account of rational choice subject to reasonable conditions to characterize the deliberations of the parties as representives of free and equal persons; and all of this within a political conception of justice, which is, of course, a moral conception. There is no thought of trying to derive the content of justice within a framework that uses an idea of the rational as the sole normative idea," "Justice as Fairness: Political not Metaphysical," *Philosophy and Public Affairs* 14 (1985): 237 n. 20.

13. "A Kantian Conception of Equality," *Cambridge Review* 96 (1975): 94–99, here 94; see also, *KC,* 521, 546; Rawls's notion of equality is therefore similar to Dworkin's notion of equal concern and respect.

14. Rawls discusses this aspect of the person as free in "Social Unity and Primary Goods," 169; for a careful discussion of this question, see T. M. Scanlon, "Preference and Urgency," *Journal of Philosophy* 72 (1975): 655–69, and Allen Buchanan, "Revisability and Rational Choice," *Canadian Journal of Philosophy* 5 (1975): 395–408; see also my discussion of this topic in chapter 4, sec. IV.

15. In response to several Marxist objections (notably, MacPherson), Rawls no longer insists upon the objective circumstance of justice (*KC,* 539); however, even with the advances of technology and science (and the freeing of production for the satisfaction of generalized interests) there is no guarantee that moderate scarcity can be overcome given the plurality of conflicting (yet equally permissible) conceptions of the good.

16. "Reply to Alexander and Musgrave," 634.

17. See "Fairness to Goodness," 537; and *KC,* 549.

18. For this criticism, see R. P. Wolff, *Understanding Rawls,* 119f.; and S. Benhabib, "The Methodological Illusions of Modern Political Theory," 64f.

19. It is important here not to confuse the "maximin rule for choice under uncertainty" with the "maximin equity criterion" or Difference Principle, which stipulates that inequalities resulting from the basic structure of society are permissible only if they are to the advantage of the least well-off and forms part of the list of possible principles of justice from which the parties in the original position must choose. See J. Rawls, "Some Reasons for the Maximin Criterion," *American Economic Review* 64 (1974): 141–46.

20. Some notable exceptions are H. Bedau, "Social Justice and Social Institutions," *Midwest Studies* 3 (1978): 159–75; Evan Simpson, "The Subjects of Justice," *Ethics* 90 (1980): 490–501; and, most recently, Thomas Pogge, *Realizing Rawls* (Ithaca: Cornell University Press, 1989), chap. 1.

21. Rex Martin, *Rawls and Rights* (Lawrence: University of Kansas Press, 1985), 31–2.

22. Nozick's failure to notice this leads him to overemphasize the extent to which principles (as end-state principles) require continual interference in people's lives (see *Anarchy, State and Utopia,* 163). Although the Difference Principle may require some intervention for purposes of redistribution, the idea is to structure social institutions from the outset in ways that will satisfy the Difference Principle. Of course, deeper disagreements exist since Nozick begins with an inviolable natural right to liberty and property for which he offers no argument. Rawls's theory is not right based in this sense: see "Justice As Fairness: Political Not Metaphysical," 236 n. 19; for a further discussion of this point, see T. M. Scanlon, "Nozick on Rights, Liberty and Property," in *Reading Nozick,* 107–29, especially p. 114.

23. Sandel, *Liberalism and the Limits of Justice* 175; cf. Rawls's remark that there is "no fixed [human] nature" in "The Independence of Moral Theory," 20; and my discussion of Sandel's objection in chapter 4.

24. This objection is developed by Alistair Macleod in "Distributive Justice, Contract and Equality," *Journal of Philosophy* 81 (1984): 709–18.

25. See Sidney Alexander, "Social Evaluation Through Notional Choice," *Quarterly Journal of Economics* 88 (1974), especially p. 604; and Jean Hampton, "Contracts and Choices: Does Rawls Have a Social Contract Theory?" *Journal of Philosophy* 74 (1980): 315–38.

26. Sandel, *Liberalism and the Limits of Justice,* 132.

27. "Reply to Alexander and Musgrave," 651.

28. Ibid.

29. I discuss Sandel's objections at greater length in chapter 4, sec. II; for a similar objection to Sandel's presentation of Rawls, see T. Pogge, *Realizing Rawls,* chap. 2.

30. See *DE,* 66; and Benhabib, "The Methodological Illusions of Modern Political Theory," 63.

31. See also Rawls, "The Priority of Right and Ideas of the Good," *Philosophy and Public Affairs* 17 (1988): 251–76, where Rawls distinguishes among five different ideas of the good and discusses the role each plays in his political conception.

32. "The Nature and Scope of Distributive Justice," in *Philosophical Papers,* v. 2 (New York: Cambridge University Press, 1985), 291; see also "Die Motive einer Verfahrensethik," in *Moralität und Sittlichkeit,* ed. Axel Honneth and Wolfgang Kuhlmann (Frankfurt: Suhrkamp, 1986), 101–39.

33. See "The Diversity of Goods," in *Utilitarianism and Beyond,* ed. A. Sen and B. Williams (New York: Cambridge University Press, 1982), 132.

34. Walzer, *Spheres of Justice* (New York: Basic Books, 1983), 15.

35. See Rawls, "The Idea of an Overlapping Consensus," *Oxford Journal of Legal Studies* 7 (1987): 3, and "The Priority of the Right and Ideas of the Good," 262.

36. To be sure, Rawls states that "justification is a matter of mutual support of many considerations" (*TJ*, 21, 579) and the various arrows in Figure 2-1 pointing from "our" point of view to the well-ordered society, the original position and the two principles are meant to show that the process of reflective equilibrium not only takes place between our considered convictions and the model-conceptions, but also between us and each of these aspects of Rawls's theory.

37. Compare *TJ*, 578, and *KC*, 568; see also Rawls's remark (in "The Domain of the Political and Overlapping Consensus," 251) that while his theory may not apply to all societies, it is not historicist or relativist since it seeks to specify a conception of justice appropriate for any modern society.

38. For this criticism, see R. Brandt, *A Theory of the Good and the Right* (Oxford: Clarendon, 1979), 20; and N. Daniels, "Wide Reflective Equilibrium and Theory Acceptance in Ethics," *Journal of Philosophy* 76 (1979): 256–82: "Coherent fictions are still fictions, and we may be only reshuffling our prejudices," 269.

39. The distinction between narrow and wide reflective equilibrium is implicit in *A Theory of Justice* (see 49), but explicitly stated in "The Independence of Moral Theory," 8.

40. "The Independence of Moral Theory," 8.

41. N. Daniels, "Reflective Equilibrium and Archimedean Points," *Canadian Journal of Philosophy* 10 (1980): 83–103, here 85–6. My own discussion of reflective equilibrium is greatly indebted to Daniels's two essays; however, unlike him, I do not include the model-conceptions of the well-ordered society and the person among the background theories appealed to in the process of wide reflective equilibrium. Rather, I see them as constructions which (like the original position) result from the process of reflective equilibrium. This seems to accord more with Rawls's desire to distinguish moral theory from other theories (and thus the model-conception of the person from theories of psychology or human nature). See "The Independence of Moral Theory," 8, and D. Little, "Reflective Equilibrium and Justification," *Southern Journal of Philosophy* 22 (1984): 373–87, especially 381.

42. Daniels refers to this as the "independence constraint." See "Wide Reflective Equilibrium and Theory Acceptance," 259–60.

43. See M. Smith, "Rawls and Intuitionism," in *New Essays on Contract Theory, Canadian Journal of Philosophy*, (suppl. v. 3): 163–78.

44. See N. Daniels, "Wide Reflective Equilibrium and Theory Acceptance," 265 for a discussion of this difference.

45. See D. Lyons, "The Nature and Soundness of the Contract and Coherence Arguments," in *Reading Rawls*, 141–67; P. Singer, "Sidgwick and Reflective Equilibrium," *The Monist* 58 (1974): 490–517, at 515; and D. Little, "Reflective Equilibrium and Justification."

46. For a critical discussion of this analogy, see N. Daniels, "On Some Methods of Ethics and Linguistics," *Philosophical Studies* 37 (1980): 21–36.

47. See "Justice as Fairness," 225, 239 n. 21; see also "The Idea of an Overlapping Consensus," 3.

48. Ibid., 234; "The Domain of the Political," 240.

49. See ibid., 237 n. 20; for a critique of this version of foundationalism, see Arthur Ripstein, "Foundationalism in Political Theory," *Philosophy and Public Affairs* 16 (1987): 115–137.

50. Ibid., 246–7; and "The Idea of an Overlapping Consensus," 4.

51. Ibid., 229–30.

52. See, for example, his remark in "The Idea of an Overlapping Consensus": "Here I assume that free and willing agreement is agreement endorsed by our considered convictions on due reflection, or in what I have elsewhere called 'reflective equilibrium'" (p. 5 n. 8).

53. "Justice as Fairness," 238.

54. These considerations also point to a weakness in David Brink's recent attempt to criticize Rawlsian constructivism from the perspective of moral realism, "Rawlsian Constructivism in Moral Theory," *Canadian Journal of Philosophy* 17 (1987): 71–90. Rawls's constructivism does not depend on an argument about the underdetermination of moral theory on the basis of appeals to ideals of the person, but on a specific conception of an acceptable public justification of political ideals and principles.

55. See, for example, Thomas Scanlon's alternative characterization of the impartial standpoint in "Contractualism and Utilitarianism" in *Utilitarianism and Beyond,* 121; Jürgen Habermas's discussion of impartiality in "Justice and Solidarity," *The Philsophical Forum* 21 (1989): 35f.; and Thomas Nagel's comments on the need for "a higher-order of impartiality" to adjudicate between different orders of impartiality in "Moral Conflict and Political Legitimacy," *Philosophy and Public Affairs* 16 (1987): 216.

56. It is important to note, however, that the notion of *modus vivendi* used here (and, I believe, by Larmore and Ackerman) differs from the interpretation offered by Rawls. Rawls describes a *modus vivendi* as a form of justification that appeals to a convergence of self- or group-interests apart from any common moral motivations and thus is closer to what I earlier described as foundationalism (see n. 49) and what Nagel has called a "convergence theory" (p. 213). The sense of a *modus vivendi* employed here is closer to what Nagel has described as a "mixed theory," that is, one that appeals to both moral conceptions *and* self- or group-interest as the situation may require (Nagel, 220). Thus, in *Patterns of Moral Complexity* (New York: Cambridge University Press, 1986), Charles Larmore states that a framework for dialogue cannot

be derived solely from a neutral model of rationality but must assume that the parties "wish to show everyone *equal respect*" (p. 61). Ackerman also rejects such an attempt to ground the framework for dialogue in a neutral model of rationality. What constitutes a *modus vivendi* for them is simply the fact that the grounds for dialogue are not found in a claim to moral truth or what Rawls calls a general and comprehensive moral doctrine. Thus, despite his own claim that a "political conception of justice" is not simply a *modus vivendi,* Rawls's "method of avoidance" appears congruous with that of Larmore and Ackerman (see Larmore's remarks on Rawls's approach, 125).

57. "The Idea of an Overlapping Consensus," 8.

58. See T. Scanlon, "Contractualism and Utilitarianism," 111, on the importance of this distinction.

59. "The Idea of an Overlapping Consensus," 7–8.

60. Ibid., 8.

61. Ibid., 8; see also, "Justice as Fairness: Political Not Metaphysical," 231.

62. See Bruce Ackerman, *Social Justice in the Liberal State* (New Haven: Yale University Press, 1980), 9, and "What is Neutral About Neutrality?" *Ethics* 93 (1983): 375; Larmore introduces a "a universal norm of rational dialogue": "When two people disagree about some specific point, but wish to continue talking about the more general problem they wish to solve, each should prescind from the beliefs that the other rejects, (1) in order to construct an argument on the basis of his other beliefs that will convince the other of the truth of the disputed belief, or (2) in order to shift to another aspect of the problem, where the possibilities of agreement seem greater" (53).

63. Nagel, 232.

64. "The Idea of an Overlapping Consensus," 19.

65. Ibid., 5, n. 7, 24.

66. "Justice as Fairness," 241; see also T. Scanlon, "The Significance of Choice," in *The Tanner Lectures on Human Values,* v. 8, ed. S. McMurrin (Salt Lake City: University of Utah Press, 1988), 173ff., and S. Freeman, "Reason and Agreement in Social Contract Views," *Philosophy and Public Affairs* 19 (1990): 151ff.

67. "The Idea of an Overlapping Consensus," 8.

68. In "The Domain of the Political and Overlapping Consensus" Rawls suggests that the "burdens of reason" (or sources of desagreement among reasonable persons) count against such a discursive model of legitimacy (238). I believe that this view misunderstands the role of consensus within a discourse ethics. Certainly reasonable people may disagree about things. The question, however, is whether, in seeking to find a reasonable basis of agreement for selecting basic principles of jus-

tice, the idea of an agreement between free and equal persons remains open and can be reflexively applied to the common basis of agreement or whether, as in Rawls's recent "political" conception, such a recursive model of reasonable agreement would be unacceptable since the determination of what is reasonable itself depends upon a prior agreement based in "common sense" or "fundamental intuitive ideas" implicit in (some) public cultures. For a similar critique, see Onora O'Neill, *Constructions of Reason* (New York: Cambridge University Press), 211.

NOTES TO CHAPTER THREE

1. For a brief but accurate account of Habermas's development, see Richard Bernstein, "Introduction," in *Habermas and Modernity,* ed. R. Bernstein (Cambridge: MIT Press, 1985); for more detailed discussions, see Thomas McCarthy, *The Critical Theory of Jürgen Habermas* (Cambridge: MIT Press, 1978); Seyla Benhabib, *Critique, Norm and Utopia: A Study of the Critical Foundations of Critical Theory* (New York: Columbia University Press, 1986); Stephen K. White, *The Recent Work of Jürgen Habermas* (New York: Cambridge University Press, 1988); and Axel Honneth, *The Critique of Power: Reflective Stages in a Critical Social Theory,* trans. K. Baynes (Cambridge: MIT Press, 1991).

2. See especially *DE* and *ME,* and Karl-Otto Apel, "The *A priori* of the Communication Community and the Foundations of Ethics," in *Towards a Transformation of Philosophy,* trans. G. Adey and D. Frisby (London: Routledge and Kegan Paul, 1980), and Apel, *Diskurs und Verantwortung* (Frankfurt: Suhrkamp, 1988); see also *The Communicative Ethics Controversy,* ed. S. Benhabib and F. Dallmayr (Cambridge: MIT Press, 1990).

3. For Hare's view, see "Meaning and Speech Acts," *The Philosophical Review* 79 (1970): 3–24, and "Some Alleged Differences Between Imperatives and Indicatives," *Mind* 76 (1967): 309–26. For a more recent statement of his moral theory, see *Moral Thinking* (Oxford: Clarendon, 1981).

4. For the criticism that his principle of universalizability achieves "formality" at the expense of "fertility," see Onora Nell, *Acting on Principle,* chap. 1.

5. Compare the discussion of the task of moral theory by T. Scanlon in "Contractualism and Utilitarianism," in *Utilitarianism and Beyond,* ed. B. Williams and A. Sen (New York: Cambridge University, 1982); more generally, see Christine Korsgaard, "Skepticism About Practical Reason," *Journal of Philosophy* 83 (1986): 5–25.

6. For Habermas's definition of the task of moral theory, see ME, 211 and *Die Neue Unübersichtlichkeit* (Frankfurt: Suhrkamp, 1985), 225. On the problem of moral conflict, see B. Williams, "Conflict of Values," in *Moral Luck* (New York: Cambridge, 1981); S. Hampshire, "Morality and Pessimism," in *Public and Private Morality* (New York: Cambridge, 1978); and the recent collection, *Moral Dilemmas,* ed. Christopher Gowans (New York: Oxford University Press, 1987).

7. On the evolution of the concepts of labor and interaction, see Axel Honneth, *The Critique of Power;* T. McCarthy, *The Critical Theory of Jürgen Habermas;* and A. Giddens, "Labor and Interaction," in *Habermas: Critical Debates,* ed. J. Thompson and D. Held (Cambridge: MIT, 1982); I offer a brief defense of Habermas's two-level approach to society in "Rational Reconstruction and Social Criticism: Habermas's Model of Interpretive Social Science," *The Philosophical Forum* 21 (1989): 122–45.

8. See "Remarks on the Concept of Communicative Action," in *Social Action,* ed. G. Seebass and R. Tuomela (New York: Reidel, 1985), 169 [hereafter, "Remarks"], and "A Reply" in *Communicative Action,* ed. A. Honneth and H. Joas (Cambridge: MIT Press, 1991), 233.

9. See, for example, Searle's "Response" to Habermas in *John Searle and His Critics,* ed. E. Lepore and R. van Gulick (New York: Basil Blackwell, 1991), 89–96. I hope that my own exposition of Habermas's position will answer some of the problems and misunderstandings in Searle's discussion, especially regarding the relation between Habermas's validity claims and Searle's analysis of the constitutive conditions of illocutionary acts.

10. "Reply to My Critics," in *Habermas: Critical Debates,* 263–4 [hereafter, "Reply"]; and *TCA* 1:285.

11. "Aspects of the Rationality of Action," in *Proceedings of the International Symposium on "Rationality Today,"* ed. T. Geraets (Ottawa, Ontario: University of Ottawa, 1979) 195 [hereafter, "Aspects"]; *TCA* 1:86–7; "Reply," 263–4.

12. *TCA* 1:285; "Reply," 264; and the discussion in S. White, 10ff.

13. Cf. *TCA* 1:70, 86, 101; "Remarks," 154.

14. For a more detailed discussion of this aspect of communicative action, see my "Rational Reconstruction and Social Criticism."

15. This distinction between a weaker and stronger sense of communicative action corresponds roughly to Habermas's distinction between "normatively secured action" (action that relies on a tacit, largely unreflective consensus) and "communicative action" (actions in which the consensus has become reflective and the validity claims explicitly thematized). Since this contrast will invariably always be one of degree (not distinct kinds), I prefer to speak of communicative action in a weaker and stronger sense; see also the helpful clarification in Nancy Fraser, "What's Critical About Critical Theory," *Unruly Practices* (Minneapolis: University of Minnesota, 1989), 139 n. 8.

16. See "Remarks," 151.

17. "Remarks," 170.

18. J. Habermas and N. Luhmann, *Theorie der Gesellschaft oder Sozialtech-*

nologie? (Frankfurt: Suhrkamp, 1971), and *Legitimation Crisis* (Boston: Beacon Press, 1975), part 3.

19. "Reply," 265, and "Remarks," 158.

20. See *The Philosophical Discourse of Modernity,* 343.

21. *TCA* 1:82; Habermas suggests that the aspect of the lifeworld as a resource is emphasized by the phenomenological approach of Husserl and Schutz, while the aspect of the lifeworld as that about which actors negotiate is emphasized in eth-nomethodological approaches; see "Remarks," 160.

22. "Remarks," 167; *TCA* 2:135.

23. *The Philosophical Discourse of Modernity,* 342; also *TCA* 2:145.

24. Tugendhat, "Habermas on Communicative Action," and Michael Baurmann, "Understanding as an Aim and Aims of Understanding," both in *Social Action,* ed. Seebass and Tuomela; see also Skjei, "A Comment on Performative, Subject and Proposition in Habermas's Theory of Communication," *Inquiry* 28 (1985): 87–122, and Allen Wood, "Habermas's Defense of Rationalism," *New German Critique* 35 (1985): 159. For a slightly different attempt to defend Habermas's distinction against these criticisms, see James Bohman, "Emancipation and Rhetoric: The Perlocutions and Illocutions of the Social Critic," *Philosophy and Rhetoric* 21 (1988): 185–204.

25. *TCA* 1:101; "Remarks," 154, and *MCCA,* 144; but admittedly Habermas is not always clear on this and sometimes, especially in connection with his discussion of Weber, he equates teleological and purposive-rational action. See for example, *TCA* 1:85–6; "Aspects," 194; and "Reply," 237.

26. As I shall argue below, however, this confusion does not present a serious threat to Habermas's project; see too Habermas's more recent clarification in "A Reply," *Communicative Action,* ed. Honneth and Joas, 240 and *Nachmetaphysisches Denken,* 68ff.

27. "Reply to Skjei," *Inquiry* 28 (1985): 108 and "A Reply," *Communicative Action,* 242.

28. Allen Wood's interesting discussion is, I believe, also in error on this point: If, as Wood argues, "acts of reaching understanding" are better classified as perlocutionary acts since they aim at persuasion (p. 162), Habermas's attempt to distinguish between persuasion and rational agreement would indeed fail. However, the aim of *Verständigung* is not to persuade but, in Austin's phrase, to "secure uptake." As Searle argues in his own earlier critique of Grice, "securing uptake" (rather than "getting someone to believe") is what distinguishes illocutionary from perlocutionary acts in that this aim is constitutive for the act being an act of a certain type, that is, an assertion, a promise, a request, etc. (see below, p. 93f.). As we shall see, Habermas believes that these "illocutionary aims" can themselves best be clarified (and classified) with reference to basic validity claims that speakers raise with their utterances.

Habermas's defense of what Wood calls "the *Verständigung* thesis" (the thesis that action aimed at reaching understanding is, in some nontrivial sense, fundamental) is indeed tied to the claim that this rationally binding/motivating force is present in illocutionary acts and that, in communicative action, all other ends are subordinate to reaching agreement with respect to these claims.

29. Giddens, in Thompson and Held, 159; for Habermas's stated view, see *TCA* 1:101, 295, 305; "Reply to Skjei," 106, and "Reply," 264.

30. "Reply," 265.

31. *TCA* 1:295.

32. Giddens, in Thompson and Held, 159.

33. Foucault, *Power/Knowledge,* ed. Colin Gordon (New York: Pantheon, 1980), and "The Subject and Power," in P. Rabinow and B. Dreyfus, *Michel Foucault: Beyond Structuralism and Hermeneutics* (Chicago: University of Chicago, 1982), 208–226.

34. See *The Philosophical Discourse of Modernity* (Cambridge: MIT, 1987), chap. 10; Nancy Fraser, "Foucault on Modern Power," *Praxis International* 1 (1981): 272–87, especially p. 283; Honneth, *The Critique of Power,* chap. 5 and 6; and the excellent discussion by C. Taylor, "Foucault on Freedom and Truth," in *Philosophical Papers,* v. 2 (New York: Cambridge University, 1985).

35. See Honneth, 298f.; McCarthy, "The Seducements of Systems-Theory, or Democracy and Complexity," *New German Critique* 35 (1985): 43, 49–50; and Nancy Fraser, "How Critical is Critical Theory?," 113–43.

36. See Habermas's own critique of H. Arendt along the same lines in "Arendt's Communications Concept of Power," *Social Research* 44 (1977): 3–24; and "A Reply," *Communicative Action,* ed. Honneth and Joas, 388.

37. A. Gewirth, *Reason and Morality* (Chicago: Chicago University Press, 1978), *Human Rights* (Chicago: Chicago University Press, 1982), and "The Epistemology of Human Rights" in *Human Rights,* ed. E. F. Paul and F. Miller (Oxford: Blackwell, 1984), 1–24.

38. On the notion of a claim-right, see chapter 1, n. 15.

39. *Reason and Morality,* 135.

40. For criticisms of Gewirth, see A. MacIntyre, *After Virtue,* 66–8; Stephen White, "On the Normative Structure of Action: Gewirth and Habermas," *The Review of Politics* 44 (1982): 282–301; A. Danto, "Constructing an Epistemology of Human Rights: A Pseudo-Problem?" in *Human Rights,* ed. E. Paul; and the essays in *Human Rights, Nomos* 23. For Gewirth's replies, see especially *Human Rights;* "Replies to Some Criticisms," in *Nomos* 23:178–90; and "Why Agents Must Claim Rights: A Reply," *Journal of Philosophy* 79 (1982). My own criticisms most resemble those of MacIntyre and White, especially p. 288.

41. Gewirth defines a prudential claim-right as follows: "Prudential rights are a species of claim rights, so that they entail correlative duties of other persons to act or to forebear in ways required for the right holder's having the object of his right." See "From the Prudential to the Moral: Reply to Singer," *Ethics* 95 (1985): 302.

42. Singer, as Gewirth notes, is thus mistaken in objecting that the right needed for deriving the correlative ought must be a moral right; see Singer, "From the Prudential to the Moral," *Ethics* 95 (1985).

43. "Meaning and Truth" in *Logico-Linguistic Papers* (London: Methuen, 1971), 170–89; see also John McDowell, "Meaning, Communication and Knowledge," in *Philosophical Subjects,* ed. Z. van Straaten (Oxford: Clarendon, 1980), 117–39.

44. See his "Truth and Meaning," in *Inquiries into Truth and Interpretation* (Oxford: Clarendon, 1984), 17–36.

45. "Meaning and Truth," 179; for similar criticism of truth-conditional semantics, see J. McDowell, ibid.; Christopher Peacocke, "Truth Definitions and Actual Languages," in *Truth and Meaning,* ed. G. Evans and J. McDowell (Oxford: Clarendon, 1976); and Simon Blackburn, *Spreading the Word* (Oxford: Clarendon, 1984), chap. 4.

46. "Meaning and Truth," 181.

47. Ibid., 182.

48. Cf. for example, D. Holdcroft, *Words and Deeds* (Oxford: Clarendon, 1978); Dennis Stampe, "Meaning and Truth in the Theory of Speech Acts," in *Syntax and Semantics,* v. 3, ed. P. Cole and J. Morgan (New York: Academic Press, 1975); and D. Davidson, "Moods and Performances," in *Inquiries into Truth and Interpretation.*

49. Davidson, "Communication and Convention," ibid., 272, 280; M. Platts, *Ways of Meaning* (London: Routledge and Kegan Paul, 1980): 88, 91.

50. See, for example, the exchange between Davidson, Dummett, and Hacking about the goals for a theory of meaning in *Truth and Interpretation,* ed. E. Lepore (New York: Blackwell, 1986).

51. See Quine, *Word and Object* (Cambridge: Harvard, 1960), and Davidson, "Radical Interpretation," in *Inquiries into Truth and Interpretation,* 125–39.

52. "Communication and Convention," ibid., 274.

53. This is the formulation of the task for a theory of meaning found in Dummett; see "What is a Theory of Meaning, I" in *Mind and Language,* ed. S. Guttenplan, especially p. 121; and "What does the Appeal to Use Do for the Theory of Meaning," in *Meaning and Use,* ed. A. Margalit (Boston: Reidel, 1979), especially p. 134.

54. McDowell, 124.

55. For a similar interpretation of Habermas's pragmatic theory of meaning and some of the problems associated with it, see Albrecht Wellmer, "Was ist eine pragmatische Bedeutungstheorie?" in *Zwischenbetrachtungen*, ed. Wellmer, Honneth, McCarthy, and Offe (Frankfurt: Suhrkamp, 1989), 318–70.

56. The phrase is from S. Blackburn's, *Spreading the Word*, 113.

57. See the critique of this strategy offered by Davidson in "Communication and Convention," 265–80; for Habermas's criticisms of meaning nominalism, see "Intentionalistische Semantik," in *Vorstudien und Ergänzungen zur Theorie des kommunikativen Handelns* (Frankfurt: Suhrkamp, 1984), and "Zur Kritik der Bedeutungstheorie," in *Nachmetaphysisches Denken* (Frankfurt: Suhrkamp, 1988), 105–135.

58. "Meaning," *Philosophical Review* 66 (1957): 377–88, and "Utterer's Meaning and Intentions," *Philosophical Review* 78 (1969): 147–77.

59. Blackburn, 111.

60. "Meaning," 383–4.

61. Lewis, *Convention* (Cambridge: Harvard University Press, 1969).

62. Lewis, 58: "A regularity in the behavior of members in a population P when they are agents in a recurrent situation S is a *convention* if and only if it is true that, and it is common knowledge in P that, in any instance of S among members of P, (1) everyone conforms to R; (2) everyone expects everyone else to conform to R; (3) everyone prefers to conform to R on the condition that the others do, since S is a coordination problem and uniform conformity to R is a coordination equilibrium in S."

63. For the notion of 'mutual' or 'common' knowledge, see Schiffer, *Meaning* (Oxford: Clarendon, 1972), 31 and Lewis, 52–60.

64. For a discussion of the problem of coordination, cf. Lewis, chap. 1, and Schiffer, 138–48.

65. Bennett, "The Meaning-Nominalist Strategy," *Foundations of Language* 10 (1973): 152; see also Schiffer, 39.

66. Bennett, 155.

67. Strawson, "Intention and Convention," in *Logico-Linguistic Papers,* 157; see also Schiffer, 17–27.

68. See the proposals in Blackburn, 115; Platts, 87; and Grice's own proposal in "Meaning Revisited," in *Mutual Knowledge,* ed. N. Smith (New York: Academic Press, 1982), 243.

60. *Speech Acts* (New York: Cambridge University Press, 1969), 46; J. Habermas, "What is Universal Pragmatics?" in *Communication and the Evolution of Society,* 8; *TCA* 1:275; and "Intentionalistische Semantik," 338.

70. See his "Introduction," to the *Philosophy of Language,* ed. Searle (New York: Oxford University Press, 1971), 10, and *Speech Acts,* 46.

71. *Speech Acts,* 47.

72. See Bennett, 162f.; see also Searle, *Speech Acts,* 49–50, for his revision of Grice's definition of nonnatural meaning or speaker's meaning.

73. Habermas, "Intentionalistische Semantik," 338.

74. Ibid., 338; see also *TCA* 1:288f., especially p. 292; Habermas has in the meantime reformulated his definition of perlocutions to bring it more into conformity with accepted usage. As he notes, however, this requires no substantial change in his argument, cf. "A Reply," *Communicative Action,* ed. Honneth and Joas, 240.

75. Austin, *How To Do Things With Words* (Cambridge: Harvard University Press, 1962), 113; and S. Davis, "Perlocutions," in *Speech Act Theory and Pragmatics,* ed. J. Searle (Boston: Reidel, 1980), 38.

76. Schiffer, 7.

77. See Bennett, 147.

78. See "Intentionalistische Semantik" and "Zur Kritik der Bedeutungstheorie," in *Nachmetaphysisches Denken* (Frankfurt: Suhrkamp, 1988), 112; for his related critique of objectivism in the social sciences, see *On the Logic of the Social Sciences* (Cambridge: MIT, 1988), and "Reconstruction and Interpretation in the Social Sciences," in *Moral Consciousness and Communicative Action,* 21–42.

79. See Schiffer, 31.

80. Consequently, Tugendhat's rebuke of Habermas's dismissal of meaning-nominalism is unjustified, cf. Tugendhat in Seebass, *Social Action,* 186 n. 5.

81. Searle, *Speech Acts,* 45; Strawson, "Intention and Convention."

82. In his article "Intention, Meaning and Truth-Conditions," (*Philosophical Studies* 35 [1979]: 345–60) R. Cummins makes a related criticism regarding the notion of convention employed in the meaning-nominalist strategy: Bennett's strategy, according to Cummins, is to explain sentence meaning in terms of primitive utterance-types that in turn are regarded as conventions of Gricean mechanisms. However, in a natural language there are an infinite number of noncomposite sentences, yet there clearly cannot be an infinite number of conventionalized Gricean mechanisms. The meaning-nominalist strategy thus fails because it cannot account for the possibility of an infinite number of noncomposite sentences.

83. Rawls, "Two Concepts of Rules," *The Philosophical Review* 64 (1955): 3–32; the idea of language as rule-following belongs, of course, to Wittgenstein.

84. *Speech Acts,* 16.

85. Austin, 147–8, and Searle, "Austin and 'Locutionary Meaning'" in *Essays on J. L. Austin,* ed. I. Berlin (Oxford: Clarendon, 1973), 158; for Austin's view that

certain illocutionary acts are bearers of truth and falsity, see his debate with Strawson, reprinted in *Truth,* ed. G. Pitcher.

86. Searle, "Austin on Locutionary and Illocutionary Acts"; for further discussion cf. Forguson, "Locutionary and Illocutionary Acts"; Strawson, "Austin and 'Locutionary Meaning'"; and Warnock, "Some Types of Performative Utterance," all in *Essays on J. L. Austin,* ed. I. Berlin (Oxford: Clarendon Press, 1973); D. Holdcroft, *Words and Deeds: Problems in the Theory of Speech Acts* (Oxford: Clarendon, 1978), and G. Bird, "Austin's Theory of Illocutionary Force," in *Midwest Studies in Philosophy* 6 (1981): 345–69.

87. Searle, "Austin," 155–6.

88. Cf. D. Stampe, "Meaning and Truth in the Theory of Speech Acts," in *Speech Acts,* ed. Cole and Morgan; D. Holdcroft, *Words and Deeds,* and "Meaning and Illocutionary Acts"; and L. J. Cohen, "Do Illocutionary Forces Exist?" *Philosophical Quarterly* 14 (1964): 118–37; see also the discussion in Wellmer, "Was ist eine pragmatische Bedeutungstheorie?"

89. Cf. Searle, "Meaning," in *Intentionality* (New York: Cambridge, 1983), and *Foundations of Illocutionary Logic* (New York: Cambridge, 1985), 3; for Strawson's view, see, in addition to "Meaning and Truth," "Austin," in Berlin, 60ff.

90. For a discussion of the relationship between performatives and truth-conditions, see G. Warnock, "Some Types of Performative Utterance," in Berlin, 65–89, especially p. 82; and the debate between R. M. Hare, "Meaning and Speech Acts," *Philosophical Review* 79 (1970), and A. Genova, "Speech Acts and Illocutionary Opacity," *Foundations of Language* 13 (1975): 237–49.

91. Austin, 114–6; Austin also introduced various grammatical criteria for distinguishing illocutions from perlocutions which I will not take up here; it does not seem that there is any unique set of grammatical rules for distinguishing them. See. T. Cohen, "Illocutions and Perlocutions," *Foundations of Language* 9 (1973): 492–503, and S. Davis, "Perlocutions."

92. See Strawson, "Intention and Convention," 152.

93. Austin, 103; Strawson, "Intention and Convention," 152.

94. Searle, *Speech Acts,* 19–21.

95. In *Words and Deeds* (p. 34f.) Holdcroft thus misunderstands Searle's claim; against Holdcroft, but with Strawson, Searle, and Habermas, Warnock argues that hinting is not properly an illocutionary act. See Warnock, "A Question About Illocutionary Acts," in *Language and Morality* (Oxford: Blackwell, 1983), 110; Strawson, "Intention and Convention," 163; and Habermas, "What is Universal Pragmatics," 40.

96. See Jacques Derrida, *Limited Inc* (Evanston: Northwestern University Press, 1988) and T. Binkley, "The Principle of Expressibility," *Philosophy and Phenomenological Research* 39 (1979): 307–25, for this objection.

97. Austin, 101; Davis, 38; and G. Bird, "Austin's Theory of Illocutionary Force," *Midwest Studies in Philosophy* 6 (1981): 357.

98. Searle, *Speech Acts,* 37; see also his "Austin on Locutionary and Illocutionary Acts," in Berlin, 151; and *Foundations of Illocutionary Logic, 7.*

99. *Speech Acts,* chap. 3 for a discussion of the constitutive rules underlying the act of promising. The following summary is drawn from this chapter. In more recent writings Searle refers to the essential rule as the "illocutionary point" of a speech act; in addition, he suggests that there ar at least twelve other criteria for identifying basic illocutionary acts. However, the four criteria discussed here remain, I think, the most important. See also, "A Taxonomy of Illocutionary Acts," in *Expression and Meaning* (New York: Cambridge University Press, 1979), 1–29, and *Foundations of Illocutionary Logic,* 12–20, 52–59.

100. *Speech Acts,* 49–50 (with minor alterations).

101. See *TCA* 1:316, 318; and Searle, *Foundations of Illocutionary Logic, 7.*

102. For a more detailed discussion, see Apel, "Linguistic Meaning and Intentionality," in *Critical and Dialectical Phenomenology,* ed. H. Silverman and D. Welton (Albany: SUNY Press, 1987), 2–53; for an alternative formulation of the relation between semantics and pragmatics, see R. Stalnaker, "Pragmatics," *Synthese* 22 (1970): 272–81.

103. *Speech Acts,* 45; more recently, however, Searle seems to have swung in the other direction, now attempting like Grice to define meaning in terms of prelinguistic intentions. See *Intentionality,* chap. 6 and *John Searle and his Critics,* ed. E. Lepore and R. van Gulick (New York: Basil Blackwell, 1991).

104. "What is Universal Pragmatics?" 38–9.

105. Habermas describes these rules as "quasi-transcendental" in "What is Universal Pragmatics," 21–2, and as "transcendental in a weak sense" in *TCA* 1:310.

106. *Speech Acts,* 186 n. 1.

107. Habermas's notion of a transcendental argument seems to be largely the same as Strawson's; for a discussion, see his "Philosophy as Stand-In and Interpreter," in *After Philosophy,* ed. K. Baynes, J. Bohman, and T. McCarthy (Cambridge: MIT, 1987).

108. *Speech Acts,* chap. 10; for a detailed discussion of Searle's argument, see Apel, *Sprachpragmatik und Philosophie* (Frankfurt: Suhrkamp, 1976).

110. "What is Universal Pragmatics?," 61; see also E. Tugendhat, *Traditional and Analytic Philosophy: Lectures on the Philosophy of Language* (New York: Cambridge University Press, 1982), 187–88, 398–99.

111. Ibid., 61.

112. See *TCA* 1:295ff., "A Reply" in *Communicative Action,* ed. Honneth and Joas, 217, and Tugendhat, 150, for remarks on the yes/no position-taking with respect to the offers contained in speech acts.

113. *TCA* 1:278, 305; see also "What is Universal Pragmatics," 59ff. Searle and other critics of Habermas are thus mistaken in assuming that Habermas's account of understanding requires agreement with the *content* of what is said, rather than agreement about the validity conditions of the utterance; see Searle, "Reply to Habermas," *John Searle and His Critics,* ed. Lepore, 92.

114. *TCA* 1:236, 278; see also T. McCarthy, "Reflections on Rationalization in the Theory of Communicative Action," *Praxis International* 4 (1984): 177–91.

115. It is important not to confuse the notion of the lifeworld with the notion of the three worlds about which speakers seek to reach an understanding: Speakers reach an understanding *against* the background of the lifeworld and draw upon it as a resource; however, they reach an understanding (and make propositionally-differentiated speech acts) *about* the three worlds; see *TCA* 1:70ff., 335f., "Remarks on Communicative Action," in Seebass, 164–9, and my "Rational Reconstruction and Social Criticism," 134f.; on the importance of "background" for meaning, see also Searle, "Literal Meaning," in *Expression and Meaning,* and "The Background," in *Intentionality.*

116. For Searle's classification, see "A Taxonomy of Illocutionary Acts," in *Expression and Meaning;* for criticisms, see Habermas, *TCA* 1:319–28; A. Martinich, *Communication and Reference* (New York: de Gruyter, 1984), chap. 3; and M. Kreckel, *Communicative Acts and Shared Knowledge in Natural Discourse* (New York: Academic Press, 1981), 43ff., 58.

117. Martinich, 12, and *TCA* 1:320–21.

118. See N. Fotion, "Master Speech Acts," *Philosophical Quarterly* 21 (1971): 232–43, and "Speech Activity and Language Use," *Philosophia* 8 (1979): 615–38.

119. *TCA* 1:326.

120. "Reply to Skjei," 111–12.

121. See *DE,* 67, and McCarthy's formulation in *The Critical Theory of Jürgen Habermas,* 326.

122. *ME,* 198; for a contrasting view of the "moral point of view," see B. Williams, *Moral Luck* (New York: Cambridge University Press, 1983), 8.

123. J. Mackie, *Ethics: Inventing Right and Wrong* (New York: Penguin, 1977), 22; in "Ethics and the Fabric of the World," B. Williams argues that Mackie improperly conflates this notion of objectivity with Kant's claim that the Moral Law is objectively valid (without, of course, endorsing Kant's view) (in *Morality and Objectivity,* ed. T. Honderich, 206); see also the interesting discussion by Jonathan

Lear, "Moral Objectivity," in *Objectivity and Cultural Divergence,* ed. S. C. Brown (New York: Cambridge University Press, 1984), 135–70.

124. E. Tugendhat, *Probleme der Ethik* (Stuttgart: Reclam, 1984), 78–9, 123–4; see also K. Ilting, "Geltung als Konsens," *Neue Hefte für Philosophie* 18 (1979): 22–50, and Habermas's discussion of Tugendhat in *DE,* 68–76.

125. See *LC,* part 3, chap. 3; and "Wahrheitstheorien," in *Vorstudien.*

126. *Virtues and Vices* (Berkeley: University of California, 1978), 157–73; see also W. Frankena, "Has Morality and Independent Bottom?" *The Monist* 63 (1980): 49ff., and Foot's reply in "Comments on Frankena's Carus Lectures," *The Monist* 64 (1981): 308ff. For an excellent discussion of this question, see John McDowell, "Are Moral Requirements Hypothetical Imperatives?" *Proceedings of the Aristotelian Society,* suppl. v. 52 (1978): 13–29.

127. *MCCA,* 130; and "Über Moralität und Sittlichkeit: Was macht eine Lebensform 'rational'?" in *Rationalität,* ed. W. Schnädelbach (Frankfurt: Suhrkamp, 1984), 218–35.

128. See *The Philosophical Discourse of Modernity,* chap. 11.

129. *DE,* 67; see also Wellmer, *Ethik und Dialog,* 45–50, 60ff.

130. *DE,* 94f.; see also "The Entwinement of Myth and Enlightenment: Re-Reading the 'Dialectic of Enlightenment'," *New German Critique* 26 (1983): 27, and Karl-Otto Apel, "The Problem of a Philosophical Grounding in Light of a Transcendental Pragmatic of Language," in *After Philosophy.*

131. R. S. Peter, *Ethics and Education* (London: Allen and Unwin, 1966), 114f.

132. H. P. Grice, "Logic and Conversation," in *Syntax and Semantics: Speech Acts,* v. 3, ed. P. Cole and J. Morgan, 41–58, here 45.

133. *DE,* 89; see "Wahrheitstheorien," 177–8, for an earlier formulation of these rules of argumentation.

134. See T. Scanlon, "Contractualism and Utilitarianism," in Sen and Williams, *Utilitarianism and Beyond,* 113–5, for a discussion of the problem of who participates in a contractual agreement.

135. See Jon Elster, *Sour Grapes* (New York: Cambridge University, 1983), for a discussion of this and other conceptions of the genesis of interests.

136. *Die Neue Unübersichtlichkeit,* 229, 241; and "Wahrheitstheorien," 174ff; see also Karl-Otto Apel, "The *A priori* of the Communication Community and the Foundation of Ethics," in *Towards A Transformation of Philosophy,* especially 276ff.

137. See his most recent formulation in his interview with T. Hviid Nielsen in Habermas, *Die nachholende Revolution* (Frankfurt: Suhrkamp, 1990), 131–3, especially 133: "Paradoxically stated, the regulative idea of the validity of utterances is

constitutive for the social facts that are brought about through communicative action" (my translation).

138. Ibid., 131.

139. "Reply," 235, and *DE*, 106.

140. See the various formulations in *DE*, 86, 92, 97, and *ME*, 198 n. 7.

141. Habermas thus differs from Apel on this point; see Apel, "The *A priori* of the Communication Community and the Foundation of Ethics" in *Towards a Transformation of Philosophy*, 258–62; Wellmer is correct to note that rules of argumentation should not be immediately regarded as moral norms, but he is mistaken in attributing this position to Habermas (see Wellmer, 102–13, 144–45).

142. This first consideration against viewing the rules of argumentation as constituting a moral principle is also emphasized by Stephen White (*The Recent Work of Jürgen Habermas*, 57); the second by Wellmer (144–45).

143. See *Communication and the Evolution of Society*, 66; *ME*, 199–200; *MCCA*, 170; and "Justice and Solidarity," *The Philosophical Forum* 21 (1989), 47–48. Stephen White also discusses the way in which for Habermas reciprocity functions as "the naturalistic kernal of moral consciousness" (*The Recent Work of Jürgen Habermas*, 58–65).

144. See *ME*, 198 n. 7.

145. "Contractualism and Utilitarianism," in Sen and Williams, *Utilitarianism and Beyond*.

146. Ibid., 107.

147. This question should also be distinguished from the question of why people don't always act in accordance with moral reasons which they acknowledge, that is, the problem of *akrasia*. The claim is rather that contractualism can provide reasons that are moral motivations; see also S. Darwall, *Impartial Reason* (Ithaca: Cornell University Press, 1983).

148. Scanlon, 110.

149. Ibid., 112: Contractualism "involves no specific claim as to which principles could be agreed to or even whether there is a unique set of principles which could be the basis of agreement."

150. See, for example, B. Williams, *Ethics and the Limits of Philosophy*, and, for a survey of the debate from the perspective of moral psychology, the essays collected in *The Moral Domain*, ed. T. Wren (Cambridge: MIT Press, 1989).

151. It would be a mistake, however, to say that discourse ethics is thus concerned only with the question of political legitimacy; the distinction between norma-

tive questions of justice (or morality) and evaluative questions of the good life is closer to Kant's distinction between *Rechtspflichte* and *Tugendpflichte* as this was presented in chapter 1, although even with respect to moral duties, discourse ethics is concerned only with the specification of a procedure through which they might be determined.

152. See, for example, J. B. Elshtain, *Public Man, Private Woman: Women in Social and Political Thought* (Princeton: Princeton University Press, 1981), and C. Pateman, "Feminist Critiques of the Public/Private Dichotomy," in *The Public and the Private,* ed. S. Benn and G. Gaus (London: St. Martin's, 1983), 281–303.

153. See *ME,* 206–7; "Justice and Solidarity," 50; and *Die neue Unübersichtlichkeit,* 237.

154. For criticisms, see Wellmer, *Ethik und Dialog;* R. Beiner, "Do We Need A Philosophical Ethics? Theory, Prudence, and the Primacy of Ethos," *The Philosophical Forum* 20 (1989): 230–243; and S. Benhabib, "In the Shadow of Aristotle and Hegel," *The Philosophical Forum* 21 (1989): 1–31. For my own interpretation of Aristotle's concept of *phronesis,* which I do not consider to be incompatible with Kant's account of practical reasoning, see "Dialectic and Deliberation in Aristotle's Practical Philosophy," *Southwest Philosophical Review* 6 (1990): 19–42.

155. Wellmer, 136–37.

156. In a response to Wellmer's critique, Klaus Günther has emphasized the importance of this restriction for the interpretation of Habermas's formulation of the principle of universalizability (p. 63ff.); Günther also makes a convincing argument that discourses about the justification of a norm will have to be complemented by discourses about the norm's application, see *Der Sinn für Angemessenheit. Anwendungsdiskurse in Moral und Recht* (Frankfurt: Suhrkamp, 1988).

157. See also Günther, 73f.

158. For some different formulations of this criticism, see Steven Lukes, "Of Gods and Demons: Habermas and Practical Reason," in *Habermas: Critical Debates,* 139–41; Walzer, *Interpretation and Social Criticism,* 11 n. 9; Iris Young, "Impartiality and the Civic Public," in *Feminism as Critique,* ed. S. Benhabib and D. Cornell (Minneapolis: University of Minnesota Press, 1987), 70–72; and Jean-Francois Lyotard, *The Post-Modern Condition* (Minneapolis: University of Minnesota Press, 1984).

159. I develop this point in more detail in "The Liberal/Communitarian Controversy and Communicative Ethics," 304ff.

160. See also Joshua Cohen, "Deliberation and Democratic Legitimacy," in *The Good Polity,* ed. Alan Hamlin and Philip Pettit (New York: Blackwell, 1989), 17–34.

NOTES TO CHAPTER FOUR

1. D. Parfit, "Later Selves and Moral Principles," in *Philosophy and Personal Relations,* ed. Alan Montefiore (London: Routledge and Kegan Paul, 1973), 137–69, and *Reasons and Persons* (New York: Oxford University Press, 1984).

2. *Proceedings and Addresses of the American Philosophical Association* 48 (1975): 5–22.

3. Ibid., 20; for a similar argument, see also Norman Daniels, "Moral Theory and the Plasticity of Persons," *The Monist* 62 (1979): 265–87.

4. Ibid., 19.

5. Ibid., 20.

6. For a further discussion of the cooperative relationship between philosophy and the empirical sciences, see Habermas, "Philosophy as Stand-In and Interpreter" in *Moral Consciousness and Communicative Action,* and the discussion in section 3, below.

7. See Samuel Scheffler, "Moral Independence and the Original Position," *Philosophical Studies* 35 (1979): 397–403, and "Ethics, Personal Identity and Ideals of the Person," *Canadian Journal of Philosophy* 12 (1982): 229–46.

8. This interpretation is also suggested by Seyla Benhabib, "The Methodological Illusions of Modern Political Theory," *Neue Hefte für Philosophie* 21 (1982): 47–74, and by Samuel Scheffler, "Moral Skepticism and Ideals of the Person," *The Monist* 62 (1979): 288–303.

9. For example, Benhabib sometimes criticizes the ideal, while at other times she seems to acknowledge the ideal and disagree more with its characterization in terms of the original position, see especially "The Generalized and the Concrete Other," *Praxis International* 5 (1986): 413, where, I believe, she conflates Rawls's model-conception of the person with the description of the parties in the original position.

10. Teitelman, "The Limits of Individualism," *Journal of Philosophy* 69 (1972): 545–56; Adina Schwartz, "Moral Neutrality and Primary Goods," *Ethics* 83 (1973): 294–307; and T. Nagel, "Rawls's Theory of Justice," in *Reading Rawls.*

11. "Reply to Lyons and Teitelman," *Journal of Philosophy* 69 (1972): 557; see also *TJ,* 584, and "Fairness to Goodness," *Philosophical Review* 81 (1975): 544, 550.

12. (New York: Cambridge University Press, 1982), 95.

13. In this context Sandel refers to Taylor's distinction between the self as a "simple weigher" and "strong evaluator" of preferences; see Taylor, "What is Human Agency?" in *Philosophical Papers,* v. I, 15–44.

14. Ibid., 180.

15. Ibid., 167, 180.

16. See MacIntyre, "How Moral Agents Have Become Ghosts," *Synthese* 53 (1982): 295–312; Sandel's description and critique of the "unencumbered self" is virtually the same as MacIntyre's critique of the emotivist self in *After Virtue* (Notre Dame, 1981), chap. 3.

17. Sandel, 179 and Taylor, "Self-Interpreting Animals," in *Philosophical Papers*, v. I, 45–76. Although Taylor has developed his model of human agency in more detail than Sandel, I do not see any significant differences in their positions— see my introduction to Taylor, "Overcoming Epistemology," in *After Philosophy*, ed. K. Baynes, J. Bohman, and T. McCarthy (Cambridge: MIT, 1987), 459–63.

18. Taylor, *Philosophical Papers*, v. I, 3.

19. See Rawls's own reservations about this in "Justice as Fairness: Political Not Metaphysical," *Philosophy and Public Affairs* 14 (1985): 239 n. 21.

20. See the essays collected in his *The Importance of What We Care About* (New York: Cambridge University Press, 1988); for an extremely helpful attempt to work out some of the problems raised by this hierarchical model, see Irving Thalberg, "Socialization and Autonomous Behavior," *Tulane Studies in Philosophy* 28 (1979): 21–39.

21. See Rawls's own description of the stages of moral development in *TJ*, 462ff.; and Habermas, *MCCA*.

22. Sandel, 78.

23. Ibid., 80; see also 132; in *Anarchy, State and Utopia*, Nozick offers a similar consideration: "Do people in the original position ever wonder whether *they* have the *right* to decide how everything is to be divided up? Perhaps they reason that since they are deciding this question, they must assume they are entitled to do so; and so particular people can't have particular entitlements to holdings (for then they wouldn't have the right to decide together on how all holdings are to be divided)," 199n.

24. Taylor suggests that the principle "to each according to his contribution" is in deep conflict with Rawls's notion that the distribution of natural talents and abilities are to be regarded as a common asset; see his "The Nature and Scope of Distributive Justice," in *Philosophical Papers*, v. II, 308.

25. See F. Hayek, "Equality, Value and Merit," in *The Essence of Hayek*, ed. C. Nishiyama and K. Leube (Stanford: Hoover Institute, 1984), 331–50, especially p. 340–41; and Daniel Bell, "On Equality," in *The Coming of Post-Industrial Society* (New York: Basic Books, 1973).

26. Taylor, "The Diversity of Goods," in *Philosophical Papers*, v. II, 233.

27. Ibid., 239f.

28. "Persons, Character and Morality," in *Moral Luck* (New York: Cambridge University Press, 1981), 19; see also his critique of Kant's notion of practical reason (or moral agency) in *Ethics and the Limits of Philosophy* (Cambridge: Harvard University Press, 1985), chap. 4.

29. For a careful assessment of William's position, see Barbara Herman, "Impartiality and Integrity," *The Monist* 66 (1983): 233–50, and Samuel Scheffler, "Morality Through Thick and Thin," *The Philosophical Review* 96 (1987): 411–34.

30. See *KC*, 545; and "Justice as Fairness: Political Not Metaphysical," 241.

31. "Rawls's Theory of Justice," in *Reading Rawls*, 178; and "Contractualism and Utilitarianism," in *Utilitarianism and Beyond*, ed. Sen and Williams (New York: Cambridge University Press, 1982).

32. "Contractualism and Utilitarianism," 121.

33. Ibid., 122.

34. See, for example, *DE*, 66, and *ME*, 198; most recently, see his characterization of the abstract normative core of socialism in *Die nachholende Revolution* (Frankfurt: Suhrkamp, 1990), 195.

35. Habermas, "Moral Development and Ego Identity," in *Communication and the Evolution of Society*, p.88.

36. "Justice and Solidarity," *The Philosophical Forum* 21 (1989): 35; see also *ME*.

37. For a more extensive discussion of Habermas's appropriation (and criticisms) of Kohlberg, see Stephen White, *The Recent Work of Jürgen Habermas*, chap. 4 and 5.

38. Kohlberg cites four general criteria for identifying hard Piagetian stages: they refer to structures, not functions; they represent an invariant sequence (i.e., there should be no regressions from higher to lower stages); the stages are structured wholes; and each higher stage comprehensively integrates and surpasses the preceding one. See "The Current Formulation of the Theory," in *Essays on Moral Development*, 2:236–50; for a similar characterization of Kohlberg's stages as hard or "natural" stages, see J. C. Gibbs, "Kohlberg's Stages of Moral Development: A Constructive Critique," *Harvard Educational Review* 47 (1977): 43–61, especially p. 44 and 47, where Gibbs claims that Piagetian stages also satisfy a fifth criterion, namely, that the development is one of "systems-in-action" and need not involve the conscious awareness of the agent. Gibbs then argues that only stages 1 through 4 in Kohlberg's theory satisfy all of these criteria.

39. See J. C. Gibbs, "Kohlberg's Stages of Moral Judgment: A Constructive Critique."

40. This suggestion is developed by Thomas McCarthy in "Rationality and Relativism: Habermas's Overcoming of Hermeneutics," in *Habermas: Critical*

Debates, 74; Habermas, in his reply in this volume, also embraces McCarthy's suggestion, 260.

41. See "Synopses and Detailed Replies to Critics," in *Essays in Moral Development,* 2:374–75, and his essay in *The Moral Domain,* ed. T. Wren (Cambridge: MIT Press, 1989).

42. "From Is to Ought," in *Essays in Moral Development,* 1:179; see also 104.

43. "The Claim to Moral Adequacy of a Highest Stage of Moral Judgment," *Journal of Philosophy* 70 (1973): 630–46, here 633; see also his statement in *Essays,* 2:223, 318, and his "Reply to Owen Flanagan," *Ethics* 92 (1982): 524–5.

44. Ibid., 634.

45. *Essays,* 2:225.

46. Ibid., 310.

47. *In A Different Voice: Psychological Theory and Women's Development* (Cambridge: Harvard University, 1982), 73f.; see also the similar criticism by Owen Flanagan, Jr., "Virtue, Sex and Gender: Some Philosophical Reflections on the Moral Psychology Debate," *Ethics* 92 (1982): 499–512.

48. Ibid., 69.

49. Ibid., 99f.

50. See his "Synopses and Detailed Replies to Critics," in *Essays,* 2:338–79; for a closer analysis and criticism of Kohlberg's responses, see Seyla Benhabib, "The Generalized and the Concrete Other: The Kohlberg-Gilligan Controversy and Feminist Theory." She interprets Kohlberg's responses as so many attempts to save a faltering research paradigm in moral psychology.

51. In addition to Kohlberg's own denial that his stages are sex-biased, the following studies also support that conclusion (although there is some debate about the research methods used in some of them): Anne Colby and William Damon, "Listening to a Different Voice: A Review of Gilligan's *In A Different Voice,*" *Merrill-Palmer Quarterly* 29 (1983): 473–81; Michael Pratt, Gail Golding, and William Hunter, "Does Morality Have a Gender? Sex, Sex Role and Moral Judgment: Relationships Across the Adult Lifespan," *Merrill-Palmer Quarterly* 30 (1984): 321–40; Judith Smetana, "Morality and Gender," *Merrill-Palmer Quarterly* 30 (1984): 341–48; and L. J. Walker, "Sex Differences in the Development of Moral Reasoning: A Critical Review," *Child Delvelopment* 55 (1984): 677–91. But, now see, D. Baumrind, "Sex Difference in Moral Reasoning," *Child Development* 57 (1986): 511–21.

52. Neither Kohlberg nor Gilligan seem to be of one mind about the characterization of their respective stages, see Owen Flanagan and Kathryn Jackson, "Justice, Care, and Gender: The Kohlberg-Gilligan Debate Revisited," *Ethics* 97 (1987): 622–37 and Bill Puka, "The Majesty and the Mystery of Stage 6," in *The Moral Domain,* 182–223.

53. *Essays,* 2:230.

54. See especially *Essays,* 2:248–9; in this connection Kohlberg also mentions his distinction between A and B substages within his own stages, see 534–6.

55. See ibid., 232.

56. *Essays,* 2:232; for a similar interpretation of Gilligan's work, see Gertrude Nunner-Winkler, "Two Moralities? A Critical Discussion of an Ethic of Care and Responsibility versus an Ethic of Rights and Justice," in *Morality, Moral Behavior and Moral Development,* ed. William Kurtines and Jacob Gewirtz (New York: John Wiley, 1984), 325–47.

57. For example, in "Moral Development and Ego Identity," he introduced the discourse ethic as a possible formulation of stage 7; however, in his more recent essays he reinterprets stage 5 as a stage of principled reasoning more generally, and equates stage 6 with the discourse ethic, see especially, *MCCA,* 172, and "Justice and Solidarity."

58. See especially "Reconstruction and Interpretation in the Social Sciences," in *Moral Consciousness and Communicative Action,* 33ff.; for a fuller account of Habermas's notion of a reconstructive science, see my "Rational Reconstruction and Social Criticism."

59. See especially *MCCA.*

60. See his discussion of Selman in *MCCA* and his discussion of the stages of social interaction in "The Development of the Self," [1977] in *Critical Theories of Psychological Development,* ed. John Broughton (New York: Plenum, 1987), 275–301.

61. See "Justice and Solidarity," 34–5.

62. T. McCarthy, "Rationality and Relativism," 74; see also "A Reply to My Critics," in Thompson and Held, 260, and *MCCA,* 173ff.

63. See especially "Justice and Solidarity," 46–48.

64. Ibid., 47–8.

65. See "Individuierung durch Vergesellschaftung," in *Nachmetaphysisches Denken* (Frankfurt: Suhrkamp, 1988), 187–241.

66. For a similar analysis of the relation between autonomy and socialization, see the extremely insightful study by Diana Meyers, *Self, Society, and Personal Choice* (New York: Columbia, 1989), as well as her earlier essay, "The Socialized Individual and Individual Autonomy," in *Women and Moral Theory,* ed. E. Kittay and D. Meyers (Totowa, N.J.: Rowman and Littlefield, 1987), 139–53; see also Robert Young, "Autonomy and Socialization," *Mind* 89 (1980): 565–76.

67. See *MCCA,* 116–194.

68. See Habermas's alternative characterization of the moral point of view in "Justice and Solidarity," 40.

69. For an analysis of some of the political implications of this insight, see Nancy Fraser, "Struggle over Needs: Outline of a Socialist-Feminist Critical Theory of Late Capitalist Political Culture," in *Unruly Practices* (Minneapolis: University of Minnesota Press, 1989), 161–187.

70. "Moral Development and Ego Identity," 93–4.

71. For this criticism, see Adina Schwartz, "Moral Neutrality and Primary Goods," *Ethics* 83 (1973): 294–307, and Sandel, ibid., 27; for a general discussion, see W. Sessions, "Rawls's Concept and Conception of Primary Goods," *Social Theory and Practice* 7 (1981): 303–24, in addition to Rawls's own extended and revised account in "Social Unity and Primary Goods," in *Utilitarianism and Beyond,* ed. Sen and Williams, 159–85.

72. "Social Unity and Primary Goods," 166.

73. Ibid., 166; see also 165 n. 5 for Rawls's explicit statement of this revision.

74. "Preference and Urgency," *Journal of Philosophy* 72 (1975): 655–69, here 656.

75. Ibid., 660.

76. Ibid., 668.

77. See Rawls's remarks in "Social Unity and Primary Goods," where he tentatively accepts Scanlon's account, 170 n. 10.

78. Ibid., 165–66.

79. For a similar formulation of this objection, see White, *The Recent Work of Jürgen Habermas,* 73–4. White defends discourse ethics by introducing a notion of "constrained indeterminism"; for my own attempt to defend discourse ethics against this criticism by introducing the idea of a variety of overlapping discourses, see "The Liberal/Communitarian Controversy and Communicative Ethics," 304f. and the discussion in chapter 3, above.

80. See Tom McCarthy, "Practical Discourse and the Relation Between Morality and Politics," in *Ideals and Illusions: On Reconstruction and Deconstruction in Contemporary Critical Theory* (Cambridge: MIT Press, 1991) and Nancy Fraser, "Struggle over Needs," in *Unruly Practices.*

NOTES TO CHAPTER FIVE

1. Some of Rawls's more recent remarks on the problem of justification *could* be read as moving in this direction, see, for example, "Kantian Constructivism," *Journal of Philosophy* 77 (1980): 516.

2. What I have in mind is hinted at in Rawls's remark (*KC*, 565) that as the knowledge ascribed to the parties in the OP changes, so too might the principles they choose there. Habermas also suggests that such a distinction is important and that Rawls's own theory might be fruitfully reconstructed along this line. See his remarks in "Life Forms, Morality and the Task of the Philosopher," in *Habermas: Autonomy and Solidarity*, ed. P. Dews (London: Verso, 1986), 204–5; for a similar remark about the importance of distinguishing between the procedure of legitimation and substantive proposals for social justice, see White, *The Recent Work of Jürgen Habermas*, 50.

3. See especially his remarks in "Justice as Fairness: Political not Metaphysical," *Philosophy and Public Affairs* 14 (1985): 229–30.

4. See especially Joshua Cohen, "Deliberation and Democratic Legitimacy," in *The Good Polity*, ed. Alan Hamlin and Philip Pettit (New York: Blackwell, 1989), 17–34.

5. "Justice as Fairness: Political not Metaphysical," 225.

6. See V. Held, *Rights and Goods: Justifying Social Action* (New York: Free Press, 1984), 127; on negative and positive liberty, see—in addition to I. Berlin's "Two Concepts of Liberty," in his *Four Essays on Liberty*—C. Taylor, "What's Wrong with Negative Liberty?" in his *Philosophical Papers*, 2:211–29, and W. Parent, "Some Recent Work on the Concept of Liberty," *American Philosophical Quarterly* 11 (1974): 149–67.

7. "Justice as Fairness," in *Philosophy, Politics and Society*, 2d ser., ed. P. Laslett and W. Runciman (Oxford: Blackwell, 1962), 132–57, here 133.

8. H. L. A. Hart, "Rawls on Liberty and Its Priority," in *Reading Rawls*, ed. Norman Daniels (New York: Basic Books, 1975), 234–6.

9. See R. Dworkin, "What Rights Do We Have?" in *Taking Rights Seriously*, for a similar objection to the notion of a general right to liberty.

10. J. Feinberg, "Rawls and Intuitionism," in *Reading Rawls;* and N. Bowie, "Equal Basic Liberty For All," in *John Rawls's Theory of Social Justice*, ed. H. Blocker and E. Smith (Athens: Ohio University Press, 1980).

11. R. Wolff, *Understanding Rawls* (Princeton: Princeton University Press, 1977), 91; see also N. Daniels, "Liberty and Its Worth," in *Reading Rawls*.

12. See also Rawls's remarks about the justification of "constitutional essentials," in "The Domain of the Political," 252f.; for a proceduralist view of constitutional interpretation, see J. Ely, *Democracy and Distrust* (Harvard, 1980); for a view of constitutional interpretation based on the notion of protecting processes of democratic will-formation, see G. Frankenburg and U. Rödel, *Von der Volkssouveränität zum Minderheitenschutz* (Frankfurt: Europäische Verlag, 1981), and, for a more general argument about the need to relate constitutional interpretation to moral principles of justification, see Habermas, "Law and Morality: Two Lectures," *The Tanner Lec-*

tures on Human Values, v. 8, trans. K. Baynes (Cambridge: Harvard University Press, 1988), 217–79.

13. For Rawls's fullest discussion of primary social goods, see "Social Unity and Primary Goods," in *Utilitarianism and Beyond*, ed. A. Sen and B. Williams (New York: Cambridge University Press, 1982), 159–85.

14. Ibid., 163; see also A. Gibbard, "Disparate Goods and Rawls's Difference Principle," *Theory and Decision* 11 (1979): 267–72; and J. Arrow, "Some Ordinalist-Utilitarian Notes on Rawls's Theory of Justice," *Journal of Philosophy* 70 (1973): 252–4.

15. In view of this interpretation it is also not surprising that Rawls states that the "simplest form" cannot settle the question of whether private property capitalism or democratic socialism will provide a more equitable distribution of social goods (*TJ*, 163).

16. *TJ*, 7; Rawls, "The Basic Structure as Subject," in *Values and Morals*, ed. A. Goldman and J. Kim (Boston: Reidel, 1978), 47–71; and H. Bedau, "Social Justice and Social Institutions," *Midwest Studies in Philosophy* 3 (1978): 159–75.

17. See also B. Barber, "The Absolutization of the Market: Some Notes on How We Got From There to Here," and T. Scanlon, "Liberty, Contract and Contribution," both in *Markets and Morals*, ed. G. Dworkin, et al. (New York: Halsted Press, 1977).

18. See D. Bell, "Equality and Merit," in *The Coming of Post-Industrial Society* (New York: Basic Books, 1973), and R. Nozick, *Anarchy, State and Utopia* (New York: Basic Books, 1974).

19. See W. Narr, "The Welfare-State as an Expression of Crisis—Not Its Solution," *Praxis International* 6 (1986): 21–31; *Liberalism Reconsidered*, ed. D. MacLean and C. Mills (N.J.: Rowman and Littlefield, 1983); *The Development of the Welfare State in Europe and America*, ed. P. Flora (London: Transaction Books, 1981); R. Mishra, *The Welfare State in Crisis* (NJ: Harvester Press, 1984); and *Democracy and the Welfare State*, ed. A. Gutman (Princeton: Princeton University Press, 1988).

20. This can be viewed as a variant of the "social limits to growth" thesis developed by F. Hirsch in *Social Limits to Growth* (Cambridge: Harvard University Press, 1976); see also, *Dilemmas of Liberal Democracies*, ed. A. Ellis and K. Kumar (London: Tavistock, 1983).

21. See Michael Harrington, *The New American Poverty* (New York: Holt, Rinehart and Winston, 1984), and R. Cloward and F. Piven, *Regulating the Poor: The Functions of Public Welfare* (New York: Vintage, 1972).

22. R. Unger, *Law in Modern Society* (New York: Free Press, 1976); *Dilemmas of Law in the Welfare State*, ed. G. Teubner (New York: de Gruyter, 1985); and *Alternative Rechtsformen und Alternativen zum Recht*, ed. E. Blankenburg (Opladen, 1980).

23. For a discussion of this problem with respect to school and family law, see *TCA* 2:368ff.; more generally, see "Law and Morality."

24. G. Teubner, "Substantive and Reflexive Elements in Modern Law," *Law and Society Review* 17 (1983): 239–85; P. Nonet and P. Selznick, *Law and Society in Transition: Toward A Responsive Law* (New York: Harper, 1978), and R. Unger, *Law in Modern Society.*

25. See "Law and Morality: Two Lectures"; for an instructive discussion of Habermas's views, see Ulrich Preuss, "Rationality Potentials of Law—Allocative, Distributive and Communicative Rationality," in *Critical Legal Thought: An American-German Debate,* ed. C. Joerges and D. Trubek (Baden-Baden, 1989), 525–56.

26. These brief remarks are, no doubt, insufficient for clarifying these difficult issues; for further discussion, see Nancy Fraser, "Women, Welfare, and the Politics of Need Interpretation," in *Unruly Practices;* Frances Olson, "The Family and the Market," *Harvard Law Review* 96 (1983); and Ulrich Preuss, "Rationality Potentials of Law."

27. Hart, in Daniels, 252.

28. A. Gutmann, *Liberal Equality* (New York: Cambridge University Press, 1980), 175–6.

29. C. Pateman, *The Problem of Political Obligation: A Critical Analysis of Liberal Theory* (New York: Wiley, 1979), 133.

30. See, now, Rawls, "The Priority of Right and Ideas of the Good," *Philosophy and Public Affairs* 17 (1988): 251–76.

31. For a critique of Rawls's treatment of political obligation, see C. Pateman, *The Problem of Political Obligation,* chap. 6, and A. J. Simmons, *Moral Principles and Political Obligations,* (Princeton: Princeton University Press, 1979), chap. 6; for a brief history of the idea of citizenship, see M. Walzer, "Citizenship," in *Conceptual Innovations,* ed. T. Ball (New York: Cambridge University Press, 1987).

32. See C. Offe, "Legitimation Through Majority Rule?" in *Disorganized Capitalism* (Cambridge: MIT Press, 1985), 259–99, and Arthur Kuflik, "Majority-Rule Procedure," in *Due Process (Nomos,* v. 18), ed. J. R. Pennock and J. Chapman (New York: New York University Press, 1977), 296–32.

33. See P. Schmitter, "Democratic Theory and Neocorporatist Practice," *Social Research* 50 (1983): 889.

34. For an excellent discussion of this problem, see C. Offe, "Competitive Party Democracy and the Keynesian Welfare State," *Policy Sciences* 15 (1983): 225–40, especially p. 232–3.

35. See, for example, the introduction and essays in *Organizing Interests in Western Europe: Pluralism, Corporatism, and the Transformation of Politics,* ed. Suzanne Berger (New York: Cambridge University Press, 1981).

36. See, for example, the essays in *Trends Toward Corporatist Intermediation*, ed. P. Schmitter and G. Lehmbruch (Beverly Hills: SAGE, 1979); *Patterns of Corporatist Policy-Making*, ed. G. Lehmbruch and P. Schmitter (Beverly Hills: SAGE, 1982); *Organizing Interests in Western Europe: Pluralism, Corporatism and the Transformation of Politics*, ed. Suzanne Berger (New York: Cambridge University Press, 1981); and Alan Cawson, *Corporatism and Political Theory* (London: Blackwell, 1986).

37. See G. Heiman, "The Sources and Significance of Hegel's Corporate Doctrine," in *Hegel's Political Philosophy*, ed. Pelczynski (New York: Cambridge University Press, 1971), 111–35, and my "State and Civil Society in Hegel's *Philosophy of Right*," *Cardozo Law Review* 3 (1989).

38. See especially P. Schmitter, "Democratic Practice and Neo-Corporatist Practice," *Social Research* 50 (1983).

39. "Interest Intermediation and Regime Governability in Contemporary Western Europe and North America," in *Organizing Interests in Western Europe*, ed. S. Berger, 285–327, here 295.

40. "Introduction," to *Organized Interests and the State: Studies in Meso-Corporatism*, ed. Alan Cawson (Beverly Hills: SAGE, 1985), 8.

41. See Charles Sabel, "The Internal Politics of Trade Unions," in *Organizing Interests in Western Europe*, ed. S. Berger, 299–44.

42. See Offe, "The Attribution of Public Status to Interest Groups: Observations on the West German Case," in S. Berger, 123–58; and "Korporatismus als System nichtstaatlichen Makrosteuerung?," 247; and L. Panitch, "The Development of Corporatism in Liberal Democracies," *Comparative Policy Studies* 10 (1977): 61–90.

43. Offe, ibid.; see also A. Cawson, *Corporatism and Welfare* (London: Heinemann, 1982), and "Functional Representation and Democratic Politics: Towards a Corporatist Democracy?" in *Democratic Theory and Practice*, ed. G. Duncan (New York: Cambridge University Press, 1983), 173–84.

44. See, for example, P. Schmitter, "Democratic Theory and Neocorporatist Practice," and J. Habermas, *Legitimation Crisis*, pt. 3.

45. For a helpful discussion of the liberal public/private distinction in connection with recent corporatist theory, see G. Gauss, "Public and Private Interests in Liberal Political Economy, Old and New," in *Public and Private in Social Life*, ed. S. Benn and G. Gauss (New York: St. Martin's Press, 1983), 183–223.

46. See especially Joshua Cohen, "Deliberation and Democratic Legitimacy"; Noberto Bobbio, *The Future of Democracy* (Minneapolis: University of Minnesota, 1987); Bernard Manin, "On Legitimacy and Political Deliberation," *Political Theory* 15 (1987): 338–68; Frank Michelman, "Law's Republic," *Yale Law Journal* 97 (1988): 1493–1537; and Cass Sunstein, "Beyond the Republican Revival," *Yale Law Journal* 97 (1988): 1539–90.

47. For a similar argument see Jean Cohen, "Why More Political Theory?" *Telos* 40 (1979): 70–94; see also Jean Cohen and Andrew Arato, *Civil Society and Social Theory* (Cambridge: MIT Press, 1991).

48. *The Structural Transformation of the Public Sphere*, trans. T. Burger (Cambridge: MIT, 1989), 27–8.

49. Habermas has always maintained that this idea of the public sphere was an ideology insofar as it was limited by considerations of class and gender; however, to the extent this idea also played a role in limiting political authority and securing constitutional rights his claim is that it was "simultaneously more than mere ideology" (p. 88). Still, even this *idea* of the bourgeois public sphere has been challenged in view of the rhetorical uses to which it has been put and the gender biases which it apparently harbors; see Joan Landes, *Women and the Public Sphere in the Age of the French Revolution* (Ithaca: Cornell University Press, 1988). However accurate some of these criticisms may be historically, their normative significance (it seems to me) must finally be judged in light of the alternative proposals for political change that they generate.

50. Kant's distinction is idiosyncratic precisely because it aligns the "public" use of reason with a person's "private" status—the "private" use of reason, by contrast, is tied to a person's public or civil office; see also Onora O'Neill, "The Public Use of Reason," *Political Theory* 14 (1986): 523–551, and John Laursen, "The Subversive Kant: The Vocabulary of 'Public' and 'Publicity'," *Political Theory* 14 (1986): 584–603.

51. Its realization, he writes, "should not be impossible on structural grounds" (p. 234), and "can today no longer be disqualified as simply utopian" (p. 235); neither formulation, however, reflects much optimism or confidence.

52. At one point he cites a suggestion that "the state's political bureaucracy" might be limited by "society's political bureaucracy" so long as this process is itself checked by a "quasi-parliamentary deliberation" (p. 234). This position suggests a more "etatistic" conception of socialism than in his later writings; see also J. Cohen and A. Arato, "Politics and the Reconstruction of the Concept of Civil Society," in *Zwischenbetrachtungen*, ed. A. Wellmer, T. McCarthy, A. Honneth, and K. Offe (Frankfurt: Suhrkamp, 1989), 482–503.

53. This is clear, for example, from his remark that Rousseau conflates the question of legitimacy with the question of institutional design, even though Habermas then makes no attempt to address the latter issue. For a similar criticism, see Jean Cohen, "Why More Political Theory?" and Philip Lawrence, "The State and Legitimation: The Work of Jürgen Habermas," in *Capitalism and the Democratic State*, ed. Duncan Graeme (New York: Cambridge University Press, 1988), 133–158.

54. For a fuller discussion of Habermas's two-tiered model of society as "lifeworld" and "system" see my "Rational Reconstruction and Social Criticism: Habermas's Model of Interpretive Social Science," *The Philosophical Forum;* Stephen

White, *The Recent Work of Jürgen Habermas,* chap. 5; and various essays in *Communicative Action,* ed. A. Honneth and H. Joas (Cambridge: Mit Press, 1991).

55. Despite certain parallels, it is important that this distinction not be too closely identified with Habermas's distinction between communicative and strategic action. As Habermas has recently emphasized, the system/lifeworld distinction becomes misleading if it is understood to imply two mutually exclusive domains of action: a sphere of pure strategic action, on the one hand, and a power-free sphere of communicative action on the other (see "A Reply," *Communicative Action,* ed. Honneth and Joas, 250–57). Power dynamics and strategic action exist within the institutions of the lifeworld, just as normatively secured or consensual action is found within the subsystems of the economy and the administrative state. Nancy Fraser's discovery of a "gender subtext" in the system/lifeworld distinction is, I believe, at least in part due to an over identification of this distinction with the distinction between two types of action (cf. "What's Critical About Critical Theory? Habermas and the Case of Gender," in *Unruly Practices*). Habermas's location of the family within the lifeworld is certainly not intended to imply that it is a power-free institution based on purely communicative or consensual relations.

56. For a discussion of these general modes of interpenetration, see Richard Münch, *Theory of Action: Towards A New Synthesis Going Beyond Parsons* (London: Routledge and Kegan Paul, 1987), 35ff.

57. According to Habermas, the rationalization of the lifeworld along these lines proceeds only to the extent that symbolic reproduction comes to rely more upon the interpretive accomplishments of participants who reciprocally raise and redeem the formal validity claims inherent in their communicative practices than upon a preexisting "normatively *ascribed* agreement" (1:340). For this reason while such differentiation "signals a release of the rationality potential inherent in communicative action" (2:146), it also brings about a situation in which symbolic reproduction is increasingly fragile and risk-filled.

58. In the following I am indebted to Andrew Arato and Jean Cohen, "Politics and the Reconstruction of the Concept of Civil Society," in *Zwischenbetruchtungen,* ed. Wellmer, et al.; see also my brief remarks in "State and Civil Society in Hegel's *Philosophy of Right.*"

59. "The New Obscurity: The Crisis of the Welfare State and the Exhaustion of Utopian Energies," in *The New Conservatism* (Cambridge: MIT Press, 1989), 64; Habermas, "Volkssouveränität als Verfahren," in *Die Ideen von 1789,* ed. Forum für Philosophie (Frankfurt: Suhrkamp, 1989), 28ff.

60. See "The New Obscurity," 64, and "Die nachholende Revolution," 199.

61. "The New Obscurity," 63; "Volkssouveränität," 28f.; see also C. Offe, "Fessel und Bremse: Moralische und institutionelle Aspekte 'intelligenter Selbstbeschränkung'," in *Zwischenbetrachtungen,* 739–774.

62. "Volkssouveränität," 30–31; "Die nachholende Revolution," 199.

63. "The New Obscurity," 67.

64. See "Volkssouveränität," 31; and "Die nachholende Revolution," 199.

65. Ibid.

66. See Habermas, "Law and Morality," 217–79 and *Faktizität und Geltung* (Frankfurt: Suhrkamp, forthcoming).

67. "Volkssouveränität," 31; "Die nachholende Revolution," 199.

68. For a similar proposal (and critique of alternative positions) see Frank Michelman, "Traces of Self-Government," *Harvard Law Review* 100 (1986): 4–77, especially p. 54ff.

69. See Jeremy Waldron, "Introduction," to *Theories of Rights* (New York: Oxford University Press, 1984), 20; see also his "Theoretical Foundations of Liberalism," *The Philosophical Quarterly* 37 (1987): 127–150 (where he argues that liberalism is best understood as a theory of justification in which "the social order should in principle be capable of explaining itself at the tribunal of each person's understanding").

70. See, for example, "The Domain of the Political and Overlapping Consensus," 244.

BIBLIOGRAPHY

Alexander, Sidney. "Social Evaluation Through Notional Choice," *Quarterly Journal of Economics* 88 (1974): 597–625.

Ameriks, Karl. "Kant's Deduction of Freedom and Morality," *Journal of the History of Philosophy* 19 (1981): 53–79.

Apel, Karl-Otto, ed. *Sprachpragmatik und Philosophie*. Frankfurt: Suhrkamp, 1976.

Apel, Karl-Otto. *Towards a Transformation of Philosophy*. London: Routledge and Kegan Paul, 1980.

Arato, Andrew, and Jean Cohen. *Civil Society and Social Theory*. Cambridge: MIT Press, 1991.

Aune, Bruce. *Kant's Theory of Morals*. Princeton: Princeton University Press, 1979.

Austin, J. L. *How To Do Things With Words*. Cambridge: Harvard University Press, 1962.

Baynes, Kenneth, James Bohman, and Thomas McCarthy, eds. *After Philosophy: End or Transformation?* Cambridge: MIT Press, 1987.

Baynes, Kenneth. "The Liberal/Communitarian Controversy and Communicative Ethics," *Philosophy and Social Criticism* 14 (1988): 293–313. Reprinted in Rasmussen.

Baynes, Kenneth. "Rational Reconstruction and Social Criticism: Habermas's Model of Interpretive Social Science," *The Philosophical Forum* 21 (1989): 122–45. Reprinted in Kelly.

Baynes, Kenneth. "Dialectic and Deliberation in Aristotle's Practical Philosophy," *Southwest Philosophy Review* 6 (1990): 19–42.

Beck, L. W. "Kant and the Right of Revolution," *Journal of the History of Ideas* 32 (1971): 411–22.

Benhabib, Seyla. "The Methodological Illusions of Modern Political Theory: The Case of Rawls and Habermas," *Neue Hefte für Philosophie* 21 (1982): 47–74.

Benhabib, Seyla. *Critique, Norm and Utopia: A Study of the Foundations of Critical Theory*. New York: Columbia University Press, 1986.

Benhabib, Seyla. "The Generalized and the Concrete Other: The Kohlberg-Gilligan Controversy and Feminist Theory," *Praxis International* 5 (1986): 402–24.

Benhabib, Seyla. "In The Shadow of Aristotle and Hegel: Communicative Ethics and Current Controversies in Practical Philosophy," *The Philosophical Forum* 21 (1989): 1–31. Reprinted in Kelly.

Benhabib, Seyla, and Fred Dallmayr, eds. *The Communicative Ethics Controversy.* Cambridge: MIT Press, 1990.

Bennett, Jonathan. "The Meaning-Nominalist Strategy," *Foundations of Language* 10 (1973): 141–68.

Berlin, Isaiah, ed. *Essays on J. L. Austin.* Oxford: Clarendon Press, 1973.

Bernstein, Richard, ed. *Habermas and Modernity.* Cambridge: MIT Press, 1985.

Bird, Graham. "Austin's Theory of Illocutionary Force," *Midwest Studies in Philosophy* 6 (1981): 345–69.

Bittner, Rüdiger. "Maximen." In *Akten des 4. Internationalen Kant Kongresses,* ed. by V. G. Funke, 485–98. Berlin: de Gruyter, 1974.

Blackburn, Simon. *Spreading the Word: Groundings in the Philosophy of Language.* Oxford: Clarendon Press, 1984.

Blocker, H. Gene, and Elizabeth H. Smith, eds. *John Rawls' Theory of Social Justice: An Introduction.* Athens, OH: Ohio University Press, 1980.

Brandt, Reinhard, ed. *Rechtsphilosophie der Aufklärung.* Berlin: de Gruyter, 1982.

Buchanan, Allen. "Revisability and Rational Choice," *Canadian Journal of Philosophy* 5 (1975): 395–408.

Cohen, L. J. "Do Illocutionary Forces Exist?" *Philosophical Quarterly* 14 (1964): 118–37.

Cohen, Jean. "Why More Political Theory?" *Telos* 40 (1979): 70–94.

Cohen, Joshua. "Deliberation and Democratic Legitimacy." In *The Good Polity,* ed. by Alan Hamlin and Philip Pettit, 17–34. New York: Blackwell, 1989.

Daniels, Norman, ed. *Reading Rawls: Critical Studies of a Theory of Justice.* New York: Basic Books, 1975.

Daniels, Norman. "Moral Theory and the Plasticity of Persons," *The Monist* 62 (1979): 265–87.

Daniels, Norman. "Wide Reflective Equilibrium and Theory Acceptance in Ethics," *Journal of Philosophy* 76 (1979): 256–82.

Daniels, Norman. "On Some Methods of Ethics and Linguistics," *Philosophical Studies* 37 (1980): 21–36.

Daniels, Norman. "Reflective Equilibrium and Archimedean Points," *Canadian Journal of Philosophy* 10 (1980): 83–103.

Davidson, Donald. *Inquiries into Truth and Interpretation.* Oxford: Clarendon Press, 1984.

Dews, Peter, ed. *Habermas: Autonomy and Solidarity.* London: Verso, 1986.

Dummett, Michael. "What Does the Appeal to Use Do for the Theory of Meaning?" In *Meaning and Use,* ed. by A. Margalit, 123–35. Boston: Reidel, 1979.

Dworkin, Ronald. *Taking Rights Seriously.* Cambridge: Harvard University Press, 1978.

Evans, Gareth, and J. McDowell, eds. *Truth and Meaning: Essays in Semantics.* Oxford: Clarendon Press, 1976.

Fraser, Nancy. *Unruly Practices: Power, Discourse and Gender in Contemporary Social Theory.* Minneapolis: University of Minnesota Press, 1989.

Freeman, Samuel. "Reason and Agreement in Social Contract Views," *Philosophy and Public Affairs* 19 (1990): 122–57.

Gauthier, David. "The Social Contract as Ideology," *Philosophy and Public Affairs* 6 (1977): 130–64.

Gibbard, Alan. "Disparate Goods and Rawls' Difference Principle," *Theory and Decision* 11 (1979): 267–72.

Gibson, Mary. "Rationality," *Philosophy and Public Affairs* 6 (1977): 193–225.

Gilligan, Carol. *In A Different Voice: Psychological Theory and Women's Development.* Cambridge: Harvard University Press, 1982.

Gregor, Mary. *Laws of Freedom: A Study of Kant's Method of Applying the Categorical Imperative in the 'Metaphysik der Sitten'* Oxford: Blackwell, 1963.

Grice, H. P. "Meaning," *The Philosophical Review* 66 (1957): 377–88.

Grice, H. P. "Utterer's Meaning and Intentions," *The Philosophical Review* 78 (1969): 147–77.

Grice, H. P. "Meaning Revisited." In *Mutual Knowledge,* ed. by N. U. Smith, 223–43. New York: Academic Press, 1982.

Günther, Klaus. *Der Sinn für Angemessenheit. Anwendungsdiskurse in Moral und Recht.* Frankfurt: Suhrkamp, 1988.

Gutmann, Amy. *Liberal Equality.* New York: Cambridge University Press, 1980.

Habermas, Jürgen. *Toward A Rational Society.* Trans. by Jeremy Shapiro. Boston: Beacon Press, 1970.

Habermas, Jürgen. "Social Identity," *Telos* 7 (1974): 112–35.

Habermas, Jürgen. *Legitimation Crisis.* Trans. by Thomas McCarthy. Boston: Beacon Press, 1975.

Habermas, Jürgen. "Some Distinctions in Universal Pragmatics," *Theory and Society* 3 (1976): 155–67.

Habermas, Jürgen. "Aspects of the Rationality of Action." In *Proceedings of the International Symposium on 'Rationality Today',* ed. by T. Geraets, 185–205. University of Ottawa, 1979.

Habermas, Jürgen. *Communication and the Evolution of Society.* Trans. by Thomas McCarthy. Boston: Beacon Press, 1979.

Habermas, Jürgen. "History and Evolution," *Telos* 39 (1979): 5–44.

Habermas, Jürgen. "The Entwinement of Myth and Enlightenment: Re-reading Dialectic of Enlightenment," *New German Critique* 32 (1982): 13–30.

Habermas, Jürgen. *The Theory of Communicative Action,* v. 1 and 2. Trans. by Thomas McCarthy. Boston: Beacon Press, 1984, 1987.

Habermas, Jürgen. "Über Moralität und Sittlichkeit: Was macht eine Lebensform 'rational'?" In *Rationalität,* ed. by H. Schnädelbach, 218–35. Frankfurt: Suhrkamp, 1984.

Habermas, Jürgen. *Vorstudien und Ergänzungen zur Theorie des kommunikativen Handelns.* Frankfurt: Suhrkamp, 1984.

Habermas, Jürgen. *Die neue Unübersichtlichkeit.* Frankfurt: Suhrkamp, 1985.

Habermas, Jürgen. "Remarks on the Concept of Communicative Action." In *Social Action,* ed. by G. Seebass and R. Tuomela, 151–78. New York: Reidel, 1985.

Habermas, Jürgen. *The Philosophical Discourse of Modernity.* Trans. by Frederick Lawrence. Cambridge: MIT Press, 1987.

Habermas, Jürgen. *Nachmetaphysiches Denken.* Frankfurt: Suhrkamp, 1988.

Habermas, Jürgen. "Law and Morality: Two Lectures." In *The Tanner Lectures on Human Values,* v. 8; ed. by S. McMurrin, trans. by Kenneth Baynes, 217–79. Cambridge: Harvard University Press, 1988.

Habermas, Jürgen. "Ist der Herzschlag der Revolution zum Stillstand gekommen? Volkssouveränität als Verfahren." In *Die Ideen von 1789*, ed. by Forum für Philosophie Bad Homburg, 7–36. Frankfurt: Suhrkamp, 1989.

Habermas, Jürgen. *The New Conservatism: Cultural Criticism and the Historian's Debate*. Trans. by Shierry Weber Nicholsen. Cambridge: MIT Press, 1989.

Habermas, Jürgen. "Justice and Solidarity," *The Philosophical Forum* 21 (1989): 32–53. Reprinted in Kelly.

Habermas, Jürgen. *The Structural Transformation of the Public Sphere*. Trans. by Thomas Burger. Cambridge: MIT Press, 1989.

Habermas, Jürgen. *Moral Consciousness and Communicative Action*. Trans. by Christian Lenhardt and Shierry Weber Nicholsen. Cambridge: MIT Press, 1990.

Habermas, Jürgen. *Die nachholende Revolution*. Frankfurt: Suhrkamp, 1990.

Hampton, Jean. "Contracts and Choices: Does Rawls Have a Social Contract Theory?" *Journal of Philosophy* 77 (1980): 315–88.

Hart, H. L. A. "Rawls on Liberty and its Priority." In *Reading Rawls: Critical Studies of A Theory of Justice*, ed. by Norman Daniels, 230–52. New York: Basic Books, 1975.

Henrich, Dieter. "Der Begriff der sittlichen Einsicht und Kants Lehre vom Faktum der Vernunft." In *Die Gegenwart der Griechen im neueren Denken*, ed. by D. Henrich, et al., 77–115. Tübingen, 1960.

Henrich, Dieter. "Die Deduktion des Sittengesetzes." In *Denken im Schatten des Nihilismus*, ed. by Alexander Schwan, 55–112. Darmstadt: Wissenschaftliche Buchgesellschaft, 1975.

Henrich, Dieter. "Ethik der Autonomie." In *Selbstverhältnisse*, 1–56. Stuttgart: Reclam, 1982.

Höffe, Otfried. "Zur vertragstheoretischen Begründung politischer Gerechtigkeit: Hobbes, Kant und Rawls im Vergleich." In *Ethik und Politik*, 195–226. Frankfurt: Suhrkamp, 1979.

Holdcroft, David. *Words and Deeds: Problems in the Theory of Speech Acts*. Oxford: Clarendon Press, 1978.

Honneth, Axel, and Hans Joas, eds. *Communicative Action*. Trans. by J. Gaines and D. L. Jones. Cambridge: MIT Press, 1991.

Honneth, Axel. *The Critique of Power*. Trans. by Kenneth Baynes. Cambridge: MIT Press, 1991.

Howard, Dick. "Kant's Political Theory: The Virtue of his Vices," *Review of Metaphysics* 34 (1980): 325–50.

Kant, Immanuel. *Critique of Judgement*. Trans. by J. C. Meredith. Oxford: Clarendon, 1952.

Kant, Immanuel. *Critique of Practical Reason*. Trans. by L. W. Beck. Indianapolis: Bobbs-Merrill, 1956.

Kant, Immanuel. *Religion Within the Limits of Reason Alone*. Trans. by T. Greene. New York: Harper & Row, 1960.

Kant, Immanuel. *The Doctrine of Virtue*. Trans. by Mary Gregor. New York: Harper and Row, 1964.

Kant, Immanuel. *Groundwork of the Metaphysic of Morals.* Trans. by H. J. Paton. New York: Harper and Row, 1964.

Kant, Immanuel. *Critique of Pure Reason.* Trans. by N. Kemp Smith. New York: St. Martin's Press, 1965.

Kant, Immanuel. *The Metaphysical Elements of Justice.* Trans. by J. Ladd. Indianapolis: Bobbs-Merrill, 1966.

Kant, Immanuel. *Metaphysik der Sitten.* Hamburg: Meiner, 1966.

Kant, Immanuel. *Anthropology From A Pragmatic Point of View.* Trans. by Mary J. Gregor. The Hague: Martinus Nijhoff, 1974.

Kant, Immanuel. *The Conflict of the Faculties.* Trans. by Mary Gregor. New York: Abaris Books, 1979.

Kelly, Michael, ed. *Hermeneutics and Critical Theory in Ethics and Politics.* Cambridge: MIT Press, 1990.

Kersting, Wolfgang. "Freiheit und intelligibler Besitz: Kants Lehre vom synthetischen Rechtssatz *a priori,*" *Allgemeine Zeitschrift für Philosophie* 6 (1982): 31–51.

Kersting, Wolfgang. "Transzendentalphilosophische und naturrechtliche Eigentumsbegründung," *Archiv für Rechts- und Sozialphilosophie* 67 (1981): 157–75.

Kersting, Wolfgang. "Kant und der staatsphilosophische Kontraktualismus," *Allgemeine Zeitschrift für Philosophie* 8 (1983): 1–27.

Kersting, Wolfgang. *Wohlgeordnete Freiheit. Immanuel Kants Rechts und Staatsphilosophie.* Berlin: de Gruyter, 1983.

Kohlberg, Lawrence. *Essays on Moral Development,* v. 1 and 2. New York: Harper & Row, 1981, 1984.

Krieger, Leonard. *The German Idea of Freedom: History of a Political Tradition from the Reformation to 1871.* Chicago: University of Chicago Press, 1957.

Landes, Joan. *Women and the Public Sphere in the Age of the French Revolution.* Ithaca: Cornell University Press, 1988.

Larmore, Charles. *Patterns of Moral Complexity.* Cambridge: Cambridge University Press, 1987.

Lehmann, Gerhard. "Kants Besitzlehre." In *Beiträge zur Geschichte und Interpretation der Philosophie Kants.* Berlin: de Gruyter, 1969.

Lepore, E. and R. von Gulick, eds. *John Searle and His Critics.* New York: Basil Blackwell, 1991.

MacPherson, C. B. *The Political Theory of Possessive Individualism.* New York: Oxford University Press, 1964.

Manin, Bernard. "On Legitimacy and Political Deliberation," *Political Theory* 15 (1987): 338–68.

Martin, Rex. *Rawls and Rights.* Lawrence: University of Kansas Press, 1985.

Martinich, A. P. *Communication and Reference.* New York: de Gruyter, 1984.

McCarthy, Thomas. *The Critical Theory of Jürgen Habermas.* Cambridge: MIT Press, 1978.

McCarthy, Thomas. "Reflections on Rationalization in the Theory of Communicative Action," *Praxis International* 4 (1984): 177–91. Reprinted in Bernstein.

McCarthy, Thomas. "Complexity and Democracy, or the Seducements of Systems Theory," *New German Critique* 35 (1985): 27–53. Reprinted in McCarthy 1991.

McCarthy, Thomas. *Ideals and Illusions: On Reconstruction and Deconstruction in Contemporary Critical Theory.* Cambridge: MIT Press, 1991.

Meyers, Diana. *Self, Society, and Personal Choice.* New York: Columbia University Press, 1989.

Michelman, Frank. "Law's Republic," *Yale Law Journal* 97 (1988): 1493–1537.

Nell, Onora. *Acting on Principle: An Essay on Kantian Ethics.* New York: Columbia University Press, 1975.

Nielsen, Kai, and Roger Shiner, eds. *New Essays on Contract Theory: Canadian Journal of Philosophy.* (1977) Supplementary Volume 3.

O'Neill, Onora. *Constructions of Reason.* New York: Cambridge University Press, 1989.

Offe, Claus. *Contradictions in the Welfare State.* Cambridge: MIT Press, 1983.

Offe, Claus. *Disorganized Capitalism.* Cambridge: MIT Press, 1985.

Parfit, Derek. "Later Selves and Moral Principles." In *Philosophy and Personal Relations,* ed. by Alan Montefiore, 137–69. London: Routledge and Kegan Paul, 1973.

Pateman, Carol. *The Problem of Political Obligation: A Critical Analysis of Liberal Theory.* New York: J. Wiley & Sons, 1979.

Platts, Mark. *Ways of Meaning.* London: Routledge and Kegan Paul, 1980.

Pogge, Thomas. *Realizing Rawls.* Ithaca: Cornell University Press, 1989.

Rasmussen, David, ed. *Universalism and Communitarianism: Contemporary Debates in Ethics.* Cambridge: MIT Press, 1990.

Rawls, John. "Outline of a Decision Procedure for Ethics," *The Philosophical Review* 60 (1951): 177–97.

Rawls, John. "Two Concepts of Rules," *The Philosophical Review* 64 (1955): 3–32.

Rawls, John. "Distributive Justice." In *Philosophy, Politics and Society,* ed. by P. Laslett and W. G. Runciman, 58–82. Oxford University Press, 1967.

Rawls, John. "Justice as Reciprocity." In *Utilitarianism,* ed. by Samuel Gorovitz, 242–68. New York: Bobbs-Merrill, 1971.

Rawls, John. *A Theory of Justice.* Cambridge: Harvard University Press, 1971.

Rawls, John. "Reply to Alexander and Musgrave," *Quarterly Journal of Economics* 88 (1974): 633–55.

Rawls, John. "Some Reasons for the Maximin Criterion," *American Economic Review* 64 (1974): 141–46.

Rawls, John. "A Kantian Conception of Equality," *Cambridge Review* 96 (1975): 94–99.

Rawls, John. "The Independence of Moral Theory," *Proceedings and Addresses of the American Philosophical Association* 48 (1975): 5–22.

Rawls, John. "The Basic Structure as Subject." In *Values and Morals,* ed. by A. Goldman and J. Kim, 47–72. Boston: Reidel, 1978.

Rawls, John. "A Well-Ordered Society." In *Philosophy, Politics and Society,* 5th Series, ed. by P. Laslett and J. Fishkin, 6–20. Oxford University Press, 1979.

Rawls, John. "Kantian Constructivism in Moral Philosophy," *Journal of Philosophy* 77 (1980): 515–72.

Rawls, John. "The Basic Liberties and their Priority." In *The Tanner Lectures on Human Values,* v. 3, ed. by S. McMurrin, 1–87. University of Utah Press, 1982.

Rawls, John. "Social Unity and Primary Goods." In *Utilitarianism and Beyond,* ed. by A. Sen and B. Williams, 159–85. New York: Cambridge University Press, 1982.

Rawls, John. "Justice as Fairness: Political not Metaphysical," *Philosophy and Public Affairs* 14 (1985): 227–51.

Rawls, John. "Themes in Kant's Moral Philosophy." In *Kant's Transcendental Deductions,* ed. by Eckart Forster, 81–113. Standford University Press, 1989.

Rawls, John. "The Idea of an Overlapping Consensus," *Oxford Journal of Legal Studies* 7 (1987): 1–25.

Rawls, John. "The Priority of Right and Ideas of the Good," *Philosophy and Public Affairs* 17 (1988): 251–76.

Rawls, John. "The Domain of the Political and Overlapping Consensus" *New York University Law Review* 64 (1988): 233–55.

Riedel, M. "Transcendental Politics? Political Legitimacy and the Concept of Civil society in Kant," *Social Research* 48 (1981): 588–613.

Riley, Patrick. *Will and Political Legitimacy: A Critical Exposition of Social Contract Theory in Hobbes, Locke, Rousseau, Kant and Hegel.* Cambridge: Harvard University Press, 1982.

Riley, Patrick. *Kant's Political Philosophy.* Totowa, New Jersey: Rowman & Littlefield, 1983.

Ripstein, Arthur. "Foundationalism in Political Theory," *Philosophy and Public Affairs* 16 (1987): 115–37.

Saage, Richard. *Eigentum, Staat und Gesellschaft bei Immanuel Kant.* Stuttgart: Kohlhammer, 1973.

Sandel, Michael. *Liberalism and the Limits of Justice.* New York: Cambridge University Press, 1982.

Scanlon, T. M. "Preference and Urgency," *Journal of Philosophy* 72 (1975): 655–69.

Scanlon, T. M. "Liberty, Contract and Contribution." In *Markets and Morals,* ed. by G. Dworkin, et al., 43–68. New York: Halsted Press, 1977.

Scanlon, T. M. "Contractualism and Utilitarianism." In *Utilitarianism and Beyond,* ed. by A. Sen and B. Williams, 103–28. New York: Cambridge University Press, 1982.

Scheffler, Samuel. "Moral Independence and the Original Position," *Philosophical Studies* 35 (1979): 397–403.

Scheffler, Samuel. "Moral Skepticism and Ideals of the Person," *The Monist* 62 (1979): 288–303.

Scheffler, Samuel. "Ethics, Personal Identity and Ideals of the Person," *Canadian Journal of Philosophy* 12 (1982): 229–46.

Schiffer, Stephen. *Meaning.* Oxford: Clarendon Press, 1972.

Schmitter, Philippe C. "Democratic Theory and Neocorporatist Practice," *Social Research* 50 (1983): 885–928.

Schneewind, J. B. "Moral Knowledge and Moral Principles." In *Knowledge and Necessity*, ed. by G. N. S. Vesey, 249–62. London: MacMillan Press, 1974.

Schwartz, Adina. "Moral Neutrality and Primary Goods," *Ethics* 83 (1973): 294–307.

Searle, John. "Austin on Locutionary and Illocutionary Acts," *The Philosophical Review* 77 (1968): 405–24.

Searle, John. *Speech Acts: An Essay in the Philosophy of Language*. New York: Cambridge University Press, 1969.

Searle, John. *Expression and Meaning*. New York: Cambridge University Press, 1979.

Searle, John. *Intentionality*. New York: Cambridge University Press, 1983.

Searle, John. *Foundations of Illocutionary Logic*. New York: Cambridge University Press, 1985.

Searle, John, et al., eds. *Speech Act Theory and Pragmatics*. Boston: Reidel, 1980.

Shell, Susan. *The Rights of Reason: A Study of Kant's Philosophy and Politics*. Toronto: University of Toronto Press, 1980.

Singer, Peter. "Sidgwick and Reflective Equilibrium," *The Monist* 58 (1974): 490–517.

Stern, Paul. "The Problem of History and Temporality in Kantian Ethics," *Review of Metaphysics* 39 (1986): 505–45.

Strasnick, Steven. "The Problem of Social Choice: Arrow to Rawls," *Philosophy and Public Affairs* 5 (1975/76): 241–73.

Strauss, Leo. *Natural Right and History*. Chicago: University of Chicago Press, 1953.

Strawson, P. F. *Logico-Linguistic Papers*. London: Methuen, 1971.

Sunstein, Cass. "Beyond the Republican Revival," *Yale Law Journal* 97 (1988): 1539–90.

Taylor, Charles. *Philosophical Papers*. New York: Cambridge University Press, 1985.

Teitelman, Michael. "The Limits of Individualism," *Journal of Philosophy* 69 (1972): 545–56.

Teubner, Günther. "Substantive and Reflexive Elements in Modern Law," *Law and Society Review* 17 (1983): 239–86.

Thompson, John, and David Held, eds. *Habermas: Critical Debates*. Cambridge: MIT Press, 1982.

van der Linden, H. *Kantian Ethics and Socialism*. Cambridge: Hackett, 1988.

van Straaten, Zak, ed. *Philosophical Subjects: Essays Presented to P. F. Strawson*. Oxford: Clarendon Press, 1980.

Waldron, Jeremy. "Theoretical Foundations of Liberalism," *The Philosophical Quarterly* 37 (1987): 127–50.

Walzer, Michael. *Spheres of Justice: A Defence of Pluralism and Equality*. New York: Basic Books, 1983.

Walzer, Michael. *Interpretation and Social Criticism*. Cambridge: Harvard University Press, 1987.

Wellmer, Albrecht. *Praktische Philosophie und Theorie der Gesellschaft*. Konstanz: Universitätsverlag, 1979.

Wellmer, Albrecht. *Ethik und Dialog: Elemente des moralischen Urteil bei Kant und in der Diskursethik*. Frankfurt: Suhrkamp, 1986.

Wellmer, Albrecht, et al., eds. *Zwischenbetrachtungen: Im Prozess der Aufklärung.* Frankfurt: Suhrkamp, 1989.

White, Stephen K. "On the Normative Structure of Action: Gewirth and Habermas," *The Review of Politics* 44 (1982): 282–301.

White, Stephen K. *The Recent Work of Jürgen Habermas: Reason, Justice and Modernity.* New York: Cambridge University Press, 1988.

Williams, Howard. *Kant's Political Philosophy.* New York: St. Martin's Press, 1983.

Williams, Bernard. *Ethics and the Limits of Philosophy.* Cambridge: Harvard University Press, 1985.

Wolff, Robert P. *Understanding Rawls.* Princeton: Princeton University Press, 1977.

Wood, Allen. "Habermas's Defense of Rationalism," *New German Critique* 35 (1985): 145–64.

Wren, Thomas, ed. *The Moral Domain.* Cambridge: MIT Press, 1989.

Young, Iris. "Impartiality and the Civic Public." In *Feminism as Critique,* ed. by S. Benhabib and D. Cornell, 56–76. Minneapolis: University of Minnesota Press, 1987.

Yovel, Y. *Kant and the Philosophy of History.* Princeton: Princeton University Press, 1980.

INDEX OF NAMES

democratic participation, 167–69
deontology, 110, 138; and discourse
ethics, 110
Difference Principle, 154, 159–61; and
basic structure, 63
discourse: actual *vs.* ideal (or counterfactual), 112–14, 150; application *vs.*
justification, 212n156
discourse ethics, 9, 77, 108–21; and
communicative action, 85; and communicative reason, 3; and Kantian
morality, 6, 108
duties: and the categorical imperative,
18, 27; perfect and imperfect (Kant),
28; of virtue and of justice, 17, 28,
187n29

equality: in Kant, 11, 41; in Rawls, 56
Equal Liberty Principle, 154; and basic
structure, 63; priority over the Difference Principle, 155

fact of pluralism (Rawls), 72, 74
Fact of Reason (Kant), 7, 15–16, 48, 112
foundationalism, 1, 72, 183n4, 183n5
freedom: of association, 163; and autonomy, in Kant, 11, 16; of citizen in
well-ordered society, 56, 128; deduction of concept of, in Kant, 15; of
speech, 158. *See also* liberty

generalizable interests, 79, 142, 149; and
impartiality, 150; and need interpretations, 151

history, Kant's teleological conception
of, 8, 12, 46, 185n5, 191n82; and justice, 22

ideology, 2
illocutionary acts, 97, 202n28; classification of, 107; and performative attitude, 103–104; *vs.* perlocutionary
acts, 93, 98; and "rationally binding
force" (Habermas), 81, 85, 90, 105;
Searle's essential rule of, 101, 103;

and "securing uptake" (Austin) or
"reaching understanding" (Habermas), 93, 202n28; and validity,
103–105
impartiality, 133–36
intuitionism, 15, 24, 70

judgment: practical, 25, 119; principle
of, in Kant, 18
justice: circumstances of, 57; *vs.* conceptions of the good, 138, 143; as fairness, the "special conception," 154;
in Kant, 11; Kant's Universal Principle of, 7, 13–24; Rawls's two principles of, 153; and solidarity, 143;
strict, 20
justification, 7, 68–76; and constructivism, 1; and *modus vivendi,*
198n56; paradox of democratic, 73,
74, 181; and practical reason, 2; and
Rawls's method of avoidance, 75;
and Rawls's "three points of view,"
53, 68; and reflective equilibrium, 7,
70; reflexive, 1, 200n68; and relativism, 8, 72

law: alternative models of, 166; and
communicative action, 166; ethical
and juridical, in Kant, 19; of freedom, in Kant, 19; as medium and as
institution, in Habermas, 166; permissive, in Kant, 32
legal regulation (*Verrechtlichung*), 163,
180
legislation, ethical *vs.* juridical, in Kant,
18–19
legitimation: procedure of, 51, 153, 158;
crisis of, 164
liberalism, 184n18; in Kant, 46
liberty: negative *vs.* positive, 155; political, 156, 159, 163; restricted for the
sake of liberty, 156; and the worth of
liberty, 156, 159. *See also* freedom
lifeworld, 82, 175, 209n115; colonization of, 165, 174; as complementary
concept to communicative action, 82;

disintegration of, 164; and formal
world concepts, 83; as resource, 82;
and social rationalization, 163, 174;
and system, 174, 224n55

maxim, 16, 25
maximin rule, 4, 60; *vs.* maximin equity
criterion (or Difference Principle),
195n19
meaning: communicative-intention theory of, 88; natural *vs.* non-natural, 90;
objectivistic approach to, 89, 95; theories of, 88–108; truth-conditional
theory of, 88
meaning-nominalism, 90–95
model-conception of the person (Rawls):
and basic liberties, 158; and construction of the original position,
125; defined, 56, 127; and moral
powers, 56; and primary goods, 125,
147
moral conflict, 79, 133–34, 136
moral desert, 131, 133
moral law (Kant): and autonomy, 14;
consciousness of, 15; deduction of,
16; and Fact of Reason, 15–16;
objective validity of, 15; and practical reason, 16
moral obligation (*Sollgeltung*), 85, 111,
114
moral personality: and autonomy, in
Kant, 14, 15
moral point of view, 124, 138, 140; and
impartiality, 133, 136; and solidarity,
143
moral reason. *See* practical reason
moral reasoning, 130, 136; and communicative action, 143; post-conventional, 137, 143; stages of, 136, 143
moral realism, 15, 74, 198n54
moral theory: and cognitivism, 109, 136;
and conceptions of the person, 123;
and deontology, 110, 138; and moral
psychology, 126, 137; and philosophy of mind, 126; task of, 79, 116,
139, 200n6

morality: and justice (*Recht*), in Kant,
21–25; and legality, 12; and politics,
11, 23; and reason, 79
mutual (or common) knowledge, 81, 95

needs and need interpretation, 5, 111,
144–45, 151. *See also* preferences
noumenal self, 4, 17, 47, 66, 143,
184n11

original position: and constructivism,
153; and justification, 51–52, 73,
153; parties in, 53; as procedural representation of the categorical imperative, 51, 53, 61; and primary goods,
146; and rational choice, 52, 195n12

person: atomistic conception of, 63,
128–30, 136; and moral powers, 56,
127; social nature of, in Rawls, 4, 63,
126. *See also* model-conception of
the person
perspective: external (or observer's),
146, 148; internal (or participant's),
80, 95; internal *vs.* external, 150; and
validity, 80
possession, intelligible and physical, 31;
original common, 37. *See also* property rights
power, 85, 178
practical reason: and agreement, 3; and
autonomy, 16, 185n7; and constructivism, 1; and justice, in Kant, 13, 46;
and justification, 2; in Rawls, 50, 51,
66; *vs.* rational self-interest, 6, 29,
47. *See also* reason
pragmatics: formal, 101; and semantics,
89
preferences, 5, 148; formation of, 178;
and interpersonal comparison, 148.
See also needs and need interpretation
primary goods, 146–51; defined, 149;
functions of, in *TJ*, 146; and generalizable interests, 151; and model-conception of the person, 147, 160